BSA TWIN RESTORATION

The essential guide to the renovation, restoration and development history of all post-war BSA Twins. Plus how to recognize parts, improve specifications and maintain this classic motorcycle

ROY BACON

OSPREY

First published in 1986 by Osprey Publishing
59 Grosvenor Street, London W1X 9DA
First reprint early 1988
Second reprint autumn 1989
Third reprint spring 1991

© Copyright Roy Bacon 1986, 1988, 1989, 1991

All rights reserved. Apart from any fair dealing for the purpose of private study, research, criticism or review, as permitted under the Copyright, Designs and Patents Act, 1988, no part of this publication may be reproduced, stored in a retrieval system, or transmitted in any form or by any means, electronic, electrical, chemical, mechanical, optical, photocopying, recording, or otherwise, without prior written permission. All enquiries should be addressed to the publisher.

British Library Cataloguing in Publication Data

Bacon, Roy H.
    BSA twin restoration; the essential guide to the renovation, restoration and development history of all 1946–72, A7/10 and A50/65/70 pre-unit and unit BSA twins; plus how to recognize parts, improve specifications and maintain this classic motorcycle.
    1. B.S.A. motorcycle
    I. Title
    629.2′275   TL448.B2
ISBN 0-85045-669-X

Design Vic Shreeve

Filmset by Tameside Filmsetting Limited,
Ashton-under-Lyne, Lancashire
Printed by BAS Printers Limited,
Over Wallop, Hampshire, Great Britain

For a catalogue of all books published by Osprey Automotive please write to:

The Marketing Manager,
Consumer Catalogue Department,
Osprey Publishing Limited,
Michelin House, 81 Fulham Road,
London SW3 6RB

CONTENTS

Acknowledgements 7
Our policy 9
1 At the start 11
2 First steps 32
3 The engine 37
4 Transmission 66
5 Carburettor and exhaust 80
6 Lubrication 92
7 Electrics 100
8 The finish 116
9 Frame and stands 129
10 Suspension 134
11 Painted parts and plated details 141
12 Wheels and brakes 159
13 Cables, controls, instruments 171
14 Petrol tank 179
15 Seating 188
16 Assembly 193
17 Paperwork 196

Appendices
1 Engine and frame numbers 200
2 Model chart 202
3 Model alterations 203
4 Finish codes 204
5 Colours 205
6 Pistons 208
7 Camshafts 209
8 Valve spring lengths 209
9 Magnetos 209
10 Spark plugs 209
11 Carburettor settings 210
12 Capacities 212
13 Transmission 213
14 Wheels 216
15 Headlamp, ammeter, switches 218
16 Part numbers 220
   Picture indexes 236
   Index 238

Acknowledgements

This is the second book in this series which was started in response to the call for more detail on restorations. The basic requirement for information on date, colour and spares still needs to be met, but now the fine detail is also needed. So, this book was written to provide identification material along with guidance on carrying out the restoration work.

As with the first book I have to thank my good friend Don Mitchell who supplied me with much of the basic data from his stock of second-hand motorcycle literature. Also Dick Lewis, the well-known BSA expert from Weybridge, who filled in some of the gaps and gave useful guidance. Specific information came from Alan Blake of Avon Tyres, Derek Dyson of Champion Plugs and Martyn Ashwood of NGK — my thanks go to all.

Most of the pictures and line drawings came from the EMAP archives which hold the old *Motor Cycle Weekly* files, for which my grateful thanks. Others were from the *Motor Cycle News* files courtesy of Jim Lindsay and a number from BSA brochures, parts lists and manuals of the era. A number of the electrical line drawings were originally from Lucas. The pictures of a 1970 Firebird were sent to me by Peter Johnson of New Zealand. He carried out a superb restoration during which we corresponded via the *Classic Bike* 'agony' column I write.

Some of the pictures carried the imprint of a professional and work came from Reg Cave, Arthur Hind, C. Mayhew and Donald Page. As usual all the pictures were returned to their files after publication and I have tried to make contact to clear copyright. If my letter failed to reach you or I have used an unmarked print without realizing this, please accept my apologies.

Finally, my thanks to Tim Parker for conceiving the idea and to Lydia, Helen and Joanne at Osprey who helped bring this one to fruition.

Roy Bacon
Niton, Isle of Wight
January 1986

BSA TWIN RESTORATION

Our policy

This book is written on the basis of a restoration back to original factory specification for the model and year. It is fully appreciated that not every reader will want to aim for this but it is the only practical way to write the words.

Restorations can range from a mild check-over to concours standard and further to add features and a finish never seen on a production machine. Alterations may be carried out and these again can range from discreet rider improvements to accepted changes to update the specification, or even total rework into a hardtail chopper.

In all cases and regardless of the final aim it is hoped that this book will assist and guide the reader to produce the machine of his or her dreams. It is also hoped that the result will be sound in wind and limb and every endeavour has been made to offer advice which is helpful and safe. However, the onus is always with the reader to ensure that any machine he or she works on or rides is in a safe and legal condition. If you decide to carry out a modification you must make certain that it will work properly.

Neither the author or publisher can accept any liability for anything contained in this book which may result in any loss, damage or injury and the book is only available for purchase or loan on that basis. *Note* It is worth noting that each chapter of this book contains both general principles and specific information. The first can really apply to any make or model, while the second is very much only applicable to particular cases, such as a part made for a model that was only available for one year.

The distinction is important. The reader will invariably find the principles in other material, but the particular appeal of this book is that it gives you the specific details that relate the general principles directly to your machine.

The 650 cc Lightning Clubman at the 1965 Blackpool show. A sporting and fully equipped model for the hardest rider

Machine year

Chapter 1 contains details of the way in which models are dated, which causes, for example, 1955 models to run from late 1954 to late 1955. It also covers the habit of using up 1954 stocks in early 1955 models to clear the bins at the factory. Because of these points the text will use the model year without constant repetition that the feature or model was introduced late in the previous calendar year. Thus a late 1954 model is referred to as 1955 because that is the specification to which it was made.

The use of old parts is ignored by the BSA factory parts list and by this book. By definition they had to interchange by form and function so any notes on parts have to bypass this area. It does mean, however, that it is possible for an all-original machine with known history to have an incorrect part. It is the owner's decision as to whether to keep it or change to the correct parts list specification.

Engine and frame numbers take precedence over model year in determining when a change took place and have been noted where necessary. Parts lists, coupled with these numbers, are always the correct way back to original specification.

Scope

This book sets out to deal with production road models from 1947 to 1972 specification.

The data quoted applies to standard UK specification machines as these are the basis from which any factory variations were derived. Thus while the data will assist when dealing with a machine to USA or any other overseas specification, it cannot be assumed to be exact. The same applies to all machines built for the police as these had their own specification and could vary in detail from one force to the next.

Neither prototypes or one-off specials are mentioned. If you are lucky enough to have such a machine I am sure you appreciate its rarity and will look after it without my help.

A 1958 A10 Super Rocket on show at the Nutley, New Jersey, service school. Jeanne Lewis (Miss New Jersey) is flanked by Edward Turner, wearing his BSA tie for once, and T. A. Hodgdon, the president of BSA Inc.

Your skills

This book is not a workshop manual and neither is it a primer on being a motorcycle mechanic. It has to assume that you know how your machine works and have a good idea as to how to maintain it. Also that you have a degree of mechanical aptitude and have worked on motorcycles to some extent.

In many cases a good restoration is a combination of skill, available tools and knowledge of techniques and tricks that get the job done. Together they equate to experience and no book can give you that. It can only advise that you don't attempt more than you can cope with and adds the suggestion that with the right information, care and attention to detail this could be more than you think. Proceed slowly but with confidence.

Address list

Always a problem in a book as they tend to be out of date by publication.

If in difficulties the 'agony' columns of the specialist magazines are there to help so you can send them your query as long as you include some method of return postage.

Specifications

Many books of this type carry extensive tables of data to the fourth place of decimals which have been compiled from endless hours of research. This does not, as much of it is in *BSA Twins & Triples* (Osprey Publishing) and the rest in workshop manuals.

It is recommended that before any restoration is attempted that data and information is collected to cover your model and its year. In many areas the four figure dimensions are of little moment as parts are reamed to fit and made to size. Part of the art is knowing which ones matter and no book can teach that any more than it can show you how to paint a masterpiece or write an opera. Well not one that is any good.

So there are no endless lists of bushes and bearings, gaps and settings or tolerances and gauges. The figures and data that are provided are there to back up the manual you should have and to help you sort out what you may have bought.

1 At the start

The BSA vertical twin was announced in the motorcycle press in September 1946, thus being one of the earliest post-war models to follow in the steps of the pre-war Turner Triumph. During its life it was built in large numbers, but was invariably viewed as a well-made, rather sober machine that was fine for commuting and touring but somehow lacked that sporting snap of other marques.

In truth BSA built fine motorcycles, and in sports trim they could match most others. The vertical twin range was built in 500 and 650 cc engine sizes for most years with a very few 750s for the USA coming in 1972. Engines were built as semi-unit at first, later as separate from the gearbox and then in unit construction form.

The electrics changed from dynamo to alternator and the cycle side varied over the years, but all models had overhead valves, a single camshaft and a continuing design theme.

History

The first A7 (a 500) had a long-stroke engine, a rigid frame and was part of BSA's 1947 model range. It remained thus for 1948 but was joined in 1949 by the more sporting Star Twin version, which was fitted with twin carburettors. At the same time a plunger frame appeared, optional for the A7 but fitted as standard to the Star Twin, or A7ST as it was typed.

ABOVE *Seen here on the 1947 A7 are the centre stand and the early timing cover which lacked the extra screw under the oil pump area*

BELOW *Drive side of the original 1947 A7 in its rigid frame with odd centre stand*

These two continued for 1950, when they were joined by the 650 cc A10 Golden Flash, which was available in rigid or plunger frames. In 1951 the A7 engines were modified to a shorter stroke so they could use many of the A10 parts, but the form of construction remained the same with the gearbox bolted to the rear of the crankcase. The A7 continued to be built in rigid or plunger frames while the Star Twin had the spring frame as standard. For 1952 all three models were fitted with the plunger frame as standard and the rigid one no longer listed.

The three models continued for 1953 and were joined by an export-only sports 650 in the plunger frame and named the Super Flash. These models continued for 1954 but were joined by versions in pivoted-fork frames, the latter for export only at first. The sports types were renamed the A7SS or Shooting Star and A10RR or Road Rocket. From 1955 only the pivoted-fork frames were in use except for the A10, which continued also to be offered in plunger form for sidecar owners. The Star Twin went from the line-up to leave a five-model range to run on through 1956 and 1957.

1958 brought changes to the machines and the end of the A10 in the plunger frame, so the basic range comprised sports and touring models in the two engine sizes. The sports 650 became the A10SR or Super Rocket and was joined by an export only Rocket Scrambler model for the USA. This model became known as the Spitfire Scrambler in due course.

The pivoted fork models all had separate engine and gearbox and the 1958 range continued to be offered to 1962. That year it was joined by the first of the unit construction machines, but for enthusiasts there was the most sporting of the earlier type, the Rocket Gold Star or A10RGS. This continued in production for 1963 and during that year a few of the A10 models were also produced. These included some A10GF machines with alternator electrics as well as A10SR and Spitfire models. 1963 was the last year for the non-unit machines and only 650s were built.

The unit construction era opened with the announcement of the A50 and A65 in January 1962. These two were joined by the 650 cc Rocket version for 1964, this being typed the A65R, and with it came sports models for the USA. For off-road use there were the A50 Cyclone Competition and A65 Spitfire Hornet, both of which came with waist-level open exhaust pipes, no lights, twin carburettors and high-rise handlebars in the US style. On the USA road they were joined by the A65T/R Thunderbolt Rocket and A65L/R Lightning Rocket, both with high bars. The first was an Americanized version of the A65R while the second used some more sporting cycle parts and was fitted with the twin carburettor engine.

The line-up became further confused during 1965 when four new models were listed for the home market using similar designations to the US machines.

The 1949 Star Twin with twin carburettors and new plunger frame, an option for the A7

AT THE START

ABOVE *First year of the A10 was 1950 during which Jim Ferriday and George Wilson did a quick round-Britain trip on this outfit*

BELOW *The 1951 A10 in its optional Golden Flash beige which made it such a handsome model*

ABOVE *Home market A10 built late in 1951 when the nickel shortage was affecting finish. Hence no chrome plating on the petrol tank which was simply lined*

LEFT *The A10 Super Flash, the first sports 650 with rather more power than the plunger frame could manage*

BELOW *First year of the pivoted fork frame shown here on a 1954 A10 complete with headlamp cowl and underslung pilot light*

The first two were the A50C Cyclone and A65L Lightning, which were twin carburettor road models for the home market. With them came the A50CC Cyclone Clubman and A65LC Lightning Clubman with downswept handlebars and racing seat to suit production racing.

Along with these newcomers the A50, A65 and A65R continued for the home market as did the A50 Cyclone Competition, A65 Spitfire Hornet and A65L/R for the USA one. In addition for that area there appeared a sports 500 for the road labelled the A50 Cyclone Road model, which was much as the A65L/R with twin carburettors. Missing was the A65T/R as few in the USA would settle for a single carburettor model if one with two was to be had.

For 1966 BSA simplified matters and reduced the range of twins to six. The smaller were the A50 tourer, which took the name Royal Star by which it had always been known in the USA, and for off-road use there was the A50 Wasp. In the 650 cc class there were four models, the first being the A65T Thunderbolt with single carburettor which replaced the earlier A65 tourer. The twin carburettor version was the A65L Lightning and the off-road version the A65H Hornet. Top of the range was the A65S Spitfire MkII, which was based on the Lightning but with the hotter Hornet internals and GP carburettors. It replaced the A65LC.

This range continued for 1967 and 1968 with the Spitfire becoming the MkIII and MkIV in turn while for 1968 the off-road 650 became the A65FS Firebird Scrambler. There was no Spitfire for 1969 as its place had been taken by the Rocket 3 (not dealt with in this book), and no Wasp, which had vanished from the parts list in 1967. This left just four models for 1969 and 1970.

1971 brought the last major changes with the advent of the oil-in-frame models in just three 650 cc types. However, by then the company was in serious financial trouble and only the A65T and A65L continued into 1972. They were joined by the A70L, which was an enlarged (750 cc) version built to provide the basis of a US dirt track racer.

Model choice

The potential owner of a BSA twin has a good range of model types, two engine sizes and many years to select from. The one chosen is down to the individual and is their choice alone. Selection may be determined by a past memory of a favourite model, a wish felt for some time or a desire to complete a collection, but for most it is determined by the money they have and the machines on offer.

Remember that some models were only made in small numbers so that their spares could be hard to find. Also that export specification models may pose similar problems even in the country they were destined for and worse outside it. A further pitfall arises where an attempt has been made either to create a rare model from a more prosaic one or to convert from one market specification to another. Very rarely will the change be totally complete so another hybrid appears and can cause headaches.

The year of the full width, light alloy hubs as seen on a 1956 A7 Shooting Star

ABOVE *Drive side of the A7SS in 1957 showing full chaincase*

LEFT *1958 brought a new style of full width hub seen here on an A10 outfit*

BELOW *The sports 650 in its 1958 form as the Super Rocket*

The BSA can be obtained in many ways, but purchase from a dealer, following up small advertisements in a local paper or specialized magazine, by word of mouth, club grapevine or personal contact are the more usual ways. Alternatively you may already have a BSA twin you wish to restore or improve in some way.

A restoration does not always start with a complete machine and many begin with a box of parts bought at an autojumble or from a local source. Often such are the hardest to complete as parts are invariably missing. The box is on sale because the last owner allowed enthusiasm to run ahead of resources, stripped the machine and then gave up or was forced to stop. He is sure it is all there but has forgotten various parts already missing, lent, lost or strayed for many reasons and every one a problem for the new owner.

The restorer must also decide what is wanted and what is possible, which may not be the same thing. A concours model may not be everyone's aim, but all should aim to get the machine in good running order to make sure it is reliable in use.

Aims can vary and may be simply to correct the faults of a machine in poor condition so it is a pleasure to ride even if its appearance is nondescript. They could be to repair damage to achieve this standard or could include changes to enhance performance, reliability or appearance. More usual is the aim to restore to original condition and in some cases beyond with more chrome, polish and sparkle than even a Small Heath show model.

The decision on the standard and style of restoration belongs to the owner just as the machine does. Whether all chrome, all original or all bituminous black it is your choice and no one else's. The decision as to what to do may depend on many factors and these include time, money and facilities as well as the owner's wishes.

Assets

Motorcycle restoration or repair requires time, money and equipment and it is necessary to have some amount of all three. Possession of a large quantity of any one reduces the need for the other two but will never remove them completely. Thus, given plenty of time the highest restoration standards can be reached using limited facilities and for minimal cost. A deep purse will allow the project to be farmed out and finished in a short time and without the need for much equipment. The ultimate on this road of just handing the model and money over to a professional may sound easy but can still call on decision making and some organizational skills. Finally, anyone with really good facilities can complete a restoration cheaply and quickly by making or refurbishing the parts and tools needed.

It has to be noted that all three assets do have to be present to some degree.

Minimal changes on a good basic design kept costs down so this 1959 A10 is much as it was five years earlier

Abilities

The BSA restorer must try to make a realistic assessment of his or her abilities. Some of us are just less well blessed with manual skills than others and it is very important to realize one's limitations early on and to plan ways round them. This can be equally satisfying as the object is to complete the project by the means that are available to you.

An example lies in the use of special tools. You must use these in certain instances and they can be bought, manufactured or parts taken to someone with them. Which method depends on the money, facilities and time already mentioned.

People's level of skill varies from job to job and this also must be allowed for. Your expertise in some areas may be to a very high standard but in others may be

Line drawing of a 1961 A7SS showing the many features common to the whole range

LEFT *Nearing the end of the line for the non-unit models was this 1960 A10 with revised mudguard mountings*

lower, so accept that fact. You must judge which areas you have the necessary competence in and those where assistance will be needed.

One answer to this problem is to lower the standard of the restoration. If you cannot do certain jobs and don't want outside help then the only answer is to settle for less than a concours finish. It is likely to be more satisfying to rebuild a basket case into a reliable machine than to attempt perfection and miss it due to personal rather than financial reasons.

ABOVE *Rarely seen left side of the 1962 Rocket Gold Star, a model with a long list of options*

BELOW *The handlebar layout, instruments and tank cap of the 1962 RGS*

AT THE START

The first of the unit construction models but the same basic mechanics at heart. A 1962 A50

The overall timescale of the job must also be considered. If the machine is needed by a particular date then the planning must allow for something to go wrong. For your first restoration it is much better not to have any deadline as even with the experience of several it is hard to estimate when a project will be finished.

It is much better to allow for delays and especially so if you are aiming for concours standard. If a straight rebuild is being done then a schedule is much easier to keep to as more of the work will be under your own control. Any schedule should include an allowance for delays, although planning ahead can often reduce them. A series of tasks that depend on one another and run in sequence should thus be started early to prevent a hold-up later on.

Wheels are the classic example as you have to despoke, dismantle, clean, paint hub, renovate rim, assemble spindle and rebuild the wheel in that order.

So the first stage of a restoration is to decide on a machine and determine the degree of restoration to be carried out. It always pays to think this through before committing oneself and proper planning not only saves time and money but makes the work more enjoyable and turns a job into a hobby.

Receipts

It pays to keep the paperwork in order from the start. This is dealt with in more detail later, but it cannot be over-emphasized that you must be able to prove that you actually own the machine which sits in the garage, shed or front hall depending on your workshop habits. Thus it is essential to obtain a receipt for the machine or, if it is built up from boxes, then get receipts for them and all the major purchases you make. It won't do any harm to keep the till receipts of even minor items and to log all these in your records. This will help prove ownership, be a useful record should you wish to sell, show a prospective customer exactly what has gone into the machine and maybe frighten you at the size of the cost of a restoration.

ABOVE *The 1964 Rocket A65R, the first of the home market sports versions of the unit range*

BELOW *Sporting US model with open exhausts, the 1964 Spitfire Hornet A65SH*

Workshop

This has been the subject of many articles that seek to describe an ideal arrangement, but for most restorers it is either their garage or garden shed. Some lucky people have better premises and some much worse and the work that comes from the shop may bear little relation to its size and facilities.

It is possible to produce a concours BSA in a small draughty shed and many people have done just this. However, the job of restoring a machine is not an easy one and the exercise is supposed to be an enjoyable hobby so it makes sense to at least be able to work in comfort.

There is seldom much you can do about the size of your workshop, but basically one can say that the smaller it is the more you need to have it well organized. Whatever the size it must be clean, dry, warm and well lit. The first job is to stop the roof from leaking and the next to check the floor and consider sealing its surface. Aside from the dust problem, which sealing greatly reduces, it also makes it much easier to find anything dropped on the floor. Normal concrete is gritty and finding small screws can be difficult.

With the roof and floor in order the walls can be seen to and a coat of white emulsion brightens the atmosphere no end and helps the efficiency of the lighting. This must be good and fluorescent tubes are essential. They should be the daylight white type and may need to be supplemented by a bench light and a hand torch or wander light. It pays to wipe the tubes over occasionally as they tend to get dirty in a workshop and any reduction in illumination is a handicap. If likely to be knocked at any time they should be protected by a guard.

Some people share a workshop and this can be a great help, but only if you get on well and can work side by side. For some jobs a pair of spare hands can save a lot of time and trouble while discussion of a problem will often solve it.

Just as important as sharing with another person is sharing the restoration site with another machine. If the same shed has to garage a machine in daily use then sooner rather than later it will come in wet and dirty. Not impossible to live with but a factor to remember when deciding what can and cannot be attempted at home.

Equipment

The workshop has to be fitted out and the first need is a bench to work on. This must be solidly built and firmly fixed in place. Next on the list is a machine bench with a means of running the motorcycle up onto it and finally come shelves of various sizes for the storage of parts, tools, equipment, spares and consumables such as oil and grease. Don't forget a place for a large, shallow box in which to store your gaskets.

The bench needs a vice and you may also wish to make up an engine stand. This can be constructed in wood or metal and its purpose is to stop the unit from falling over on the bench and maybe damaging itself. To be really useful the stand needs to be clamped down to the bench and the same effect can be achieved by holding the engine, or gearbox, in the vice. This then leaves both hands free to do the work but does emphasize the need to fix vice and bench securely. Needless to say the vice must be fitted with smooth jaws to avoid marking the castings.

The 1965 Cyclone A50C which was built in this sports form and as the Cyclone Clubman for production racing

ABOVE *Top of the road range in 1966 was the MkII Spitfire with GP carburettors and all the goodies*

BELOW *Street scrambler guise for this 1966 Wasp model A50W without lights but with low level silencers*

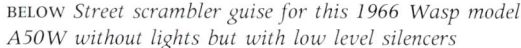

Sports Lightning A65L in 1967 with finned rocker cover

Hand tools are best stored on a board so they are easy to reach, but keep files beneath the bench to avoid any chance of metal particles getting into the works. Your hand tools are likely to have been accumulated over the years and may be of variable quality. Now is a good time to get ruthless with them and separate the good from the rest.

Spanner types are legion but the rules are basically to only use ones that fit and that are made from a good steel. My preference is for combination spanners with a ring and open end of the same size at the two ends, a set of $\frac{1}{4}$ in. drive sockets which give me feel on most motorcycle fixings, and a selection of $\frac{1}{2}$ in. drive sockets. Mine have been bought as needed to suit specific jobs so that thanks to the changes from Whitworth to Unified to metric threads a fairly full set is to hand. But it took many years to acquire and each of the big sockets were bought for a job.

The $\frac{1}{4}$ in. drive is thought light by many but its slimness is an asset in many situations. Often a nut may be slackened by a heavier tool and then run off with the smaller one, which can tuck in better.

In addition to the hand tools for taking things apart you will need some for making things. It is at this point that you have to decide how much work you will attempt and what to farm out as the equipment becomes more specialized and expensive. Possession of a good electric drill is taken as granted and it is not too hard to adapt this to a pillar drill and to a bench grinder to sharpen drills. A flexible shaft will help with port work but the next items come into another league.

There are two pieces of equipment to consider and their relative importance depends to an extent on the work you intend to do. If you will be making spacers, machining parts and working to a greater degree on the mechanics then a lathe becomes essential. With a good set of tools and attachments a whole new world of possibilities opens up and parts can be made at a speed undreamed of. Should you intend to concentrate rather more on the cycle parts then welding equipment is essential. Standard oxy-acetylene gear enables parts to be brazed, welded, filled, loosened, bent and re-formed. An alternative that helps with the engine and a good deal of the cycle part work is a butane torch. In all cases when using a mobile heat source be careful where you point it and remember what items you have warmed up. A fire extinguisher of the correct type is an essential purchase.

For serious restoration work both are really essential although a great deal is possible without either. One area where both can help is in making special tools for working on the machine in general and the engine in particular.

A further piece of specialized equipment well worth considering is a hydraulic press, which can be constructed using a car or lorry jack. Remember to disconnect the overstroke release if it has one as otherwise you can lock the press up solid and it will stay that way until a seal goes.

Also worth putting on your shopping list is an air compressor. It does not have to be new, and often it and the motor to drive it may be bought separately, but it can be very useful even if you have no intention

1968 touring A65T Thunderbolt with one carburettor and side reflectors as part of its USA style

of doing any paint spraying. What it will do is enable you to check oilways, pipe lines, carburettor jets and the like for obstructions. Also, an air-line will blast your cleaning agent off the parts and can save lots of time drying with a cloth.

The equipment you decide to acquire will depend on many factors and relates to your earlier assessment of your abilities. There is no point in having more tools than you can handle, but don't confuse lack of confidence with this. If welding or machining is unfamiliar to you read about them, consider attending an evening course at the local college and above all practise before working on anything expensive or hard to replace.

Data

Just as important as tools for the workshop is data for the mind. Before laying a tool on your BSA there is a good deal of information to be collected if you want the best results. Even if you are only after a good working machine you still need certain basic engine settings, while for a concours job the data needed is far more detailed.

In all cases the first step is to establish what you have by checking engine and frame numbers for year and model type. The latter can be further checked against the machine specification and often this can reveal discrepancies. It is all too easy to fit an A7 engine into a B31 frame and trust that the buyer will not notice. There are many other changes that can be made and some may date from early in the machine's life, long before the classic machine revival.

Hybrids are a common problem with any make that remained in production for many years with minimal changes to basic dimensions. Some were built years ago because the parts were to hand. Maybe an old BSA was bought to make a Tribsa and years later fitted with another engine unit. Others came from autojumbles as a number of parts bought from many sources. With a rising interest in machines in original specification it is inevitable that some will be built up from spares while the numbers are added to by those that had an engine change simply because of a major blow-up.

The magazine agony columns indicate that this is a common happening with most makes and so

Last Spitfire model, the A65S MkIV of 1968 with the twin leading shoe front brake of that year

something to be aware of and to check. For the machine to be a hybrid may be a good thing rather than bad for it may have a worthwhile improvement. The important matter is knowing exactly what you do have.

Dating is complicated by the English industry tradition of starting its model year in August or September. Like most confusion it arose from good intentions and came about because the works switched to making the new models when they returned from the annual holiday. Production thus was well under way with stocks in the warehouse or at the dealers when the new models were announced in the press in the run-up to the Earls Court Show. This was held in November and thus you could view in London and the next day collect your machine from your local dealer. In theory.

Thus the maker's year was out of step with the calendar so that it is quite possible to find a machine first registered in October of the year before its style. Further complication for the restorer lies in the change-over of parts, which may not coincide with the start of a new model year. Often stocks of old parts would be used, where feasible, until run down before the new ones were phased in. In many cases the change is internal and out of sight, but some are on the outside and can cause real confusion.

The only answer is to work from the engine and frame numbers using the relevant parts book. This list is a most useful publication and really an essential for the restorer along with a workshop manual. In some ways the parts list is the more important for anyone striving for originality as it lists every part used on the machine with its part number and quantity.

Other literature that will help and which can be obtained from specialist book dealers is the rider's handbook in case it can add to the data in the manual, and a sales brochure, often the only indication of the colours of the machine and its component parts.

A marque history is well worth having as it will fill out the background and I am biased to recommend *BSA Twins & Triples* as I wrote it. You should also be reading the specialist magazines, *Classic Bike* and *The Classic Motor Cycle* on older machines and *Performance Bike*, which covers modern techniques, to note addresses and articles that could be useful to you. The addresses to take note of are any that look to be good and helpful, those close to you and the ones offering a special service likely to be needed. Plating, painting, wheel rebuilds and crankshaft regrinds are common needs, but you may also need someone to help with seat renovation, electrics or instruments so a knowledge of helpful addresses can be vital.

This type of firm is not here for two reasons. The first is the general need for them to be local. It is one thing to send a dynamo away for repair but quite another if you have 40 items for stove enamelling. The second is that firms are built up of people and their expertise. A good reputation may be due to the owner ensuring it is so or the workforce being skilled or a combination of the two. It can easily change if one or more men leave so recent recommendation is the best guide.

It will also be useful to join the BSA Owners Club as they offer a unique combined experience. No other body has quite the same outlook and members are in the best position to carry out very real evaluation tests on machines, modifications and their effects. There is also the Vintage Motor Cycle Club in Britain (with others elsewhere), which offers a further source of data, a marque specialist, and from their work has come a transfer scheme now available to all.

Yet another source of information is the show in its various forms. This may be a straight exhibition that includes the older machine, a classic machine show, a rally or a race meeting with events for older machines. All provide an opportunity to study other machines, talk to owners, gather information and find out where to get parts. Autojumbles, which are often combined with other events, can become an important part of the restorer's life for they offer the opportunity to seek out elusive spares, data and services. Local and not so local ones should be attended with dates and venues found in the specialist press pages.

Work plan

This is the grand title for you tearing the engine out and apart in the first flush of enthusiasm. Unfortunately, come winter, this fades and the mix-up of parts you now have in many boxes, bags and tins becomes very unattractive. Before long another basket job hits the ad columns which is both sad and unnecessary.

Before you pick up the first tool have a long look at yourself, your facilities and the machine. *Think*, painful though it is. Make sure that you have decided what *you* want to do and that this is within the capabilities of you and your gear. Now you have to think again and decide how that happy dream of a concours win, sweet-running machine, or whatever, is to be reached.

In essence you have to decide whether to deal with the machine as a whole or by major parts. The first is usually quicker but requires more fortitude. Once

ABOVE *Firebird scrambler A65FS of 1969 with its twin waist level exhausts on the left*

ABOVE *American style A50 Royal Star for 1969 with its image a good deal changed since 1962*

New petrol tank style for the 1970 Lightning A65L. New clutch cable entry for that year

apart you will seem to have a vast number of parts all needing attention and long before you get to the assembly stage you can run out of interest. The alternative is to take a major unit and renovate that alone. It will take longer to complete the whole machine but this method does reduce the storage space needed and you do feel that you are getting somewhere as each major lump is completed. Whichever way you go you need notes, photographs and sketches in large numbers. If you are going to rely on photos you will need to take plenty and they must be good close-ups. It is possible to do this with a very basic camera but for the best results you really need a decent SLR, which can focus down to three feet or less. Unless you can get that close you just won't record the detail you need. Good lighting will help to get good photos, and a wide-angle lens could be a useful asset.

Notes and sketches are a good alternative and mean that you can safely proceed without wondering if your film is going to develop satisfactorily. A pad of paper should be kept handy for rough notes in the workshop and these tidied and written up cleanly the same day. It is all too easy, especially with cycle parts, to forget the order in which parts fit onto a stud, which way round a bolt goes or even where the horn is fitted when you come to put things together months later. Plenty of labels and plastic storage bags will make life easier.

Even if the assembly you start with is wrong it is useful to record it as a basis to work from. Do not think that you can remember it all as you cannot and neither is it always obvious as to how the parts should be. Mudguard stays in particular can cause problems as often the apparently same part is used on both sides of the machine and can be fixed in four alternative ways in each position. Four? Yes, as it can be turned over or end to end, but only one way and one position will get it back where it came from. In theory this may not matter, if the stays are all the same, but in practice they always seem happier if replaced as they were. This no doubt arises because of small distortions that the parts have accommodated and if switched round they will have to begin again.

If you start with someone else's disaster as a basket case then the problem becomes more difficult as you will have to determine what each part is, where it goes and if it needs attention or was made in its present shape at the factory. A common difficulty with basket

ABOVE *Drive side of the touring Thunderbolt in 1970, very similar to both Lightning and Royal Star*

RIGHT *Timing side of a 1970 Firebird scrambler rebuilt to a very high standard in New Zealand*

End of the road? Posed picture of the A65L in 1971 with new frame, forks and hubs

cases is rogue parts from another machine that have crept in and can give you hours of fun and frustration. These can include parts from another machine, which is no trouble for you if they are stamped AJS or Norton but could be a small headache if marked Triumph. If you have a late BSA they may belong; or they may not! A larger headache is the appearance of real BSA parts that happen to come from a single – or another model twin but not compatible with yours.

You must also beware of parts that changed in detail over the years but remained very similar in appearance, changes of thread form from Whitworth to Unified, changes brought about by metrication and some pattern parts. Of the last, some are very, very good but others can be awful. On the factory changes the threads altered over several years which can confuse, but fortunately not much was changed to metric sizes.

Another headache can be proprietary parts that were common to many English machines and some of which happened to fall in with your basket. A handful of petrol taps might be useful but not if they all came from some other machine.

AT THE START

Lists

Some people live by lists, others abhor them, but in restoration they really are an essential and should form part of your note taking. Starting from a complete machine parts can be listed as they are dismantled with notes as to whether they need to be repaired, treated or both. By working with a parts list missing items can be highlighted and a shopping list compiled. On this will go consumables as well.

When starting with a basket case a parts list is really an essential and one or more photocopies well worth obtaining at the start. Using one as a master the parts can then be checked off one by one down to the last nut, bolt and washer. What is left on the list at the end becomes the shopping list and any parts not identified are, or ought to be, rogue.

While checking the list you can begin to establish the work needed on the parts you have depending on how much you are short and how essential the missing items are. How you fulfil the shopping list depends on your aims, money and the items themselves. You may have a good selection of nuts and bolts that would be fine for the job even if not correct to concours standard. If your aim is a good working machine then use them. The same philosophy can apply to many other items.

At the end of this operation you will have dismantled the complete machine and listed all the parts that require your attention or their purchase. This may have happened in stages if that is your way of working, but happen it has. With this knowledge the restoration work will be easier to organize and the assembly straightforward to carry out.

Security

Classic motorcycles and their component parts are valuable and in some cases nearly irreplaceable. One professional restorer is quoted as saying, 'What man has made, man can make again', which is perfectly true, but only at a price.

Therefore security has become a point to bear in mind. This is especially true if you are forced to use a lock-up garage as your workshop and the necessary steps should be taken before the machine is on the premises. Avoid publicity as the word can quickly get about, so don't leave the doors open if the premises face onto the street.

Working at home reduces the problem but may not remove it so again discretion is a good idea. It could also avoid an argument with the local council through a neighbour thinking you are using your home as a repair business.

A method used by some restorers to at least cut down their risk once a machine is partly dismantled is to store the parts in different areas of their home. This is a particularly useful way of protecting the smaller, more delicate, rather expensive and fairly universal items. These minor assemblies, such as magneto, dynamo, speedometer and carburettor, all lend themselves well to this arrangement and benefit from the household heating.

1971 and final version of the Firebird Scrambler with matt black exhausts and pale frame

2 First steps

Clean machine

Now that your 'before' pictures are safely taken work can begin on your project, but not in the workshop. The very first thing is to take the machine outside and give it a good clean to remove dirt, grime, grease and oil. There are a number of cleaning agents to help with this task and the aim is to get the bulk of the dirt washed away and the machine dried before it enters the working area.

Transfers

While this chore is in hand care must be taken not to damage the finish or any transfers as reference to them may be necessary. In fact once the machine is clean and back in the workshop it is a good time to go round it and make notes as to the exact position of all the transfers with dimensions from fixed features.

If you are just overhauling the model then the transfers are unlikely to be of any major concern but for a full restoration they are. The position of the oil tank level and the piled arms on the tool box for instance are each at a fixed dimension from some other point and for a concours job should be correct.

First removals

The initial steps are to remove the parts that are fragile and easily damaged or which impede access to the major items. The first step is the fuel tank, but before touching it have a look at the control cables and note how they run. Whether they are to left or right of the steering head and above or below the fixing lugs.

On some models you cannot remove the tank without taking the seat off first so if this is the case tackle it that way without forcing anything. If any of the bolts involved hold something else as well then you must note the order the parts are in as well as which way round the bolts go.

Note also the run of the petrol pipes while the tank and taps are in their correct location and watch the handlebars as you shift the tank. It is all too easy to catch the front of it on something and have the bars swing round and clout it to produce a dent or a nasty scratch.

Now get the machine up on the bike bench and make quite sure it is secure. If it is on a stand check that the feet cannot slide off the edge of the bench even when you lean on it with a tool. Check what will happen as you dismantle the machine. Most with a centre stand will keep their front wheel on the ground but if there is any doubt force a piece of wood under the back tyre to ensure stability. To have the whole machine rock back just as you try to lift the engine out can really put you off your stroke. Or worse still you might dive to save the model and knock it over.

So aim for stability until you have the major weighty items out and then jack up the front and take the wheel out. Do it the other way round and you have too much mass balanced on too short a wheelbase for safety. Remember this for when you come to assemble.

With the bike up in the air and secure continue with the dismantling by removing the exhaust systems, which may fall away or could stick. If the latter occurs don't tip the bike over while hauling on the pipes, just try to work them off a little at a time.

Cleaning down before starting work. The bench should be tidied up before going much further and the front brake is worn out

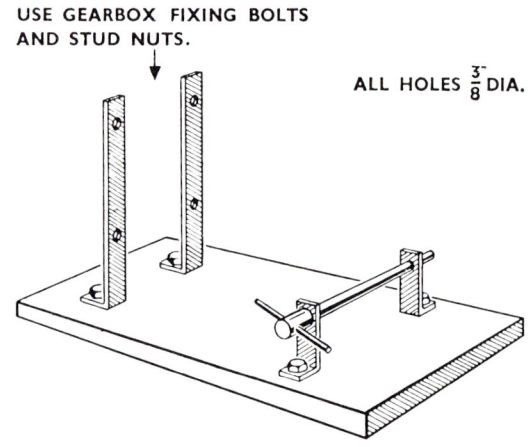

Handy bench fixture for the early semi-unit engine once separated from gearbox

FIRST STEPS

Tackle tight systems from the rear, a section at a time. Keep the pipe fixings tight and just remove the silencer bolts and clips. Work at the silencer to ease it back and off and then move on to the pipe, which should respond to the same treatment.

Now attend to the fragile items, which start with the headlamp rim with its glass, reflector and bulb. Place something soft over the front mudguard so the assembly can rest while you disconnect the wires or pull out the bulb holders. Store with care and add the rear light lens and bulb.

Next are the speedometer and rev-counter, if fitted, noting which is to left or right. Watch the bulb holder fitted in the back of the instrument and remove the bulb itself. Tie the parts so they stay together at the end of the wire and don't slide off into the main harness. The same trick is often worth doing with the instrument drive cable to restrain the knurled end fitting. A clothes peg can be used temporarily and the run of the cables must be noted.

Remove the carburettor(s) and float chamber, drain off petrol and store. If a complete strip is intended the slides could be removed from the cables and kept with the carburettor until attention is turned to that item.

The wiring is next on the list along with the control cables for they may well be linked by clips and tape holding them to the frame. More notes are needed before they are released. Then disconnect the battery and remove it. Don't hide it as it will need immediate attention if to act as a case or regular attention if it is to be used further.

The cables, suitably labelled, come off first and the label should indicate which end is which if not obvious. The wiring is usually best detached working from the rear of the machine forward to the headlamp switch. Depending on the year of the machine it may be best to detach the wiring from the switches and other electrical parts or it could be simpler to leave it joined and to take the parts off. Some, a dip-switch is an example, don't leave you any choice. More notes of course, but also check along the harness as you remove it for any points where it has been rubbed or shows signs of damage. They are areas to do something about on assembly to prevent problems occurring.

It is likely that the rectifier will have been removed during this operation but not necessarily the regulator if one is fitted. It is fragile so take it off for storage.

With the delicate details and the tangled mass of cables and wiring out of the way the machine will look a lot cleaner and easier to work on. You can now really see what you are doing and can get at it without fear that you may damage something both fragile and costly. No reason not to take care of course.

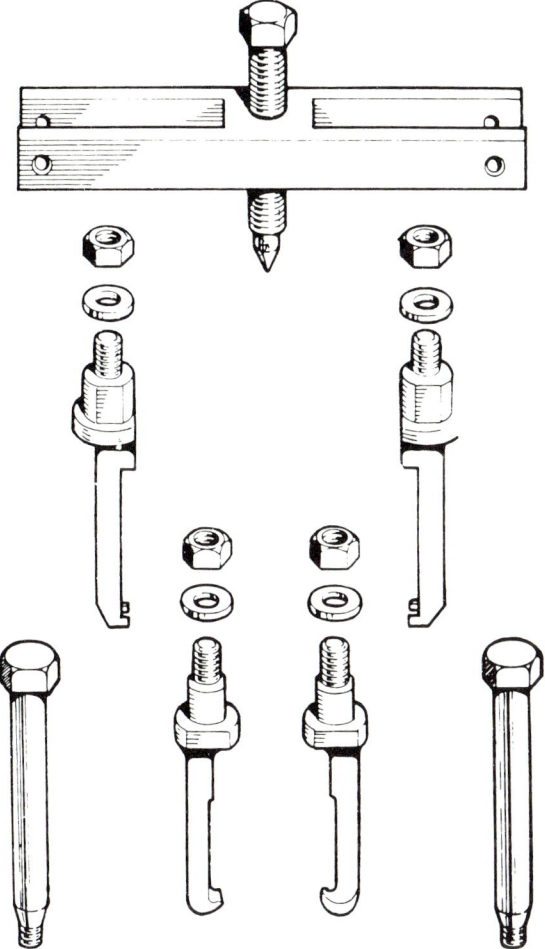

ABOVE *Typical extractor needed when dismantling engine*

RIGHT *Not the way to do it. The head fin is not the place to store nuts and washers which will surely drop down under the magneto*

Basket case

Where your BSA has come in boxes you start your restoration with the assembly of shabby components. It is well worth cleaning the contents of each box as this will make them nicer to work on, but nothing special is needed at this stage as they are going to need a lot more work and another, and better, clean before the final assembly.

What you have to do is to build up your collection of parts, each checked off against the parts list, into a complete machine. There are three problems in doing this. First is that it may not all be there. If the missing items are mainly bolts and fixings then anything from stock can be pressed into temporary service, but if you lack structural items it becomes more tricky. Second, some parts may be damaged and ill fitting, even distorting other parts. Allowance must be made where this occurs. Finally there are rogue parts, which may throw you off course.

At this stage keep everything. This is a sound move with any part from any older machine. No matter how tired or worn it may be, at some time you or someone else will want to use it because it is the best one available. If you don't use it yourself you may be able to swop it for something you do need and many a rebuild has been completed on this basis. Sometimes the swops involve three or four people but usually all will finish up with the parts they need – often at little or no cost.

With a basket case you have to build the complete machine up as you get the parts. It is valid to leave, say, the gearbox internals out as their space is defined but beware of any assumptions with the cycle parts. It is only too easy to think all is well, begin final finishing and then have to destroy that with further fitting work.

This is why a basket case always takes so much longer to complete and tries the worker's patience as it is ages before any progress at all seems to be made.

From this first assembly exercise should come a list of missing parts and those needing attention. Once you are satisfied that it is all there and will all go together then you can continue along the same lines as someone fortunate enough to start with a complete machine.

You can now take it all apart again.

Restoration

This is another word for repair and is closely linked to service and maintenance. The philosophy is the same whether you have a 1947 A7 or a 1972 A65L and the work involved and techniques used are similar or the same for both machines. The problems will vary enormously with no regard to the age of the machine and only spares availability will relate to the years to any degree.

The essence of the job is that the machine is reduced totally to its component parts. That means studs out of

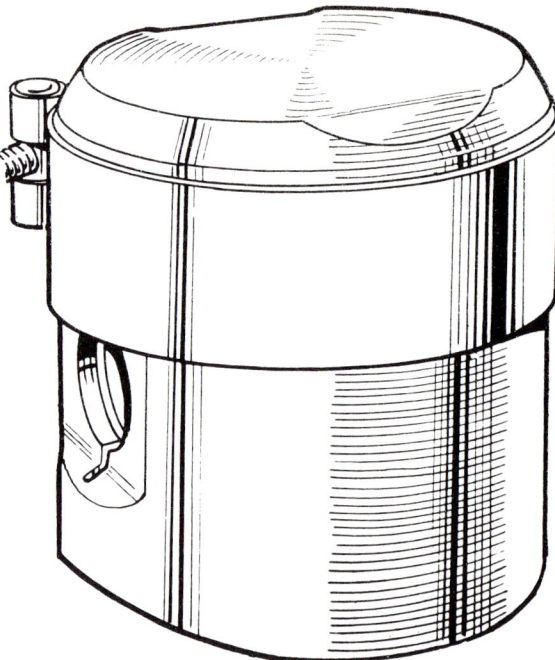

Piston clamps which really do make it easy to refit the block without breaking a ring or two

castings, spokes from wheels, seat cover from frame and so on until you are down to a single piece of metal, rubber or plastic for just about any item. Ball races and rectifiers you do not dismantle if you want them to continue living, but most assemblies will come down to individual pieces.

Once in pieces each of these has to be checked and then mended or replaced. The first operation may be as simple as running a die down a thread or as complex as metal spraying followed by grinding to a very close tolerance. Or it could be a specialist welding process plus careful freehand cutting using a flexible drive followed by a milling operation.

Replacement can be by a new spare or by an uprated part from a later machine which improves the performance. Or it can be by a modern component that does the job in a better way; tyres, shock absorbers and electronic ignition are just three examples.

After mending or replacement comes finishing when the outer coat goes onto the piece part and may be paint, plating or polish. In all cases they mirror the base material and reflect its preparation. You can then put it all together again.

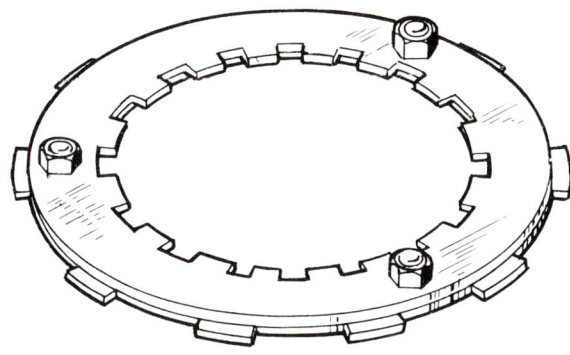

Clutch locking tool made by bolting two plates together. An inner with a handle will work better

Dismantle

There is a whole special technique to taking things apart and if you want to restore successfully you need to learn it. The first aspect is to soak things in penetrating fluid. If anything is stuck this is the opening move – and time. Let the fluid soak well in, give it another dose and come back days rather than hours later.

Try to move it. If there is any sign of a shift, you are winning; give it another soak, more time and bit by bit it will come. Rush it and it will snap.

Stubborn, well rusted nuts and bolts holding cycle parts together call for another method. If they are too far gone for further use, if they hold solid sections and if the parts are none too strong don't try to undo them. You can easily do real damage to nuts, bolts, the major parts and your fingers either with the spanners or the saw if you try that method. You won't be able to hold the fixing still to saw it so it will damage the parts.

The answer is to just do them up. For once get out the ½ in. drive socket and wind it on until it goes bang. If the bolt is largish, drill a hole up its centre first, but don't try this on bolts fixed to tapped holes – ever.

Timing cases often respond well to an impact driver, but if you go that route two rules apply. First is that the blade must fit the screw and second is to hit it good and hard. A series of taps is no use, it has to be one good blow. One of the very best motorcycle men I have known told me once that this distinguished the pro from the amateur. The latter would tap at a puller to jump a taper apart and either shift nothing or damage parts. The pro would decide it was tight, select a four pound club hammer and hit it once, good and square as direction is as important as the force behind the blow.

It always pays to think before playing the heavy hand as often parts won't part because you have not undone all you should have. Particular care is needed when dealing with castings or mouldings as both are brittle and respond in the same way if put under a bending strain. They crack. So if it's stuck check against the parts list as this may indicate a screw you have missed, either because it is hidden down a dirty counter-bore or due to it assembling from the other side to the rest of the fittings. The nut in the mouth of the A7/A10 crankcase is a classic example and leaving it in has broken many a case.

Checking

At this point you really start to find out how much work you have let yourself in for. You need to go over each part to establish if it can still be used, if it needs mending and if it needs finishing. More lists I fear.

Whether a part can still be used will depend on what it is, its material and whether it is bent, cracked, broken or badly worn. If in any or all of these conditions it will need mending or replacement. Bent parts will have to be straightened using heat and a press on occasion, cracked and broken ones may be welded and worn ones reclaimed.

It is while you are checking parts that you will find the bodges that have been done over the years to keep the machine running. Often these are the greatest problem and you are left to think that if only the owners of the past had just repaired the model your troubles would be minimal.

Sparking plug feelers and gap setting tool. You will need a full set of gauges to cover all situations

Mending

You are thus left to return parts to their original standard and it can often take all your ingenuity to deal with the past horrors. Some of the worst concern studs and threaded holes, the first often broken off in the second. Removal means making a drill bush, drilling into the stud and using an extractor to wind it out.

One thing with cover screws is that if all else fails you can drill the head off and by this means release the cover, which will expose enough screw for it to be easily removed.

Threaded holes in castings or the frame are another source of problems and thread inserts can be one solution. Normally there is enough material available to accommodate them, but for success the maker's instructions must be followed carefully.

Mending also includes getting joint faces flat. To do this all the studs will need to be removed and it is worth checking round the hole that each screws into. Often the metal will have pulled up a little so needs to be counter-sunk and then the whole surface made flat. If you have to machine it keep it to a minimum as modern gasket sealants can help a great deal in keeping oil where it should be.

Welding or heating equipment is often vital for dealing with the cycle parts that need to be warmed up before being straightened. It also allows holes to be filled up and redrilled where really needed so is very handy for some rear mudguards. It is not unknown for several sets of holes to exist for various pillion pads of the past, all long gone, so the holes need removal as well.

It is possible to take parts to a shop for welding as individual items but the need for a heat source in your own workshop may be emphasized if some assembly is out of line. Getting everything straight really can call for the parts to be in place and this makes it difficult for the job to be taken elsewhere other than to a restoration specialist.

Finishing

Once you are satisfied that a part is correct and will assemble as required then it needs to be finished. This may be as simple as a coating of oil to prevent rust for engine and gearbox parts. Or it can be a complex sequence of plating, painting and lining for a tank.

Castings may be bead blasted or polished, cycle parts are mainly painted, details are plated and in many cases parts will need to be masked to protect threads and holes.

The specialist electrical assemblies and others of the same delicacy all go through their own special processes as detailed later, but their basic mechanics may need the same mending and finishing as everything else.

Then all you have to do is to put it all together again.

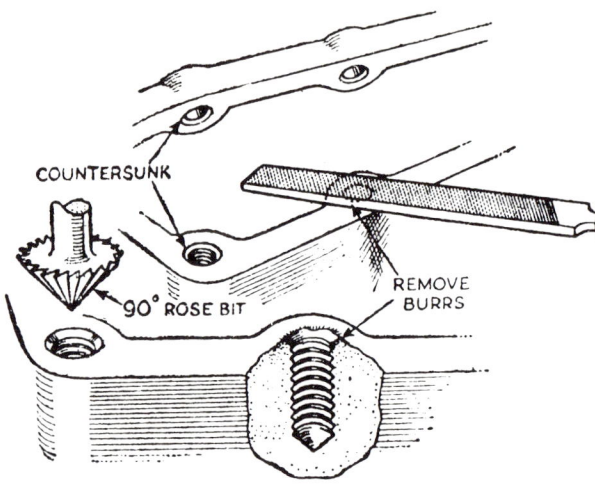

ABOVE *All machines need the casting holes cleaned up to prevent oil leaks. Same problem, same solution, common drawing*

Aiming point for the concours class. A 1950 A10 shined up for sale to the Persian Gulf

Note

From now on I will assume you are either starting from a complete machine or have loosely hung your basket job together and have collected most of the major parts needed. This is to avoid needless repetition of this assumption together with the notes relevant to it and already mentioned.

3 The engine

Most people start with the engine because it is of the greatest interest to them, and it is also likely to be the easiest area to restore.

The exact procedure you follow will depend on whether you have a unit or pre-unit model and on your working style. The first job is to take the engine, or engine unit, out of the frame and then to dismantle it. Before removing it a decision needs to be made about the large, tight nuts that are used in various places.

The purist approach to large nuts is to use a suitable tool to hold the part they are attached to and undo them. However this can be a problem in the number of special tools that may be needed and it may govern the sequence of operations.

At this stage all that is needed is for the nuts to be loosened and common practice is to do this with the engine in the frame and connected to the rear wheel and brake. With the machine in top gear, each nut is attacked in turn starting at the engine and working through the transmission to the rear wheel. A combination of jammed-on brake and clouted spanner will usually prevail unless the clutch slips.

This method means that the timing cover has to come off at what is really too early a stage in order that the internal nuts can be slackened. The alternatives are less messy in their approach and enable parts to be dealt with as desired. The first is to use tools to hold parts still and a further option, given the equipment, is to use an impact spanner. If you do go that latter route do ensure that all the parts will take the shock.

Engine types

BSA engines divide into three basic forms, these being semi-unit, pre-unit, and unit construction and all were built in two capacities plus a third right at the end. The semi-unit type dates from 1947 in the 500 cc size and 1950 for the 650 cc, which ran on to 1957. From 1954 the pre-unit style, in pivoted fork frame, began to appear and continued in both touring and sports form in both capacities, the 500 to 1962 and the 650 to a year later.

Unit construction came in 1962 in both sizes and developed into a range of models in the mid-1960s. It shrank again when the oil-in-frame models were launched in 1971 to contain only 650 cc machines and for 1972 these came down to two road versions plus another with the engine stretched to 750 cc.

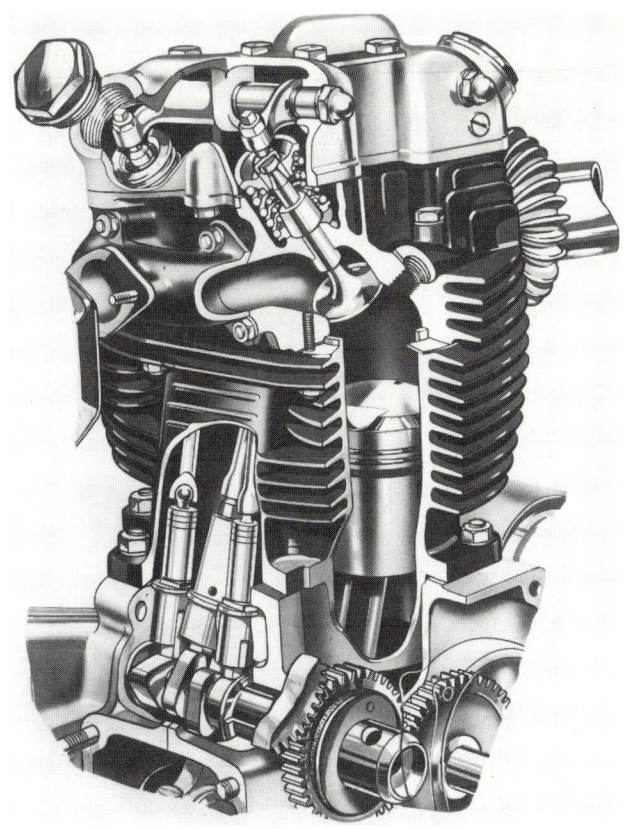

ABOVE *Cutaway drawing of the 1947 A7 engine top half showing original tappet housings and use of rocker box caps*

BELOW *1947 A7 engine drive side. Note magneto cut-out button on end cap and mileometer rewind knob under tank*

BSA TWIN RESTORATION

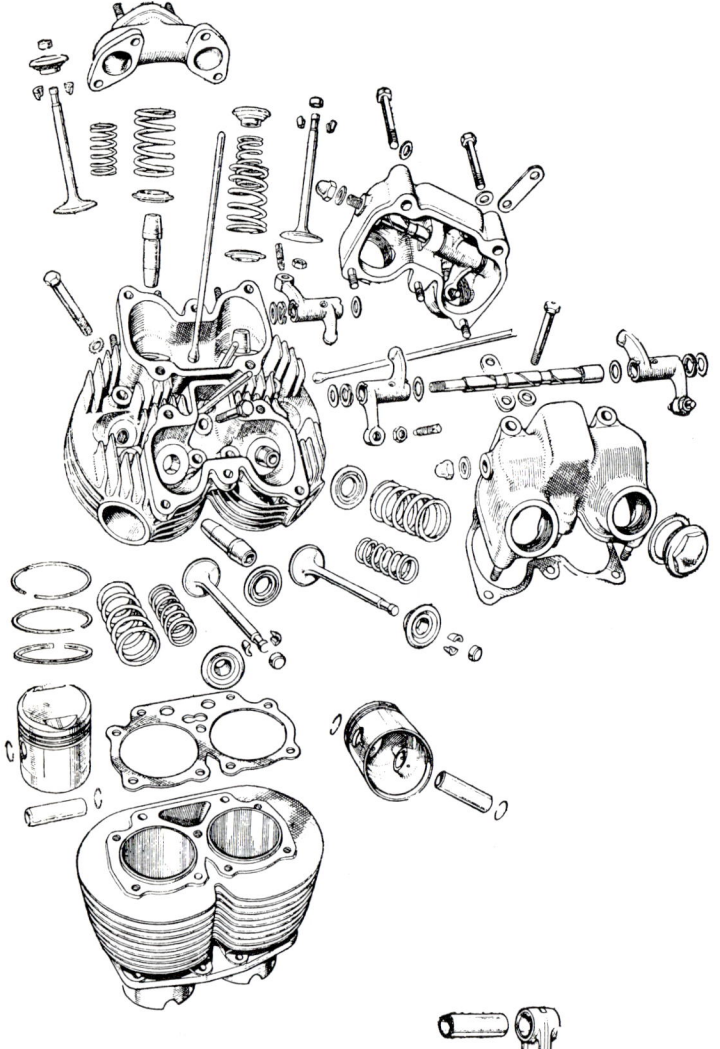

Exploded drawing of the early A7 showing the original crankshaft design with one piece rods

By 1973 BSA had gone and although a parts list exists for a Thunderbolt T65 for that year it is in fact a Triumph with the name on the tank changed.

All BSA twin engines share many common features with a single gear-driven camshaft mounted high at the rear of the crankcase, oil pump skew driven by the crankshaft and a common line, especially for the earlier ones. Variations concerned the electrics and many detail points.

Removing the engine

The procedure depends on the basic engine type and your lifting strength. The unit engines and semi-unit with gearbox weigh about 130 lb so complete removal is really a job for two or entails the use of some form of lifting tackle. The pre-unit engine is lighter and will come out by itself or complete with gearbox, but the latter is a two-man job and the former a struggle for one.

For many the solution is to take off some of the heavier items while the engine is still in the frame. It is easy enough to remove the top half of the engine, the primary transmission and the gearbox internals; this reduces the weight to manageable proportions. Of course, you will have to reverse the procedure on assembly, which may not be quite so tidy as building complete units on the bench.

Whichever way you go, start by draining the oil from both the tank and the sump. Then replace the sump plate as you are bound to stand the engine on it. Also drain the primary chaincase and gearbox while you have the trays to hand. During your first steps you should have detached the control cables and wiring, if you have not then now is the time to do so.

The external oil pipes can come off with the main

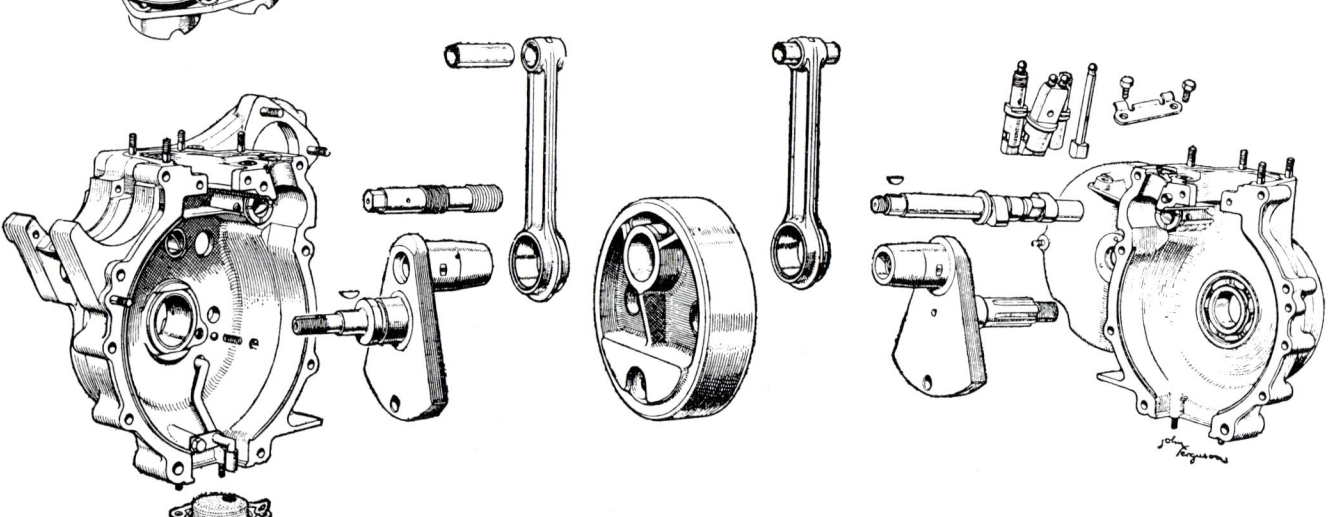

THE ENGINE

ones being the connections between oil tank and engine. Also remove the rather small pipe that feeds the rocker gear and take care when undoing the banjo bolts that hold it to the rocker box. It is all too easy to find that the bolt has stuck to the pipe union and is carrying it round with it, which puts a nasty kink in the pipe. You must hold the union to prevent this. Store the pipe with care so it does not get distorted.

You will have already removed the exhaust pipes and silencers so can now take off the footrests and rear brake pedal.

The primary transmission is the next area on pre-unit engines unless you are removing everything as one lump. With the outer case off you can undo the engine sprocket nut using a C spanner and jarring it undone. The clutch spring nuts vary in type and their removal releases the clutch plates. You then have to undo the clutch centre nut, and to hold the centre still will either have to rely on the rear brake, use an old clutch plate with handle attached, or lock the clutch centre and drum together with a plate of each type bolted to one another. You can use a piece of bent steel strip to form a scotch but this is not recommended as it puts all the load in one place.

Having got the nut off the shaft you can remove the centre and drum to just leave the hub. This is threaded and an extractor is the best means of removing it. Use it, rather than a hammer, to break the taper.

Remove the inner chaincase and make a note of any distance tube behind it on the pre-unit models. There is usually one and if you leave it out you can easily crack the case on assembly. Also check it is the correct length and does fit the space it should.

You are now ready for the big heave. Remove the engine torque stays, slacken all the fixing bolts and studs, slide out all the minor ones and then support the engine weight with either a box or a jack. Pull out the remaining bolts in turn to remove all the distance pieces and note their position. A diagram and their length will help. Then pull the bolts and take the engine out. Note that with the early rigid frames this may allow the frame halves to move a little so watch out for this as it may stop the studs coming out. If necessary arrange for the weight to be taken by another jack or hung from a girder in the roof.

Pre-unit dismantling

Hold the engine in the vice by its front mountings and add a support at the rear if this is needed. Make quite certain it is really secure and the unit is held firmly. You can now take it apart, but don't rush it and do observe as you go. It is well worth checking the valve timing before you remove anything in case the markings are missing or the assembly wrong. Use a degree disc clamped to the drive shaft, set the valve gaps as prescribed and make your notes. Also check the ignition timing on full advance and retard while you have the disc in place.

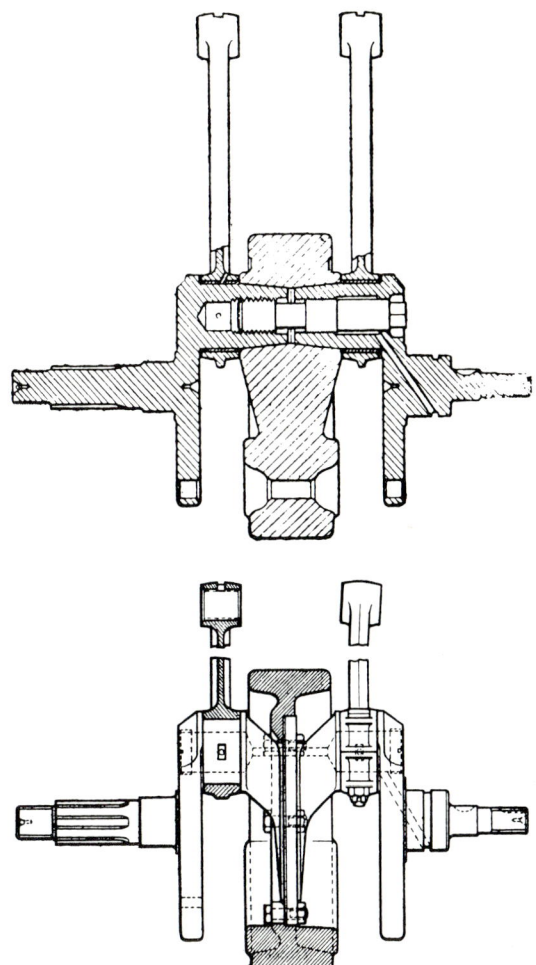

Cross-section of original crankshaft and the replacement forged in one piece with bolted on flywheel

The engine will come apart easily enough and on anything unknown the golden rule is to check everything, assume nothing and take it all apart. It may seem less trouble to leave a crankshaft in, but only full examination will show if it is really fit or just on the point of failure because the sludge trap is full.

Start at the top and remove the rocker box lids and then the rocker box, remembering that at least one valve is open and could be leaning on it. Turn the engine to minimize this effect and collect the pushrods once the box is off.

Next remove the remaining head bolts, which will release the cylinder head, and note which way up the gasket is. Leave the head assembled for the time being as it and the rocker box reduce to a good few parts, many small and easily lost.

Undo the cylinder block nuts, run the pistons up to top dead centre, give the block a sharp blow with a rubber mallet to break the joint and lift. Pack rag in the gap to catch debris and protect both rods and pistons. Lift off block and gasket.

BSA TWIN RESTORATION

BELOW *The A10 engine shown exploded and in its early form with bolted on gearbox*

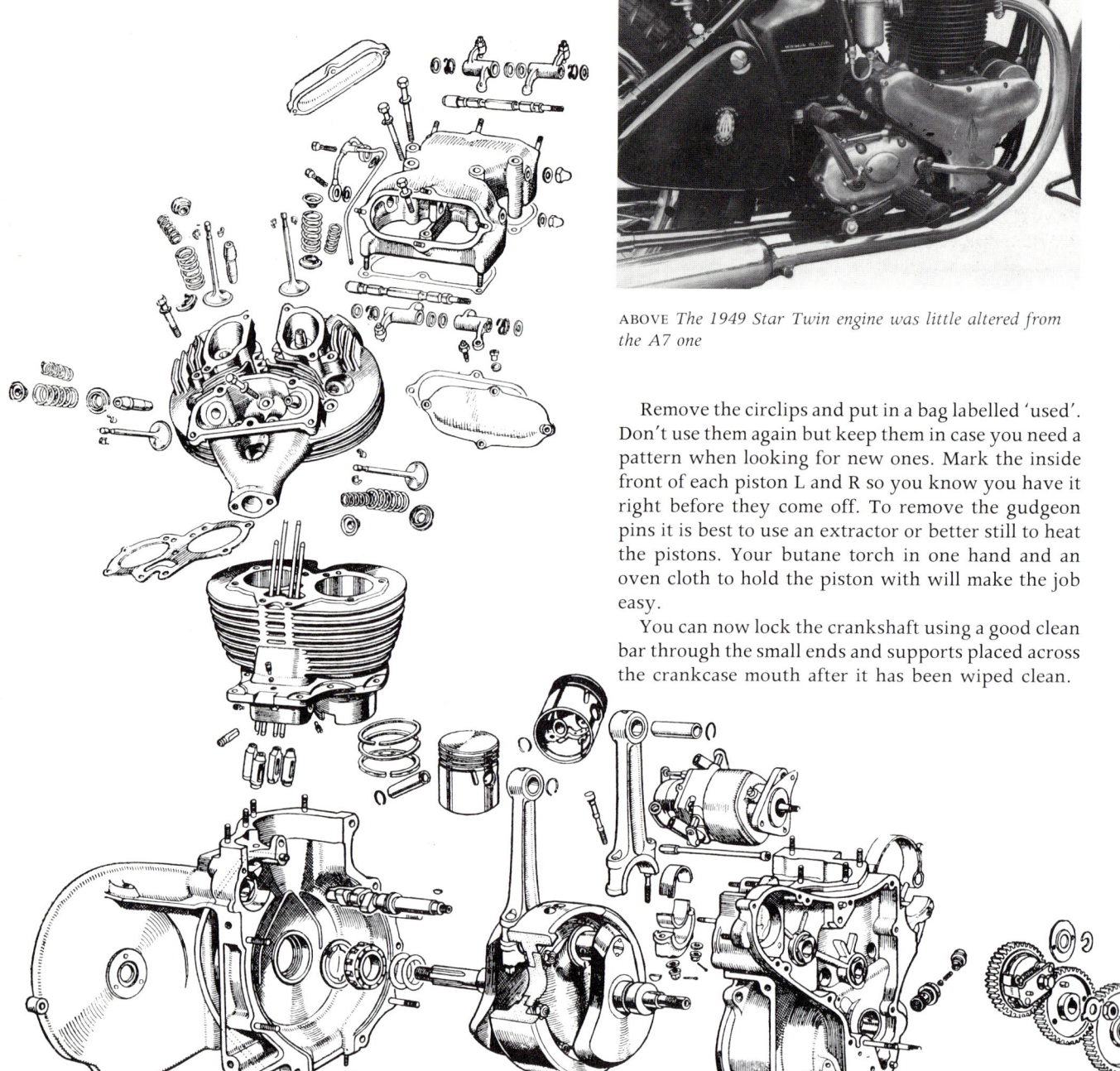

ABOVE *The 1949 Star Twin engine was little altered from the A7 one*

Remove the circlips and put in a bag labelled 'used'. Don't use them again but keep them in case you need a pattern when looking for new ones. Mark the inside front of each piston L and R so you know you have it right before they come off. To remove the gudgeon pins it is best to use an extractor or better still to heat the pistons. Your butane torch in one hand and an oven cloth to hold the piston with will make the job easy.

You can now lock the crankshaft using a good clean bar through the small ends and supports placed across the crankcase mouth after it has been wiped clean.

THE ENGINE

The A10, in 1951, which was much as the first A7 but represented a major detail design change

Drive side of the 1951 A10 engine with handsome chaincase

The outer timing cover is next followed by the dynamo chain and its two sprockets. This will allow the inner cover to be removed, but all cover screws may need an impact driver to release them. As the inner cover comes away hold the idler gear in place and don't let the breather fall out. Check the gears for the alignment of their dot and dash marks, after which they can be removed.

The magneto gear is self extracting when auto-advance is used but the manual ones need a threaded puller. DON'T hammer the magneto armature unless you have plenty of money. The camshaft gear has two tapped holes for a puller and something can readily be devised from the scrap box for this one but not the magneto.

The idler just comes away, but before the crankshaft pinion can be removed the oil pump gear needs to come off. This is screwed onto the shaft with a left-hand thread and retained by a lock washer. It is also an odd size across flats at 20 mm (but measure yours to be sure) and you may find a $\frac{25}{32}$ in. A/F socket will also fit if you have one. Only use a $\frac{1}{2}$ in. drive socket on this one as an open-ended one could do damage. Any other size could cost more than the tool.

Also remove the oil pump and note the washer under the third stud. Leave it out on assembly and you could damage the pump by bending the drive spindle housing. Prise the gear off; this may need a puller. Remove the dynamo and all its clamps if still in place, also the magneto.

You are now ready to split the cases. Start by removing the single nut in the case mouth. Many don't and fracture the casting. Next remove the sump plate and filter and then all the other studs and bolts. Split the cases apart and lift out crankshaft and camshaft.

You now have the major parts ready for your attention.

Semi-unit dismantling

This varies from the pre-unit in that the gearbox must be removed before the crankcase can be split and to do this the whole of the primary transmission must first come off. In addition, the early A7 engines as built up to 1950 had a number of variations from the later types although a good few parts remained common. Changes that affected dismantling were two separate rocker boxes with two valve caps in each, the tappets, which

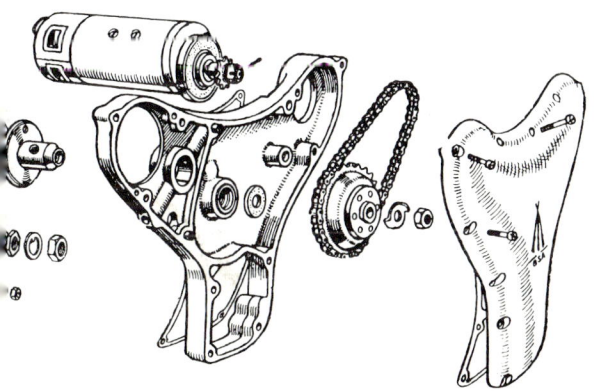

41

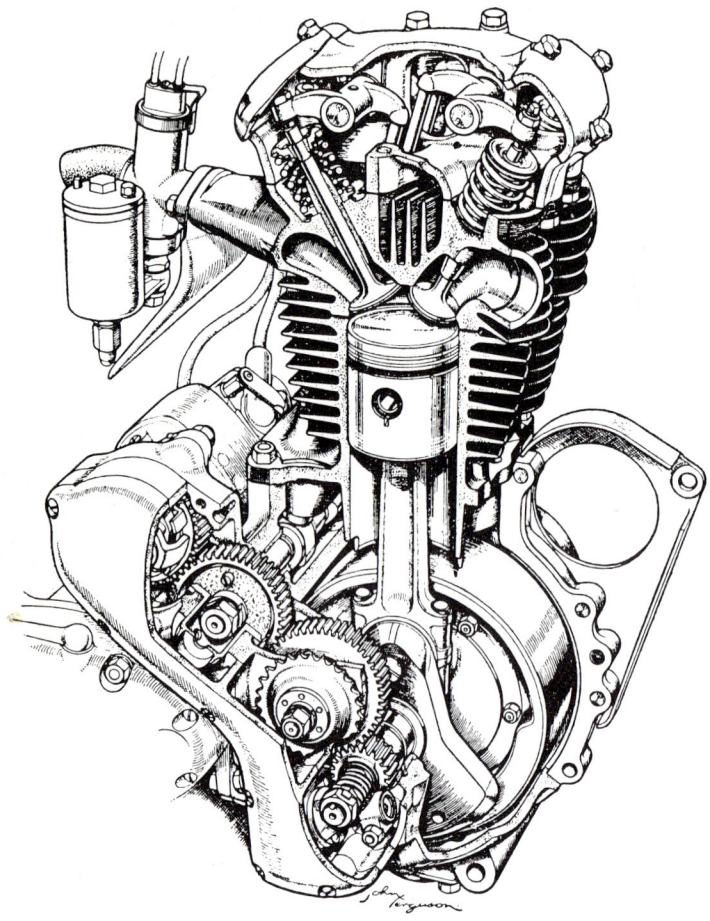

ABOVE *The A10 engine showing its basic design that remained for all twins*

BELOW *The A7 power unit in 1951 when it adopted many of the A10 parts and detail design. Dynamo is clamped to the front of the crankcase*

were clamped in the crankcase rather than the block, and, most important, the centre head bolt. This bolt is inclined at a small angle and thus MUST come out before any of the others are removed. It also must go back last. Note also that there were two studs at the rear of the head with nuts between the block fins.

Unit engine dismantling

In the main the unit engine comes apart in the same way as the pre-unit engine without the gearbox intruding to any real extent. In essence it is carried within the right crankcase half as a unit but cannot be fully removed until the clutch is off.

The main change in construction comes from the electrics, with all models being fitted with an alternator within the primary chaincase. The ignition system was by coil and points and the points plate was mounted in the timing cover and the cam driven by the timing idler gear. Removal of the auto-advance is by using a bolt screwed into the cam spindle and an impact puller on that if it fails to extract the mechanism as it should.

The timing side is as before with gear-driven camshaft but less the dynamo drive.

Aside from the presence of the gearbox, whose large nuts should have been slackened, and the ignition electrics, the engine can come down much as a semi-unit.

Detail changes were to the breather, tappets, and valve gear. The breather became a timed disc at the left end of the camshaft and the tappets located against each other in the block with simple circlips to hold them. The rockers went on spindles mounted in supports cast into the head so only a simple lid was needed to enclose them.

Thus the engine comes down much as the others as regards the top half and the timing side. Removal of the primary transmission allows the gearbox to come out, although it could remain as long as the clutch is off. The crankcase again has a fixing nut in its mouth which must be removed along with all the others before the cases are split as before.

Again the major and minor parts await your attention.

Crankshaft

The first 500 A7 models were fitted with a special two-part crankshaft with one-piece connecting rods. The crankpins of the two halves fitted into the central flywheel and were clamped into tapers by a through bolt with two different threads cut on it. In the nearside it was 12 tpi and in the off 20 tpi was used. Assembly was aided by an alignment bar and holes in each part and began by screwing the bolt into the offside half until the head stood out from the cheek by 0.50/0.515 in. From this point it had to pick up the nearside thread and of course advanced into that at a faster rate by 0.033 in. per turn.

THE ENGINE

It worked well, but BSA only used it up to engine XA7-600 and then changed to a more conventional design with split rods. A few of the built-up crankshafts went out also with split rods just before the changeover. All assemblies interchanged so few of the original ones can now exist.

From then on all BSA twins used a one-piece crankshaft with the crankpins at 360 degrees and a bolted-on flywheel. The method of fixing the flywheel changed once, but at first was by six nuts and bolts on the shaft axis, which held it in place after it had been pressed onto its central locating diameter.

For Road Rocket engines and the A10 from 1958 the bolts were reduced in number to three and fitted radially. This form of construction was used for all unit engines. All engines had plain big ends with replaceable shells and crankshafts turned in a plain timing-side main bearing and a ball or roller drive-side one. In all cases mark and note exactly how the parts are assembled and then remove the connecting rods.

The crankpins must be inspected for wear and damage. It is feasible to remove light scores, marks and even surface rust with fine emery cloth, but if they are worn they will need regrinding. A micrometer or vernier is an essential here, but some idea of the degree of ovality can be obtained using callipers and feeler gauges to detect variations.

If the crankpins need grinding the reduction in diameter was in 0.010 in. steps from the nominal to a maximum of 0.030 in. The finish and end radii are important and have a bearing on big end life and crankshaft reliability.

The mainshafts also need to be inspected as they must be a good fit in the main bearings and their threads must be in good condition. If there is any sign of trouble its cause must be located and remedied. At the same time check the main bearing journal surface in the same way as the crankpins. If worn or damaged it may be ground down 0.010 in. and an undersized bush fitted.

If the journals have already been taken down as much as is permitted then they will have to be built up by metal spray and then ground to standard size. Metal spraying is a process where minute metal particles are heated and directed onto the hot surface of the parent part so they fuse to it. The process requires special equipment and a degree of skill to achieve the right result but it can save parts otherwise damaged beyond repair.

On all crankshafts you MUST clean out the sludge trap and make sure that all oilways are unimpeded from entry to exit. Once assembled all crankshafts should be primed with oil to make sure there is no obstruction to its flow to the crankpin.

1955 Shooting Star A7 with light alloy cylinder head and separate inlet manifold

ABOVE *The Star Twin version of the A7 in 1952. Appearance very much as the touring model with just the single Amal*

Six-bolt crankshafts

There are three types of these and the first was used in the A7 from 1947 to 1950. Its stroke was 82 mm and a sludge trap was formed in each side and closed off by a plug. A small hole connected the two cavities to allow the oil to reach the drive-side crankpin.

This was joined in 1950 by the A10 type, which had an 84 mm stroke and remained in use up to 1957. It turned in a different drive-side main with a 30 mm bore rather than the 1.125 in. of the early A7.

The third type was that used by the A7 from 1951 to 1962 with the stroke reduced to 72.6 mm. It also went into the sports versions, the early Star Twin and later Shooting Star, and continued to have two sludge trap plugs.

On all these assemblies the flywheel is held in place by high-tensile bolts and after the nuts have been tightened they should be peined over to lock them. Pessimists can use Loctite as well.

Once assembled, prime the crankshaft with oil.

Three-bolt crankshafts

This type first appeared on the Road Rocket and was adopted by the A10 from 1958. It differed from the earlier design in that the flywheel was a tight fit on the centre crankshaft web and was locked to it by three radial bolts.

The sludge trap became a single good-sized hole across the crankpins and was sealed at each end by a plug. That on the drive side had a small spigot onto which the sludge trap tube located as for most of its length it was smaller than the hole it went in. It swelled out to fit the hole on the timing side to form an annulus and the oil thus flowed into the tube and then into the annulus via a pair of holes. These were drilled to be in the side closest to the crankshaft axis so that any dirt present would be centrifuged away from them. The tube was located in this rotational position as well as axially by an extension spigot formed on one of the flywheel securing bolts.

The oil tube sludge trap must be cleaned out in all cases and all the oilways checked for free oil flow. To remove the trap drill out the locking punch mark and unscrew the plug using an impact driver. Remove the flywheel bolt which located into the tube, fish out the tube with a wire hook and clean everything to perfection. Unless the flywheel has to come off the bolt can go back and locate the tube, but otherwise leave off, remove the other two and press the flywheel off after marking it.

Renovate the crankshaft as for the early pre-unit and reassemble. The flywheel has to be heated to get it to fit and 80 degrees Celsius should do the trick. Wear oven gloves to handle it and remember that it will stay warm for ages. Make sure all three bolts go in properly and then fit each using Loctite and torque up. Dispense with any washers as Loctite will be fine. If you have to replace the bolts remember that they

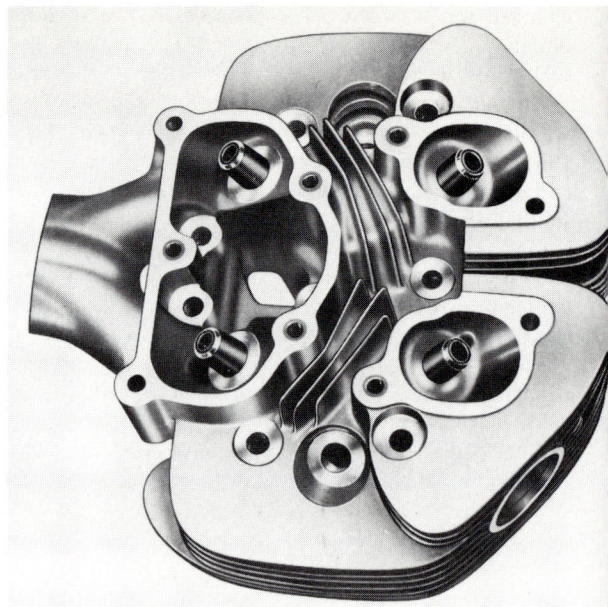

The alloy head used by the Super Rocket from 1958 on

Powerhouse of the 1956 Road Rocket with TT carburettor and light alloy cylinder head

changed for 1963 and the A70 used different ones. Finally, refit the plug using jointing compound to seal it and lock by centre punching.

The A10 type continued with the 84 mm stroke and was joined by a 74 mm version for the A50 and A65 in 1962. In 1965 the design was modified for the off-road and sporting models such as the Cyclone and Hornet so that the drive-side plug lost its spigot and the sludge trap tube was altered.

This crankshaft changed again for 1966, when the sludge trap became a blind hole with a single plug on the timing side. This was the one used on the drive side in 1965 and the tube was also that used in the previous year. A further alteration for 1966 that affected the crankshaft was a change to a roller drive-side main and the introduction of a thrust washer between the crankshaft and the timing-side bush. With that the A50 and A65 models ran on to 1972 and their end. That final year saw the A70 make its brief appearance with an 85 mm stroke for its crankshaft.

The A50 and A65 began with a common flywheel, but this soon changed, with the original staying on the 650 and a new one appearing on the 500. Both changed for 1966, when they gained a timing notch, and again in 1969, when this became a hole. For 1970 the 650 wheel was modified and for 1971 it was lightened and cut away around part of the periphery on the crankpin side. The A70 had its own flywheel.

The three-bolt crankshaft with its sludge trap held by two plugs. Used by 650 cc models only

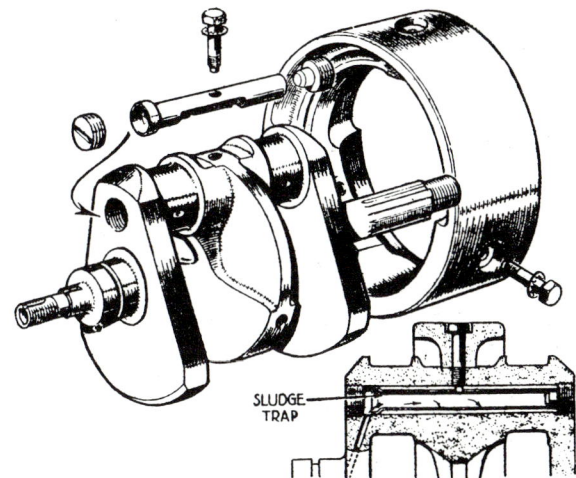

BELOW *1957 Shooting Star with manifold cast with head and usual drip shield over magneto*

Connecting rods

Most BSA rods were forged in light alloy with separate caps and shell big end bearings. Exceptions were those fitted to the A7 models from 1947 to 1950, which were steel stampings.

All connecting rods must be carefully handled at all times and not allowed to knock against other items. This includes the crankcase mouth when working on the engine. All must be carefully inspected for any signs of damage, which should be polished out. The rods may also be inspected for alignment if there is any chance they are out. If there is any doubt about a rod it should not be used; a snapped rod will totally wreck an engine and is not worth the risk.

For repair the normal practice is to fit undersize shells after grinding the crankpins and for most years these were offered in three sizes.

It is good practice to renew the rod bolts even on the cooking engines and mandatory on the sports ones. If you do intend to use the existing bolts check them with care for any signs of stretching or thread distortion. In all cases fit new nuts. Those should be done up evenly and in steps to the torque figure, which must not be exceeded for the alloy rods. Do not do the steel rod ones up to stretch the bolts beyond their yield point.

Rod types

The first few A7 engines with the built-up crankshaft had one-piece rods, after which a single steel rod was used from 1947 to 1950. Alloy rods were first used for the A10 in 1950 and in the A7 from 1951. The A10 rod centre distance is 6.469 in. and that of the A7 rod is 6.00 in. During 1951 the left rod was modified with an oil hole drilled in it to encourage oil flow to its big end and the discharge was directed at the left cylinder. To allow the oil to escape the upper big end shell was drilled, so for some years a set of shells included this one odd one. Although the rods differed the shells were the same for both engine sizes and the undrilled one was that used from 1947.

It went in 1954, when the drilled one was used in all four positions and a new pair of rods appeared for both the two 500s and the A10. When the Road Rocket was introduced it was fitted with its own pair of rods and big end shells, although it retained the A10 rod centre distance.

The 500 cc models remained unchanged to 1962 as did the Rocket 650 cc engines. The A10 adopted the Rocket rods in 1958 and both changed to a new type of big end shell the same year.

The introduction of the unit construction engines in 1962 meant a new rod of 6.00 in. centres. The left one was modified in 1966 but otherwise there was no change until 1970, when a new pair of the same centre distance were introduced. The A70 had its own special rods, again of 6.00 in. centres, and also its own big end shells. All the other unit engines used the same shells

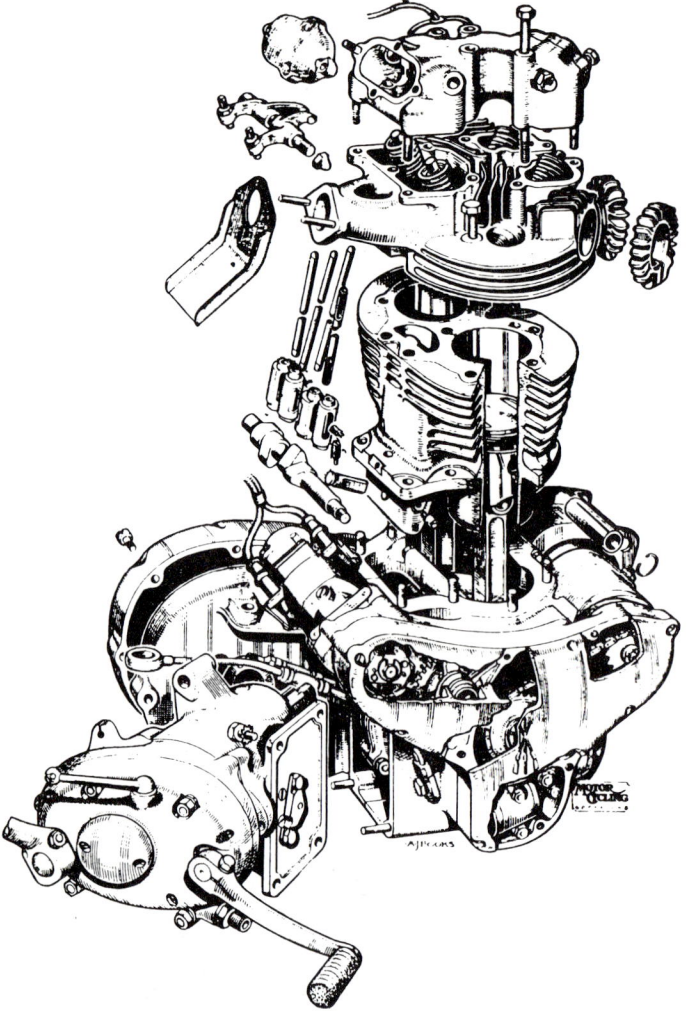

ABOVE *Line drawing of A10 engine with bolted on gearbox as used by the plunger framed models to the end of 1957*

BELOW *The Road Rocket in 1957 with rev-counter drive taken from the magneto gear nut*

THE ENGINE

as fitted to the pre-unit 650s from 1958 on.

The connecting rod bolts used in the A7 from 1947 to 1950 had castellated nuts locked with split pins. The advent of the alloy rods saw this practice continue with revised parts plus a washer under the nut to spread the load. One or other may need filing to get the pin hole to align and this has to be the method to use to ensure a correct torque setting.

The bolts changed again for 1954 and the Rocket engine had its own but used the same nut and washer. In 1958 the A10 changed to the Rocket bolt and for 1960 new bolts were introduced for both 500 and 650 cc engines. That used by the 650 went into the unit engines and was used by all models except the A70 in 1972 which had its own special bolts.

ABOVE *Touring A7 in 1958 with revised hubs, brakes and front fork nacelle*

Small end bush

There were essentially three bush types used in BSA twins. The first went in the A7 from 1947 to 1950 and the second from 1951 to 1962. The third was used by the A10 and all unit engines except for 1958–59, when an alternative was fitted.

If worn they can be pressed out using a new bush but line the oil hole up first. Then ream to give a nice slide fit on the pin. Avoid reaming by hand if possible as a guided machine reamer will do a much better job. Check the oil holes again and put to use.

Pistons

Before worrying about the condition of the pistons you should see if the block needs boring as if it does you will fit new ones anyway. If you plan to keep the existing ones they do need to be closely inspected. They must be examined for cracks in the skirt or around the gudgeon pin bosses, while the ring grooves must be in good condition as must be the pin holes and circlip grooves.

There are a number of pistons that were available for each engine size and while many remained constant during their production line the existence of options means that a check should be made if there is any doubt. Check the compression ratio by measuring the combustion chamber volume and doing a small sum. Also compare the valve head diameters with the cutaways in the piston crown to see if they are compatible as this may provide further evidence.

Due to the variety of pistons used they have been listed in an appendix with the nominal compression ratio they gave and their years of use. Most were available around the same time as an option for other models and nearly all could be obtained in a range of oversizes.

If you replace the piston use a quality make and keep to the standard compression ratio for your model. Any attempt to raise this could bring a major disaster in its train as the middle-aged or old engine objects to the added loads. Should you find yourself with a sports engine fitted with the touring cast-iron

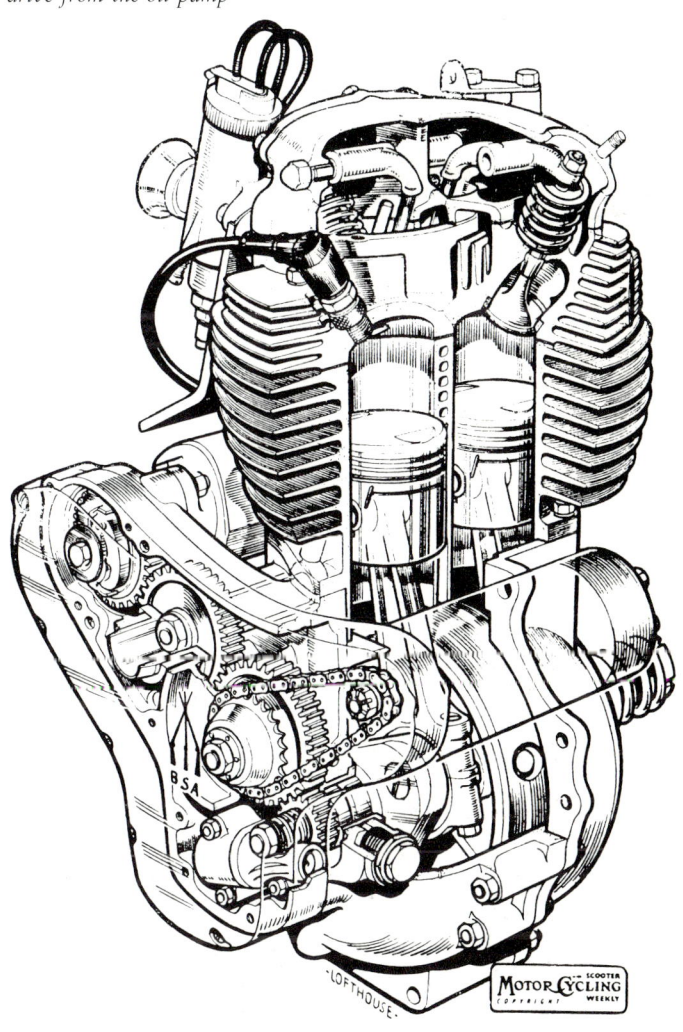

BELOW *Line drawing of the 650 cc engine in its 1960 touring form with auto-ignition advance and no counter drive from the oil pump*

Unit construction engine in its early 1962 form with star badge on points cover. This soon vanished

cylinder head go for the touring pistons otherwise the engine will overheat.

If you keep the existing pistons except to renew the rings, in which case you may need to remove the glaze from the bores with a specialist tool or medium to coarse emery cloth. Check the gaps on the new rings and do fit the taper ones the right way up or you will have a plug oiling problem.

The original A7 gudgeon pin was only used from 1947 to 1950 and then changed to a type fitted up to 1962. The A10 had just one pin type and this continued in use in all unit 650s from 1962 to 1972. The 500 cc unit engine had its own pin type. Only two types of circlips were used, one for the 500 cc pre-unit engines from 1947 to 1962 and the other for all 650s and all unit engines of all sizes.

The pins should be checked for ridges and changed if not in really good condition. The clips you change as a matter of course.

Cylinder block

This needs to be checked for damage and wear as either may have occurred. Damage may be to the fins, the top and bottom mating surfaces or to the threads. Wear occurs in the bore. From 1950 on the tappet housings became parts of the block and must also be inspected. Finally the block may need to be finished to restore its appearance.

Damaged or broken fins may be repaired by welding or brazing but it is not easy to get back to the original appearance. If you have the broken part this will help but it is a tricky job to do. If a middle fin has gone you may have to cut others away first and then refix them once the broken one is fixed. Be careful about heating the block and let it cool slowly. Do all this work before any rebore or machining that may be needed.

Check the gasket surfaces for burrs and distortion. At the base these may only cause an oil leak but at the top could lead to a blown gasket, which could mean burn damage to both head and barrel. If extensive it may need machining to clean up but this must be kept to a minimum. However, it must be done or the trouble will reoccur. If high compression pistons are fitted it may be prudent to check the piston to valve clearance when you assemble the engine.

All blocks have tapped holes in their top surface. These should be inspected to ensure that the theads are in good condition and not pulling up around the holes. If they are they must be machined flat, the holes lightly countersunk and the threads cleaned up.

Bore wear is best checked with a Mercer gauge, which will provide exact measurements. An idea of the position can be gained by feeling the wear ridge at the top of the bore, but judgement as well as an oily finger is needed. Alternative methods if you don't possess a Mercer or an internal micrometer are available. One is to use an internal bore gauge, which can be set to the unworn diameter at the bottom of the bore and used with feelers to find the wear at the top. Internal calipers can do the same job but a more delicate touch is needed to get accurate results without measuring caliper spring. More homespun techniques are to use the piston and measure the skirt clearance at several points, or a piston ring and check its gap in the same way.

If the bore is worn it will have to be bored and before this is done two other points need attention. First you must establish whether it is on standard or oversize at the moment. This will indicate what you have to go out to. Second you *must* get the new pistons before having the bores machined in case there is a supply problem.

All blocks can be taken out to plus 0.040 in. but no further or there is a chance that they will be weakened. A liner can be fitted to get back to the standard dimension and start all over again.

Finishing

When the block is mechanically fit for use it needs to be finished. This process will have begun with the cleaning it received before work began but this now needs to be completed. The block will need to be masked and sand blasted to get all the dirt out of the crevices between the fins.

It then needs to be painted black and stove enamelling is to be preferred to get the tough finish needed. An alternative is a modern air-drying paint,

RIGHT *Drawing of the unit engine which shows the A10 ancestry of the mechanics*

THE ENGINE

but to get between the fins a spray gun is needed. A trick that sometimes works is to use a piece of felt, stiffened with wire, but a brush is most awkward to use for this job so is best forgotten.

Let the paint dry fully and then remove the masking and check carefully for blasting grit in all holes. If you have masked properly there won't be any, but make certain.

Block types

The first check in determining which block you are holding is the bore size. The standard figure for the early A7 up to 1950 was 62 mm, after which it became 66. All A10 models were 70 mm, the A50 series, 65.5 mm and the A65 was 75 mm. The A70 retained the A65 bore. In addition to the standard BSA blocks Devimead have produced their own Jumbo one with

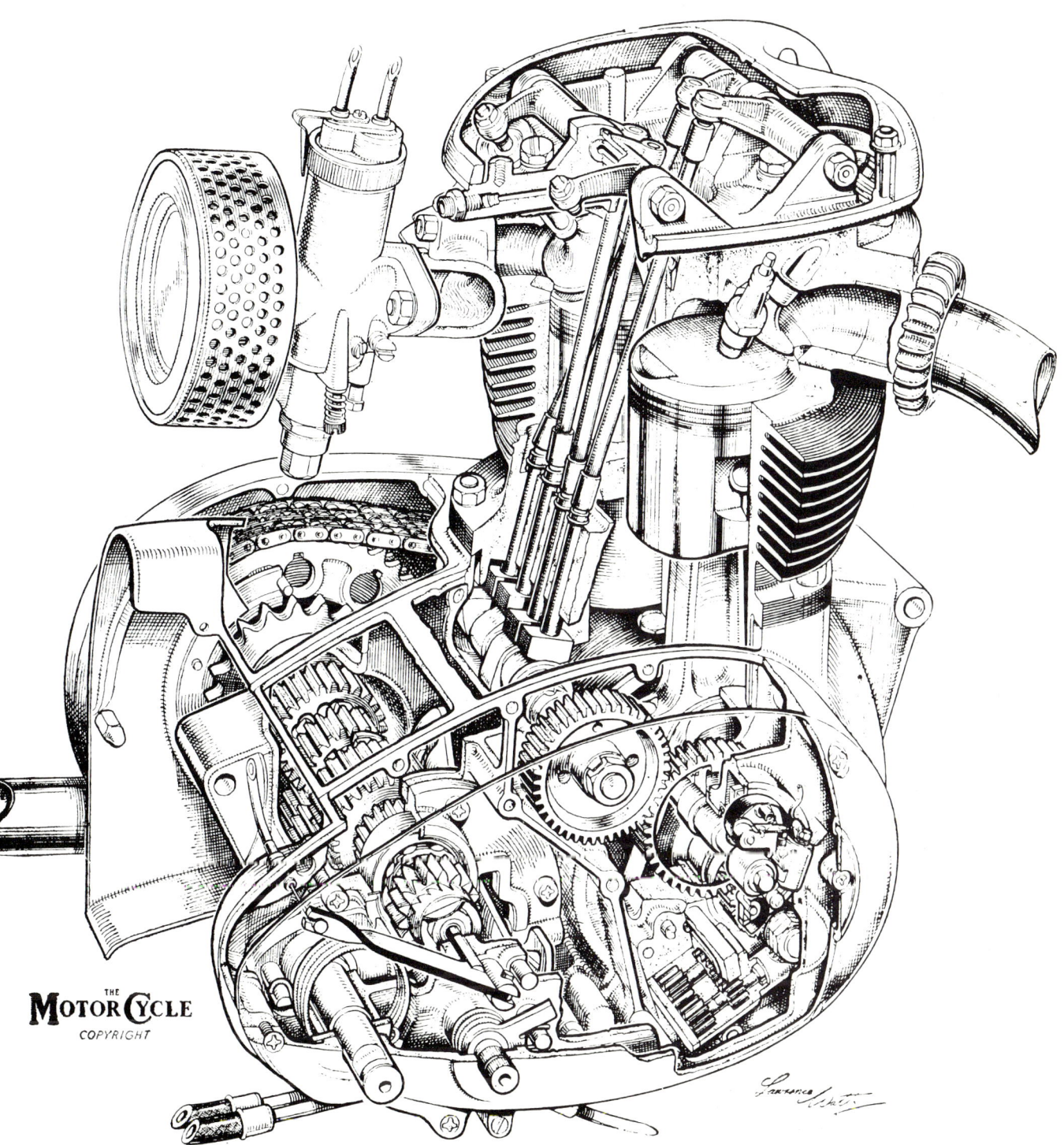

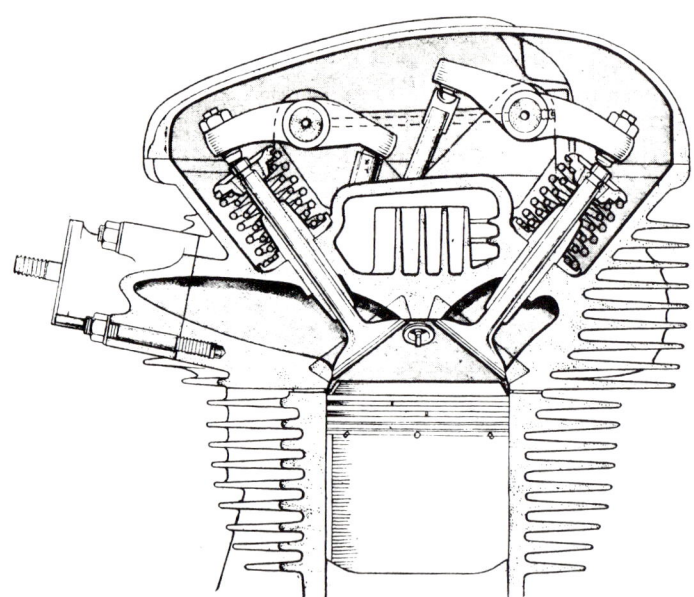

ABOVE *1964 Lightning Rocket A65LR for the USA with small tank and high bars*

LEFT *Cross-section of the unit engine head showing valves and rocker gear*

BELOW *The hot Spitfire engine in 1966 when it was built in MkII form with twin GP carburettors*

79.5 mm bore which takes the capacity out to 735 cc. With the A70 crank as well it is possible to get up to 844 cc on the standard bore and 854 on maximum oversize.

The early (up to 1950) A7 blocks also differ in not including the tappet guides, which were fitted into the crankcase. All other blocks were cast with the tappet housing at the rear beneath the mounting face. Blocks of this type were introduced for the A10 in 1950 and A7 in 1951 with both changing for 1954 to increase the fin area. Due to this the top fin gained a pair of notches in its front edge to allow the exhaust pipes to clear of it.

The A7 block was unchanged from then to 1962 and also went on the Shooting Star. The advent of the Road Rocket brought a new 650 block with the base flange thickened by $\frac{1}{8}$ in. to $\frac{1}{2}$ in. This went onto the A10 for 1958 and continued on all the larger twins to 1963.

New barrels were cast for both the A50 and A65 and these were modified in 1968, when a solid copper head gasket was adopted. They changed again for 1970, when the fixing studs increased in diameter from $\frac{5}{16}$ in. to $\frac{3}{8}$ in. and the 650 block was altered in detail for 1971. The same block went onto the A70.

Tappet guides

These were only used on the A7 engine up to 1950 as after then the tappets worked directly in the cylinder block. They seldom wear to any extent and an idea as to their condition can be found by rocking the tappet and measuring that for wear.

The central exhaust guide is clamped between the two crankcase halves and can be removed by slackening the upper case fixings. The separate inlet guides are a press fit in the case and should be removed with care using a puller rather than a hammer to avoid breakages.

Assembly is a reversal of dismantling and before the case halves are finally bolted up the guides should be aligned across the case with a rule. They are then locked by a plate.

All parts remained the same from 1947 to 1950.

Cylinder head

You may find this a victim of misguided enthusiasm with valve seats cut back due to years of keen but unnecessary valve grinding. Each owner may have done this 'to put the sparkle back' with the result that the valve heads are now well masked. The only answer will be an insert – a job for a specialist.

The first job with the head is to remove the valves and clean it thoroughly. If iron this can be done using a caustic soda solution, but *never* use this for aluminium parts. These can be done in a hot household detergent. In either case, after immersion the head must be well washed with hot water, dried off and the iron or steel items oiled or greased to prevent rust.

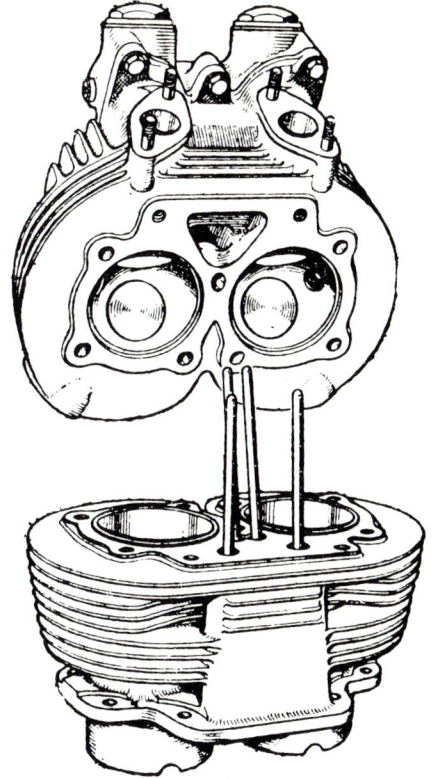

The top half of the 1947 A7 showing the air flow round the pushrod tunnel, a feature still used in 1972

Inspect the valve guides. If they are worn or cracked they must be replaced and this is best done with the head evenly heated. Unless the valve seat has been damaged the fitting of new guides is normally the only occasion when the seats need cutting. Even then a *light* cut only is needed followed by a minimum of valve grinding with the valves it is intended to fit.

Check the plug thread and fit an insert if it is in poor condition. Check all the other holes and fit inserts if required. Make sure the internal oil drains are clear. Inspect the head joint area for any signs of gas leakage and the top for damage. Deal with this.

Finally complete the head in the same way as the block in either natural or paint finish. Bead blasting is most effective for the light alloy heads.

Cylinder head types

Two types were used for the early A7 models up to 1950, the original for the A7 itself and a very similar one for the Star Twin. As a bolt on inlet manifold was used both came from the same casting with the sports version just altered in respect of inlet port size and combustion chamber finish. Both were cast in iron.

The A10 was also fitted with a cast-iron head when launched for 1950, but it differed in design with two exhaust valve wells in place of one and cast-in inlet tract. This supplied both cylinders from a single carburettor. The same style was adopted by the A7 and Star Twin in 1951 and again the sports engine used the standard casting with minor modification as did the A10SF in 1953.

There was a change in 1954 to increase the fin area for the A7, Star Twin and A10 with all models retaining iron heads. For the new Shooting Star and export-only Road Rocket came light alloy heads with that for the 650 modelled on the A10 style with integral inlet tract. The Shooting Star was fitted with a twin port head and separate inlet tract at first but from 1956 used the same one-piece style as the other models.

ABOVE *Head steady and exhaust pipe brace on a 1966 Thunderbolt*

BELOW *The A10 cylinder head, a classic design of its period*

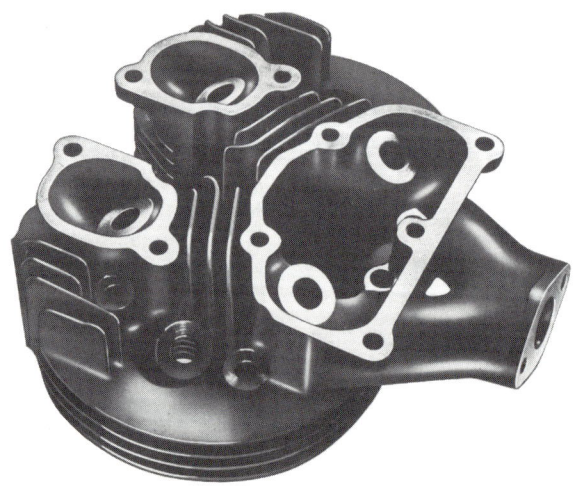

From then on the A7 and A7SS heads were unchanged but 1960 brought revision to the 650s with the fitment of bigger carburettors and thus enlarged inlet tracts.

The unit twins used light alloy heads for both A50 and A65 when launched and the two items continued on the road models to 1965. Both had a separate inlet manifold which fed parallel inlet tracts, but when the Cyclone and Lightning models came along in 1964 they were fitted with heads with splayed inlet ports to which twin carburettors were fitted.

In 1966 it was all change for all models as all inlet valves increased in diameter. For the twin carburettor machines an inlet balance pipe was added so the underside of each tract gained a tapped hole for the pipe adaptor. A change of valve guide came with modified heads in 1967 for all except the single carburettor 650 and there was a further change in 1968 due to the fitment of a new valve spring cup and a solid copper head gasket. The final change came in 1971, when a number of details were revised including the valve guides, valve collars and head gasket.

Valve guides

From 1947 to 1950 the A7 exhaust guide differed from the inlet, but for 1951 the inlet one was used in both applications. A new pair appeared for the A10SF in 1953 and one new one for the Shooting Star and Road Rocket in 1954. From 1958 on they all used the original A7 inlet one, which thus became common for all engines to 1963.

The unit twins began with common guides but the exhaust was changed soon after the model's introduction. Both guides changed in 1967 and again for 1971.

Inlet manifold

These were all cast in light alloy and are often highly polished. They should be examined for damage, flatness of the mounting faces both in and out and for the condition of the threaded holes that take the carburettor studs.

Many pre-unit BSA twins had the manifold cast as part of the head, but not the earliest ones. They used a single carburettor to feed both cylinders and the manifold had the head studs angled in so the upper ones were closer together than the lower. This part went on the A7 from 1947 to 1950 and was joined by another for the Star Twin in the last two of these years. This carried twin carburettors and had parallel intakes.

The only other pre-unit machine to use an inlet manifold was the Shooting Star for its first two years from 1954. In this case the attachment holes for the head studs splayed out. From 1956 the model was fitted with a cylinder head with integral manifold for one carburettor. All the single carburettor unit engines had a manifold and the mounting studs for them splayed in at the top. One went on the A50 and another on the A65, but neither were altered during their production runs from 1962 to 1970 and 1972 respectively.

Valves

Unless these are in very good condition they should be replaced, especially the exhaust, which has a hard time. Grind the new valves in lightly without taking too much from the seat.

There were not too many changes in valves over the years. The A7 had one pair up to 1950, another from 1951 to 1957 and a third for 1958 on. The Star Twin and later Shooting Star followed the same sequence from 1949 and from 1958 on used the A7 parts. The original A10 pair only changed once for 1958 and the Super Flash and Rocket engines kept to the same exhaust for all years but changed the inlet from 1960 on.

The unit engines had one pair of valves for each capacity and these all changed just once for 1966 on, when the inlet size was increased.

Valve springs

These should be replaced as a matter of course. All models used twin springs on each valve and in all cases the inlet and exhaust used the same pair. The original pair went onto the A7, Star Twin and A10 up to 1950 and were then changed for another which remained in use to 1963. The Super Flash and Rocket

The twin carburettor head developed for the unit twins in 1964

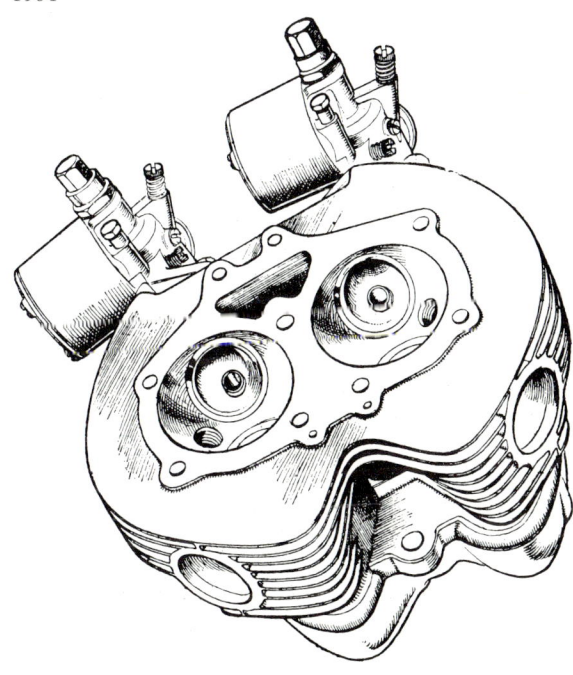

The rather bland lines of the unit engine show up on this 1967 Thunderbolt with odd added electrical component

engines each had their own pair of springs.

The unit twins used the same pair for both A50 and A65 and the original outer was quickly altered for another. The next change came in 1967, when a new pair were adopted for all models except the Wasp, which had a new pair of its own. 1968 brought a new outer, 1970 a new inner and 1971 yet another new outer, so the final two years saw the twins with springs different from earlier times.

Valve caps, cups, cotters and collars

Valve caps were only fitted to the 500 cc engine from 1947 to 1950 and for the other items in the pre-unit engines there was little variation. Just one type of cup, cotter and collar was used on all except the Super Flash and Rocket engines from 1947 to 1963. The Super Flash and Rockets had their own common cups and cotters but used different collars from one another.

On the unit twins the cotters and collars changed only once, for 1970, when their working taper altered. It is imperative that what is used matches. The valve cups were altered for 1968 and once again for 1971.

All these small detail parts require cleaning and careful inspection for any signs of damage or cracking; if there are, replacement is the only answer. Be sure there is no sign of collar collapse or cotter pull-through.

Rocker boxes

From 1947 to 1950 two rocker boxes were fitted, but with the advent of the A10 a one-piece one appeared which made location of the pushrods harder. This continued for all pre-unit engines, but for the unit models the rocker spindles were supported by pillars and the assembly simply enclosed by a lid.

It is possible to inspect the boxes without taking them apart, which is acceptable for servicing but not a full restoration. For the latter a full check is necessary so everything must come apart. Note carefully the sequence of washers and check that it is as it should be. Normal practice was a thrust washer at the inside of each rocker with a spring or thackeray washer outside plus a second thrust washer outboard of that.

Rocker spindles should be inspected for wear and oilways checked for obstruction. The rocker box or boxes need to be checked for cracks or damage, faulty threads or poor mating surfaces and these items refurbished as required. The rockers themselves need the same treatment together with their ball ends and adjusters.

THE ENGINE

ABOVE *The 1967 Spitfire Mk III with twin concentrics and rev-counter drive*

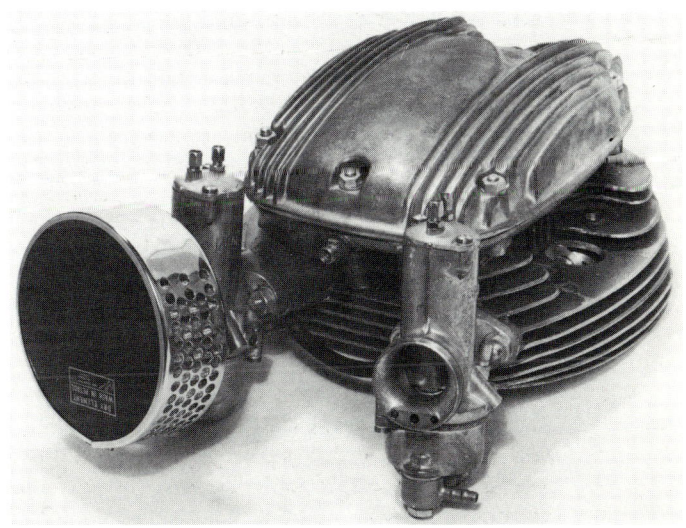

Twin carburettor cylinder head with finned rocker cover as used from 1967

The A50 Royal Star of 1968. Blanked off counter drive and US styling

Rocker box types and details

Most of the detail parts remained the same for a machine series with one set of rockers used from 1947 to 1950 in the A7 engines, another from 1950 to 1963 and a third for all unit machines. The rocker spindles began with no oil feed into either, but from engine XA7–450 in 1947 the exhaust one was supplied with lubricant. For 1949 the inlet one was also oiled so a common spindle could then be used and stayed with the models to 1963. The unit engines used just one spindle for both locations and all models.

The first A7 engines had a pair of rocker boxes each fitted with two caps to give access to the valve adjustment. These caps changed after engine XA7-600 in 1947 but otherwise the parts were unaltered up to 1950. The A10 one-piece rocker box was sealed by a pair of lids and these remained common to 1963. The box itself was joined by a similar version for the pivoted-fork models in 1954 and by two more for the Shooting Star and Road Rocket. In 1958 they all changed, with one for each sports engine and a third for the A7 and A10.

The unit engines merely had a lid over the valve gear and the original was used from 1962 to 1966. For 1967 it was replaced by a finned version using the same fixings and in 1971 this gained two tapped holes near its centre so needed a new part number.

Tappets

These should be examined for wear on the foot, which could be heavy on early A7 engines, and for their fit in their guide.

One type of tappet served all four valves on the A7 from 1947 to 1950, but two were used on the A10 and other pre-unit engines from 1950 to 1963. With the unit motors the design reverted to a new single type, which remained in use to 1972.

Pushrods

These need to be checked for straightness by rolling them on a flat surface such as a sheet of glass. Examine the ends for cracks or undue wear.

All models have different inlet and exhaust pushrods as a result of the valve and rocker geometry arising from the single rear camshaft. The original pair of 1947 were used in the A7 to 1950, joined by a new pair for the A10 that year and replaced in 1951 by another pair dimensioned to suit the later short stroke A7.

A new pair of pushrods went into the Shooting Star in 1954, but were changed for 1956 by a pair that also went into the Road Rocket. From 1958 these sports engines used the same two pairs as the tourers, thus reverting to the 1950 and 1951 parts.

The unit engines used two pairs of pushrods from 1962 to 1972, one for the 500 cc engines and the other for the 650s.

Camshafts

BSA kept to a small range of camshafts for their twins and in all cases they need inspecting for wear on the cams and the bearing surfaces. Make sure the keyway and nut thread are fit and there is no obvious damage. Check the breather drive of the unit engine camshafts and that their axial breathing hole is clear.

Although there are not too many camshaft types it is important to know what you have. The only way to be sure of this is to check the timing it gives, which is done with the gaps set at 0.015 in. in most cases.

In general it is best to run what is specified for your model and set it to its correct timing for the year. If you have a sports camshaft in an iron engine use the original gaps, which are set by expansion rates and not cam timing, but remember to keep an eye on any non-standard set-up while it is settling down.

The A7 from 1947 to 1950 used one camshaft (67-695) after engine XA7-600 and this went into the Star Twin as well. A new one (67-334) was brought in for the A10 in 1950 and went into the A7 in 1951. For the Star Twin there was a more sporting cam (67-356) and this went into the Super Flash, Shooting Star and Road Rocket in turn. For 1959 it was also adopted by the A7 and A10, while the Spitfire scrambler was fitted with a hotter cam still (67-357). In 1960 this cam was listed for the Super Rocket, but it seems that this could have been for export only with home models continuing with 67-356. For 1962 the 67-357 cam was used for Super Rocket, Rocket Gold Star and Spitfire.

Only two camshafts were listed for the unit twins, these being 68-103, with timing much as 67-356, and 68-473, with the same figures as 67-357. The first was used in the A50 and A65 for 1962 to 1965, the road A50C in 1965 and the A50 Royal Star from 1966 to 1970. The 68-473 camshaft went into all the rest, starting with the A65R in 1965 and finishing with the A70 in 1972.

Timing gears

Care is needed with these to avoid damage to them during removal or installation. The camshaft and crankshaft gears are both good fits on their shafts and a puller is likely to be needed. On the pre-unit engines the magneto gear has a self-extraction device if automatic advance is fitted, but a puller is needed for the manual ones.

The crankshaft gear is held in place by the oil pump worm, which screws onto the shaft with a spacer between it and the gear. It is a hardened part and must be turned with the correct size of socket spanner. It is locked by a nut and a lockwasher goes between the two for security. Both worm and nut have LEFT-hand threads on all engines.

You will have noted the timing marks on the gears while taking the engine apart and for the pre-unit models this operation has to be preceded by removing the dynamo drive. This also calls for a puller and some care to avoid a damaged or bent idler pinion shaft.

All parts need to be cleaned and inspected for wear, which should be minimal. If the gears do show signs on the teeth it may be necessary to change all of them as one new one in an old train will quickly wear to match the old teeth.

In general the timing gears and associated parts changed little over the years. The camshaft gears amounted to a total of three to cover the early A7 from 1947 to 1950, the pre-units from 1950 to 1963 and the unit engines. There were also three crankshaft gears with the first two for the early A7 and then the pre-unit and unit engines from 1950 to 1972. The third gear was solely for the A70.

Just one type of nut, spacer and lockwasher was used to retain the gear from 1947 to 1972 with a special spacer for the A70. The oil pump gear did change with one for the pre-units and another for the unit engines.

The idler gear varied a little more with one type for the early A7 and another for the A10 and other engines from 1950 on. A new part was introduced for the unit engines in 1962 and changed for 1968, when a new advance unit and fixing bolt came in. For 1969 it changed again to suit an alteration in its bearings. The oil seal set in the casting outboard of the gear was the same in all pre-unit engines with a new type introduced for the unit ones. It changed for 1969 to

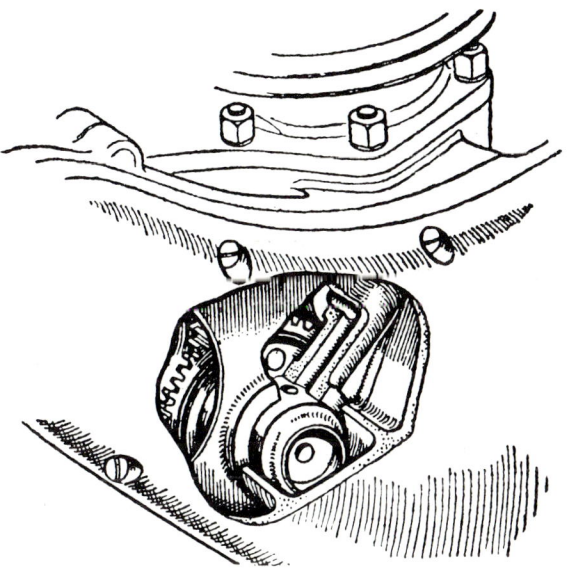

Timing cover modification introduced for 1952 to improve the engine breathing

suit the revised idler shaft and again for 1970.

The inner bearing for the idler shaft was unchanged from 1947 to 1963 but the outer one was altered for 1951 on. A new pair went into the unit engines from 1962 to 1968, but for 1969 a new part was used in both locations.

Dynamo drive

This is by chain from the idler gear spindle with the dynamo clamped to the front of the crankcase by a strap. Both chain and sprockets need to be cleaned and examined along with the clamping details. If the latter are bent they can be awkward to remove and in bad cases may need to be cut away.

The drive gear was the same for all models, but the driven was altered for 1949 on and the chain itself for 1950 on.

Timing covers, inner and outer

These need to be inspected for joint flatness, clear oilways and good thread condition. Most owners polish to a high degree as well. Check them for cracks and the condition of any bushes fitted, also the oil seal for the idler gear shaft.

The 1947 inner and outer cases only lasted to engine XA7-600 as then an extra screw was added at the bottom of the chest beneath the oil pump. A modified outer went on the Star Twin in 1949 and a new inner and outer on the A10 in 1950. These were adopted by the 500 cc engine for 1951 and remained in use to 1963, with the addition of a shroud round the breather from 1952 for the outer one.

1969 Lightning A65L with exhaust balance pipe and twin horns

THE ENGINE

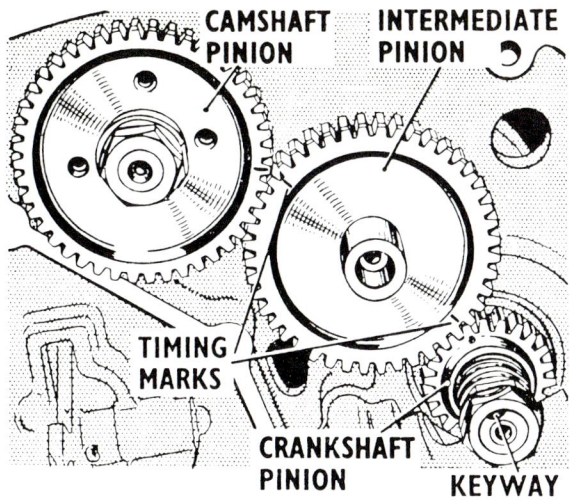

For the Super Flash and Road Rocket plus anyone else who fancied a rev-counter, an alternative outer cover was offered to which a drive box could be bolted, itself driven from a special magneto gear nut. Where this box was dispensed with a blanking plate was available.

This arrangement lasted to 1959, but for 1960 the Super Rocket was built with a modified inner cover so the rev-counter drive could be taken from the oil pump. Again a blanking plate was offered should it be needed, while a standard outer cover was fitted. The cable speed altered with this change as it had been half engine speed before thanks to the half-speed magneto drive and a 1:1 ratio drive box. The oil pump ran at one-third engine speed so the counter head had to be changed to suit.

The unit engines had totally different covers made

ABOVE *The marks used on the timing gears of the twins to set the camshaft. If in doubt check with a degree disc*

BELOW *The Thunderbolt in 1969 with BSA cast into the points cover*

to blend in with the combined casting. The outer carried a small cover over the contact points and there were a good few changes to the inner cover over the years.

The 1962 inner was changed for 1964 by the addition of an extra fixing screw. It was also joined by a modified version for the A65R which had provision for driving the rev-counter from the oil pump in the style used by the late pre-unit Rockets. Once again a blanking plate was offered and made available from 1965 to 1971.

For 1966 the speedometer drive was taken from the rear wheel so the gearbox parts previously used were deleted and a new inner provided without the drive hole. This changed for 1967, when it gained a filler cap hole in its top surface, and for 1969, when the idler gear bushes changed. And yet again for 1970 to accommodate a new clutch lift mechanism of the three-ball ramp type which replaced the lever used up to then. Finally, for 1971 extra screws were added in the area beneath the kick start.

The outer cover remained more static but changed for 1970 for the revised clutch mechanism when it gained a cable stop hole in the top and an access plug in the side. For 1971 it was changed to add the extra screw holes.

The 1962 points cover was held by four screws and carried a suitably coloured star badge for either the A50 or A65 retained by two more screws. Within a short time the cover had become an anonymous disc held by two screws, although it retained the same part number. Its only other change came for 1969, when it gained the letters BSA cast into it and therefore needed to be fitted the right way up.

Gaskets

The cylinder head gasket is most likely to need replacement, except where a solid copper one was used. In this case it should be examined for distortion or burning, but if in good condition it can be used again if annealed. This is done by heating it evenly to a cherry red and either allowing it to cool or by quenching it in water, which may produce a slightly softer material. Make sure the gasket fits over the head bolts cleanly and that continued re-use has not reduced its thickness materially.

Block and rocker box gaskets should be renewed or replaced with a modern silicone jointing compound, but keep this clear of any oilways.

The original head, block and rocker box gaskets were used up to 1950 and joined that year by those used on the A10 and, for the block, used up to 1963 by all models. An A7 head gasket joined the A10 one in 1951 and these remained unchanged to 1963. The rocker box lids used one gasket from 1950 to 1963 but the boxes changed their gaskets from 1960 on.

For the unit engines there were rather more changes. Different head gaskets were listed for the two capacities and these were revised for 1967. In 1968 they become solid copper and the 650 cc one was further modified in both 1971 and 1972. The block gasket was common to all models and was not changed until 1968 when the crankcases were revised. In 1970 it changed again to suit the increase in diameter of the fixing studs and it was modified once more for 1971. The rocker box lid gasket changed in 1969, although the lid was interchangeable back to 1962, and again for 1971.

Crankcase

These will need cleaning well and checking for damage, cracks, poor threads and obstructed oilways. To remove or refit main bearings the case around them should be evenly heated after which they should drop out. The useful way of checking the temperature is to spit on the bearing housing. If it spits back it's ready.

A ball or roller race must be completely cleaned before checking and if in doubt renew. A bush is less likely to need to be changed, but if they do the oil holes must line up.

The internal oil scavenge pipe must be secure and

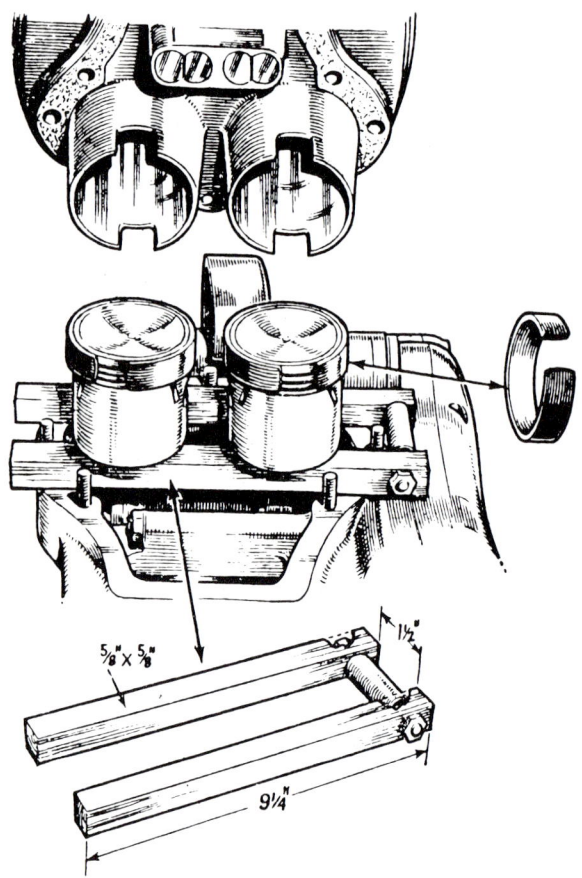

Using a piston steady and a pair of clamps to help assemble the block to the crankcase. Makes an awkward job fairly easy

oiltight. Check for cracks as any leak may stop the pump scavenging, which means a full engine strip to rectify.

The main bearings will benefit if held in place by Loctite. Replacement ones must be wiped clean before being dropped into place in the hot case. Don't forget any washers or shims that go with some mains.

Crankcase types

All the rigid and plunger frame engines had the gearbox bolted to the back of the crankcase, which thus had a substantial flange cast into it for this purpose. The earliest pair lacked the additional tapped hole at the bottom of the timing chest so a revised timing side case appeared at engine XA7-601 during 1947.

These original cases were joined by a new pair for the 1950 A10 but these were all superseded in 1951. For that year the 1950 cases were modified to improve the lubrication and were used by all semi-unit engines from then on until they were dropped in 1957.

With the advent of the pivoted fork frame came separate gearboxes and new crankcases without the rear flange. At the same time the inner primary chaincase became a separate item and no longer formed part of the drive side crankcase half. Two pairs of cases were introduced, one of which was used by the A7 engines from then on to 1962 and by the A10 up to 1957. The second pair were for the Road Rocket and were adopted by the A10 from 1958 onwards.

For the unit engines one case assembly did duty for both 500 and 650 cc capacities, but a total of seven types appeared over the years. The first was used from 1962 to 1965 and for 1966 gained the timing plug aperture in the right case with blanking plate held by two bolts. 1967 brought a hollow dowel hole around one of the chaincase screws plus changes in the bolts clamping the two halves together.

In 1968 the alternator bolted straight to the left case without a separate location casting so that side was revised while the gearbox filler cap was moved so its tapped hole in the top of the right casting went. 1969 brought wider mating faces and a single tapped hole in the front of the right case for a timing plug. Finally 1970 saw the larger diameter block studs, while the A70 had its own crankcase.

The Lightning in 1970, the last year in the old type frame

Sump plate

This bolts to the underside of the crankcase and should be carefully inspected for faults, which could allow oil to leak out. Incorporated into it is the filter, which protects the scavenge side of the oil pump, and this also must be in good condition and a close fit to the pick-up pipe.

A single type of assembly was used on all models from 1947 to 1969, but for the last three years it was split into two parts. One was the cover, which retained its external shape, and the other the filter plate, which became a separate part fitted to the same four studs as the cover. It was thus necessary to use two gaskets to ensure an oil-tight assembly.

Main bearings

All engines have a bush for the timing side and either a ball or roller race on the drive. The pre-unit engines had a timing bush of 1.375 in. nominal bore and the very first type was only used on engines up to number XA7-600, after which the crankshaft design changed and the bush with it. The new one had a larger flange and was not changed until 1958, when one of the same dimensions but with a lead-bronze bearing surface replaced it.

The unit engines had a timing bush with 1.500 in. bore and the original was changed for 1966, when the drive-side race also changed. With the change came a thrust washer between the timing-side bush and the crankshaft web, which remained in use up to 1972. The timing-side bush was itself modified for 1967 and the A70 copied the design but with its own bush and thrust washer.

On the drive side the A7 began with a ball race to locate the crankshaft. Its dimensions were $1\frac{1}{8} \times 2\frac{13}{16} \times \frac{13}{16}$ in. and it was used up to 1950. For the A10 that year and the A7 the next a single lip roller race of $30 \times 62 \times 16$ mm dimensions replaced it and remained in use to 1963. With it came a shim selection to restrict the crankshaft end float to 0.003 in.

The unit twins used the original $1\frac{1}{8}$ in. bore ball race from the early A7 from 1962 to 1965. With it they also used a shim cup plus a selection of shims rather than clamp onto the bearing. For 1966 the race became a single lip roller of the same dimensions and new shims and a shim cap were called up. This design continued in use to 1972 and also went into the A70 with a revised set of shims.

Most engines also had an oil seal fitted outboard of the drive-side main bearing. The first type was used from 1947 to 1950 in the A7 engines but did not get into the A10 or any motors from 1951 to 1953. For 1954 a new lipped seal was fitted and continued in use for all engines from then to 1972.

The famous BSA pushrod tool number 67-9114 which is nearly an essential when assembling non-unit engines

Bearing improvements

It was never good engineering practice to use a lipped roller to take end thrust of a continuous nature and this is what it can be called upon to do in the BSA twin engine. In theory the crankshaft spins freely between the roller and the timing bush, which only have to guide it from time to time, but in practice the reaction from the oil pump drive or any primary chain misalignment can throw all the load in one direction.

At high power and speed this can have a dramatic effect as many Spitfire owners have testified. The load wears the shims so the end float increases, then the thrust washer breaks up due to the greater load it has to take, the timing bush moves, the oil feed is reduced and something seizes which can put a rod through the crankcase.

Feeding the oil through the main bearing also means that the pressure at the big ends is dependent on the fit of the main and that the oil has to force its way into the centre of the mainshaft against centrigual force. Thus the left big end in particular is likely to suffer from lack of oil.

These problems were implicit in the first A10 but the design could cope with its power of 35 bhp at 5800 rpm. By the time the Spitfire was in production figures of 55 bhp and 7000 rpm were being quoted and the basic design errors began to show through.

To remedy this two firms, Devimead and SRM Engineering, produce kits to remove the problem once

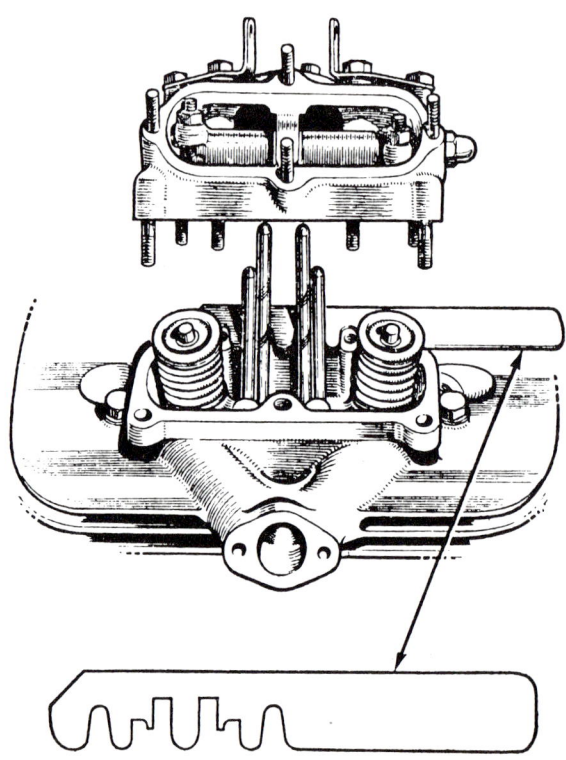

THE ENGINE

Thunderbolt from 1970 with small US tank. Lines much as 1962

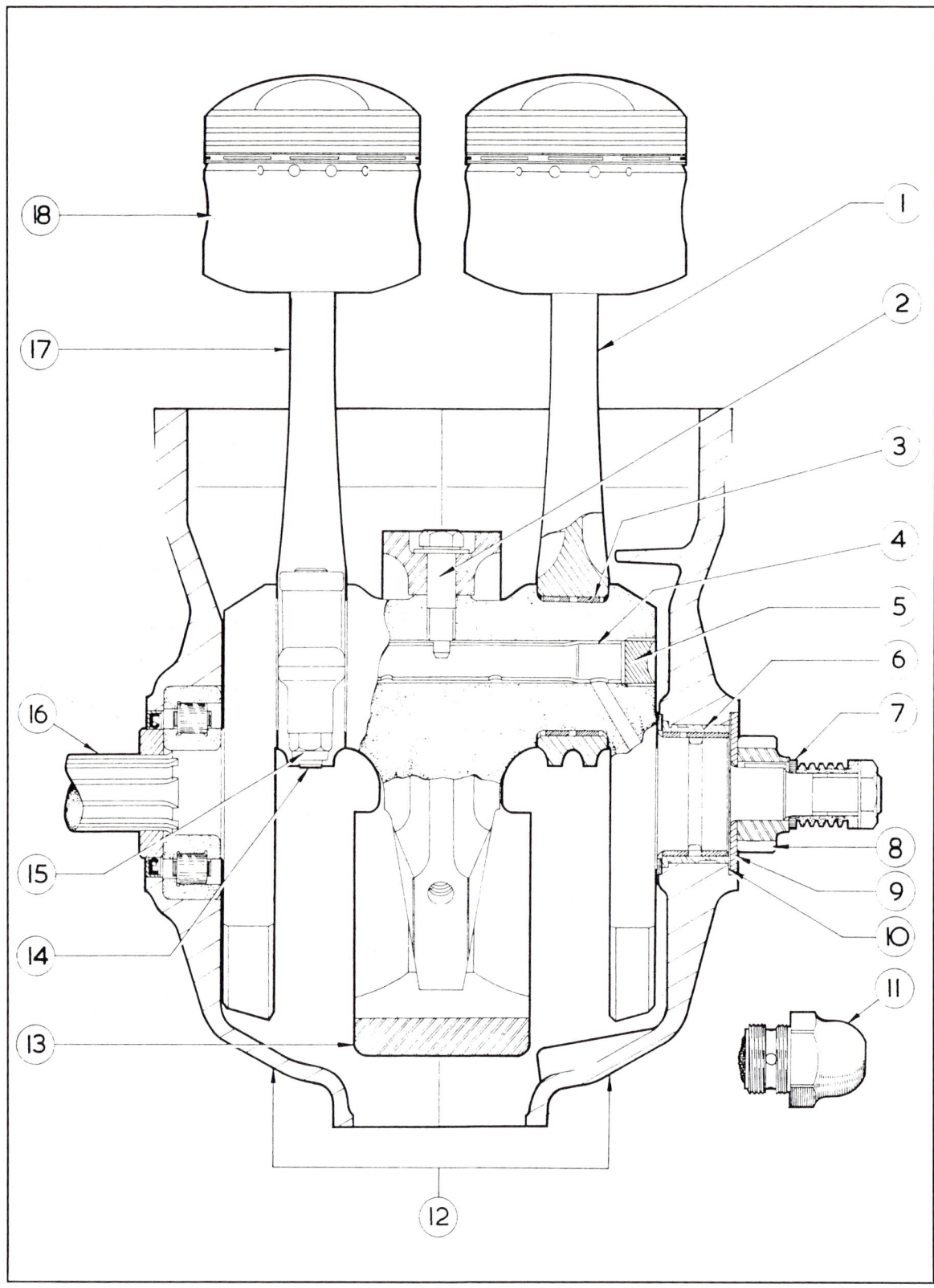

Drawing of the A70 indicating the parts not common to the A65. Not an easy conversion

and for all. This is done by fitting a combined race on the timing side that will take both radial and axial loads so the lipped roller on the drive side only carries the radial loads it should.

This change cuts off the oil supply, so a new one is arranged to end feed into the crankshaft, which aids that aspect. The alterations are well proven and have been carried out on many engines, so are to be recommended.

Camshaft bushes

The twin engines have three of these and for 1947 and from 1951 to 1963 all were the same. For 1948 to 1950 there were two of these plus one with an oil groove round the outside instead of a cross hole. The unit twins had their own set of bushes and in similar manner had two of one sort and one of another. The pair were flanged and went into the right crankcase while the odd one was plain and supported the left end of the camshaft.

Alternator housing

This casting was only used in 1966 and 1967 to support the stator and locate it to the crankcase. Prior to that the stator was mounted on studs and from 1968 located directly to the crankcase.

The housing should be inspected for damage and a check made for distortion as the part has to hold the stator concentric to the rotor to a close tolerance.

Assembly

Generally to be done as set out in the manual with some alteration to acknowledge the use of modern sealants and fitting compounds and the sequence to be used to lock up the larger nuts.

Slow and steady is the guiding rule so you make sure everything is well at one stage before going on to the next.

Start by laying out the first components needed and check that all your tools are clean. Fit the crankshaft to the drive-side case and the camshaft with the breather valve under it where fitted. Assemble and check for end float. Paint jointing compound onto the case face and fit. If it does not go home easily find out why. Fit all the screws and Loctite the nut in the crankcase mouth to make sure. Check that everything goes round.

Fit the timing gears and set the timing to the marks if this is already established. If the valve timing has to be set from scratch you can do this using a degree disc.

Then lock the crank and tighten the nuts in the timing cover. Fit the pistons, warm, followed by the block. Grease the head gasket and fit the head followed by the rocker boxes with the pushrods as dictated by the engine type.

Fit and time the magneto or the points in the timing cover. Fit the oil pump, paint jointing compound on the timing cover, bolt up and add points when applicable.

Complete the assembly by adjusting the tappets and fitting the covers. You will have oiled parts during assembly and with the crankshaft charged with oil this should look after the surfaces while you deal with the rest of the machine. Don't seal it completely if you have to store it for any time and do turn it over occasionally.

Not a standard unit but a 650 modified to twin carburettors for record taking on the Bonneville Salt Flat in 1951

4 Transmission

The transmission covers all the mechanical parts from the engine crankshaft to the rear wheel sprocket. It thus encompasses two chains, four sprockets, a clutch and a set of gears. Included with the gears is the kickstart mechanism and ancillary to them are the gearchange mechanism, clutch lift and the gearbox shell.

Attention
Articles on the restoration of a machine often state that the owner has not stripped the gearbox but is using it as found. In many cases it is apparent that the box history is not known and this practice must be condemned.

Unless you check you cannot be certain that a gear tooth is not about to fail or an errant part about to jam the gears. In the timescale of a restoration the period spent on inspecting the gears is minimal, and even on a straight rebuild the time will be well spent if you thereby make sure the box is not going to lock up on you.

BSA transmission
All twins had a four-speed gearbox with footchange pedal and kickstart lever on the right. Primary and

Primary side of the early A7 with bolted on gearbox. Clutch also has a cover dome so runs dry, or should

final drive was by chain and a multi-plate clutch was used. At first the transmission shock absorber went on the crankshaft, but the advent of the alternator meant that it had to move into the clutch body.

All rigid- and plunger-frame models had semi-unit construction with the gearbox bolted to the engine, but from 1954 a separate gearbox was used for models with a pivoted-fork frame. Unit construction was adopted from 1962. For many years a wide-ratio gearbox was available for the semi-unit and pre-unit models, while close-ratio gears were listed for the unit machines from 1965 to 1972. The Rocket Gold Star was fitted as standard with the extra-close ratio RRT2 Gold Star gearbox but was thus by definition available with any of the ratio sets that could be fitted into that box shell.

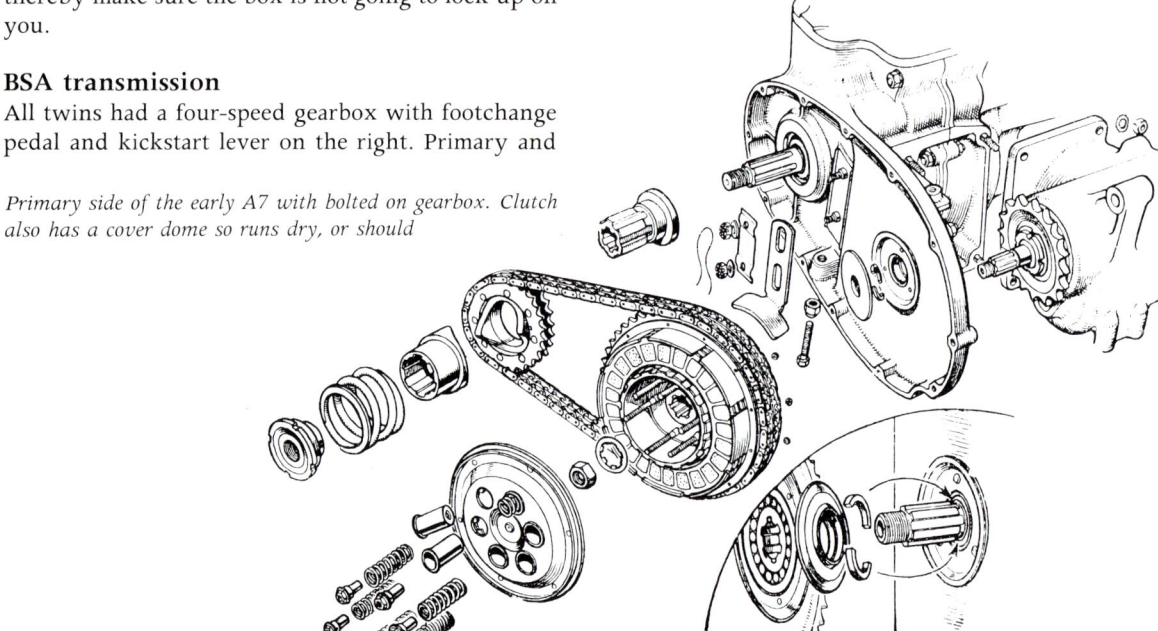

Torrens, actually editor Arthur Bourne, of The Motor Cycle *out on the new A7 in 1947*

Engine sprocket

The semi- and pre-unit twins had this mounted together with a shock absorber, but for the unit models this item moved to the clutch to make room for the alternator.

All semi-unit engines had a duplex chain and sprockets with a triplex chain listed as an option and fitted to the Super Flash. The pre-unit engines had single-strand primary chain and the unit engines fitted triplex.

In all cases the sprockets need to be checked for their fit to the crankshaft, the condition of their teeth and the smoothness of the absorber ramp. If healthy, continue to use, but if in doubt change along with the chain.

The semi-unit engines used a 27-tooth duplex sprocket with absorber ramp from 1947 to 1957, while the unit engines had a 28-tooth triplex one from 1962 to 1972. For a few years it was joined by a competition version, still with 28 teeth, which went into the off-road models and suited the special alternator rotor fitted to them.

Pre-unit models used the engine sprocket, along with gearbox and rear wheel, to adjust the gearing. The single-strand sprocket was machined with absorber ramp and was a free fit on the driving sleeve. All 500 cc models used 18 teeth, as did A10 models when with a sidecar, while the A10 Spitfire used 17 teeth. The solo A10 and Rocket models used 21 teeth, while the RGS used 23 at first and then 22. At any time most of the sprockets were available as an option for any model.

The greatest change to the single-strand sprocket came in 1955, when the shock absorber was altered to the two-lobe form, so the four-lobe type was only to be found on 1954 models.

Shock absorber – engine

This system was only used on semi- and pre-unit engines, but only one item appeared in both applications and for only one year in one of those. In all cases the engine sprocket ran free on a sleeve splined internally to the crankshaft and on the outside for a slider. This and the sprocket had matching cam ramps and were held together by a spring. If the sprocket turned on the sleeve the ramps forced the slider along the splines against the spring to provide the absorbing effect.

Minor damage to the parts may be stoned out, but check that this is not finishing off the hard surface or that it will make one ramp bear more load than the other.

The semi-unit parts had a change of spring for 1951 and in either case they should be replaced if they have shortened. The only other change was to the splined sleeve in 1954. The pre-unit design began in 1954 with a four-lobe cam and the semi-unit spring. All parts changed for 1955, when a two-lobe cam was adopted and the sleeve, its ramp cam and fixing nut changed again for 1956.

Shock absorber – clutch

This was only used by the unit engines. It went into the clutch centre and comprised a spider with vanes which lay inside the centre and its vanes. Between the metal parts went drive and rebound rubbers and the assembly was enclosed by front and rear plates secured by screws. The assembly should be checked and the rubbers changed if they seem at all hard.

The design used from 1962 to 1965 had four vanes on the spider and a total of eight rubbers with the drive ones fatter than the rebound. It was superseded by a three-vane type for 1966 and this continued to be fitted to 1972. In 1970 the centre was modified, as was the spider in 1971.

Primary chain

Expect to change this unless you find it in perfect condition. Semi-unit engines used $\frac{3}{8}$ in. duplex chain with dimensions of 0.375 in. pitch × 0.250 in. roller diameter × 0.225 in. between inner plates for all models, which all had 80 links. A triplex chain of the same dimensions was offered as an option and fitted to the Super Flash for 1953 to 1954 and this triplex chain of 80 links went into all unit engines.

All pre-unit engines used 0.5 × 0.335 × 0.305 in. single-stand chain, this being commonly referred to as $\frac{1}{2} \times \frac{5}{16}$ in. The number of links varied from 67 to 70.

Primary chain tensioner

These devices were fitted to the semi-unit engines for 1947 to 1957 and all unit motors. The two engine types had completely different arrangements although both used slipper blades to control the tension.

The early engines had a curved blade with hard chromed working surface. The blade was able to slide up or down to set the chain tension and this movement was stiffened by a spring so the blade tended to stay where put. It was pushed up to set the tension with a

The drive side construction of the unit twins as introduced in 1962 with alternator outboard of primary chain

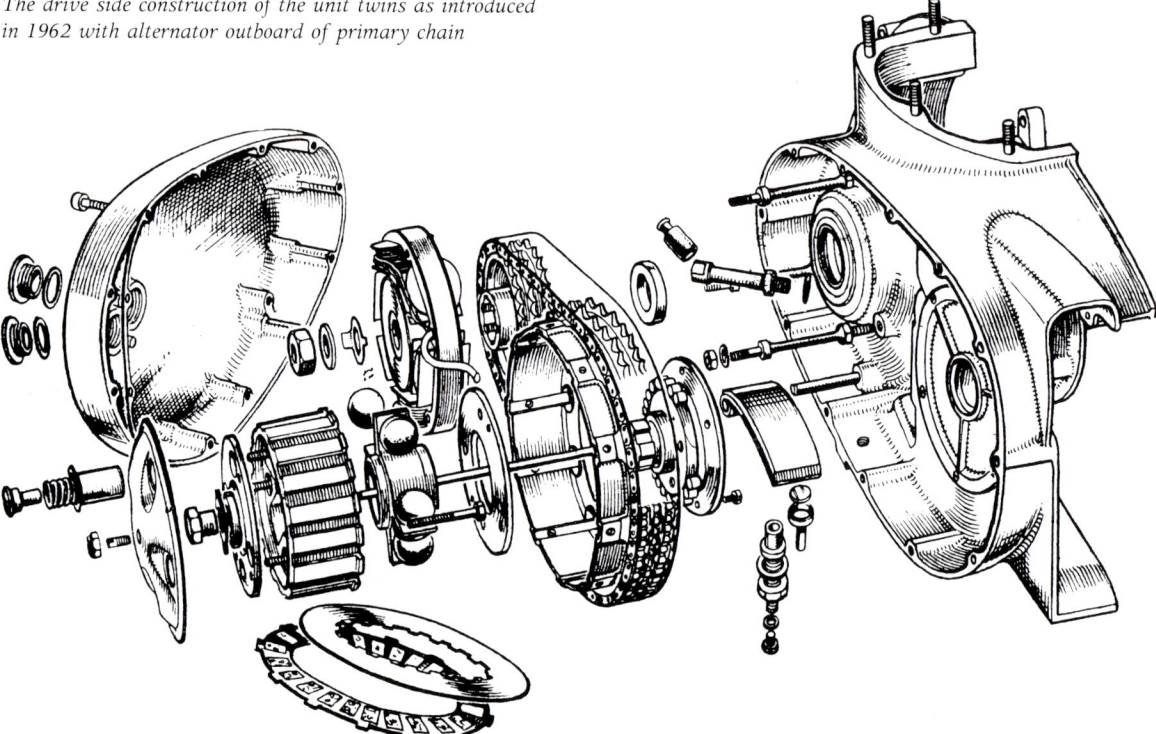

jack screw set in the underside of the chaincase. This was the only part that changed, with early versions having a standard hexagon bolt head which changed to a slotted stud end from 1951.

The unit engines used a curved blade pivoted at the front and held up against the chain by an adjuster. The details varied rather more over the years and the first change came during 1962 after engine numbers A50-159 and A65-654, when the pivot with threaded end became a pin and a distance tube. The aim of the design of the adjustment was to allow a thin rod to be inserted from below to gauge the chain tension. The screw and its locknut changed early on when the design lost a loading spring and gained a cap nut to protect the screw from dirt as well as lock it. For 1967 the cap nut went and it was back to the original plain nut. At the same time the screw was altered so its bearing pad fitted directly into its head instead of into a peg which went into the screw head. The cap nut reappeared in 1968, when the screw was modified, while it was the turn of the tensioner blade in 1969. In 1971 the cap nut gained a pair of spanner flats in addition to its hexagon, but for 1972 was changed again so it reversed its installation and its hexagon was at the closed end and furthest from the chaincase. Throughout all this and despite other changes to Unified threads the screw retained its BSF thread.

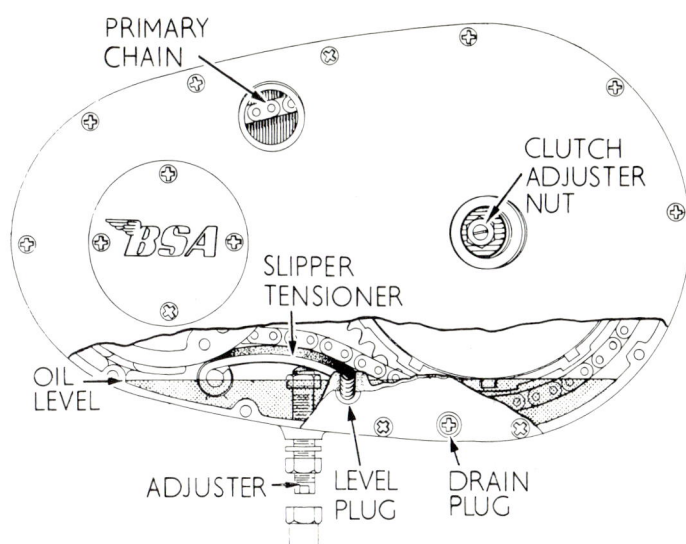

The unit engine primary drive showing the slipper tensioner and other features as in 1970

Drive side of the A7 Shooting Star in 1955

Clutch

All BSA twins were fitted with a multi-plate clutch but the design varied over the years. The semi-unit models had a clutch enclosed by a dome bolted to the chain wheel and this was mounted directly to the gearbox mainshaft. Pre-unit models used two clutch types, the first with six springs and the second with four. Unit engine clutches differed in that a shock absorber was built into the clutch centre and the original four-spring type was changed to three springs from 1966.

The clutch parts should all be cleaned and examined for wear or damage. Normal wear points are the tongues of the plates and the slots in the drum, the hub bearings and the springs, which may tire. Plates should be checked for flatness and the late type clutch nuts for the locking nib under the head.

For most parts replacement is the normal course of action. On most models the housing race can be pressed out and renewed but may need grinding once in place, which requires an engineering workshop. Expect to replace the bearings and fit a new lockwasher on all models that have one. Fit new springs if they are much below the normal free length.

The clutch springs must be adjusted so that the pressure plate lifts squarely and turns truly. If it does not the clutch will drag and spoil the gearchange. It is for the same reason that the plates must be able to slide sideways in the slots and that they in turn must be free of burrs or notches.

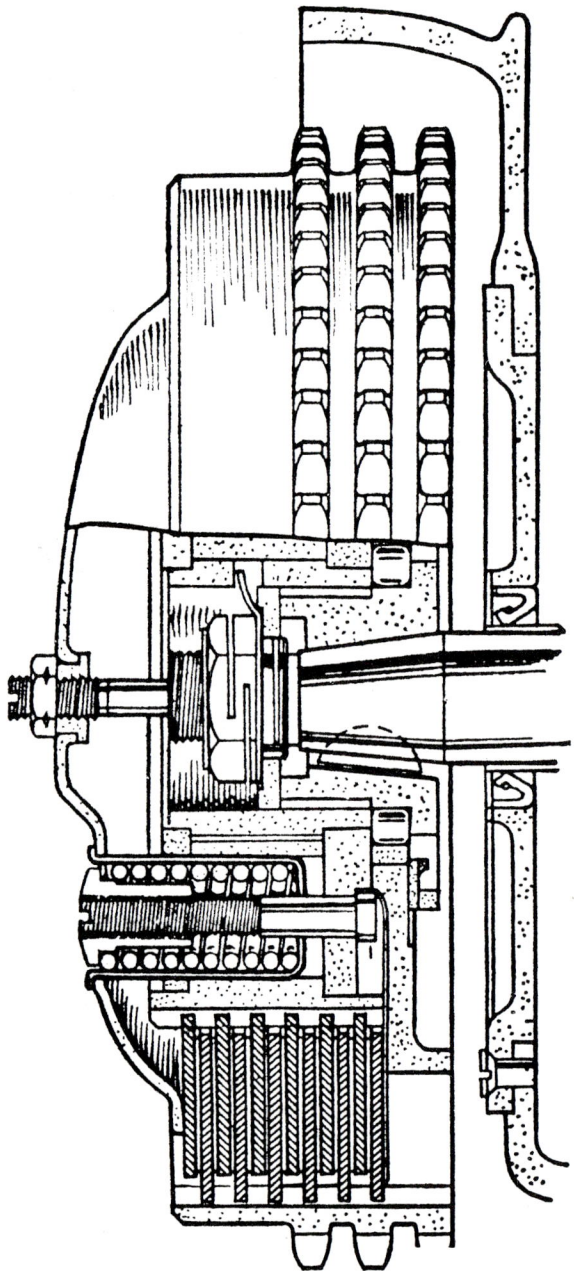

Cross-section of the six-plate clutch adopted in 1966. A needle thrust race in the pressure plate is a worthwhile modification

Clutch hub

This was first used in 1954 with the pre-unit engines and was fixed to the gearbox mainshaft on a taper and located by a key. One key was common to all pre-unit machines and another to all unit ones. The hubs varied, for a new one was introduced in 1960 for the four-spring clutch.

For the unit engines the hub was changed after engines A50-951 and A65-2301 in 1963 and again for 1966, when the three-spring clutch was adopted. It changed once again for 1970.

The hub or centre was held by a plain nut at first which was modified for 1949 and continued on all semi-unit models. It was locked by an internally serrated washer. Pre-unit machines had a different nut with built-in clamping washer and this was locked by a dished washer. The four-spring pre-unit type used a sleeve nut to retain its hub and this had both plain and lock washers. For the unit engines there was a plain nut with plain and lock washers. From 1966 the nut form changed and sat on a single thick plain washer. The nut was revised in 1968.

Clutch centre

The original centre went on all semi-unit models and had six studs fixed to it. It had multiple slots machined into its periphery to drive the clutch plates and was splined to the mainshaft. A revised centre was introduced for the pre-unit models, which retained the six studs but only had six driving slots. It fitted to the hub and it should be noted that other centres exist that will fit but are of different plate capacities and stud length.

A revised six-spring centre was fitted from 1958 and in 1960 was joined by a four-spring centre on the lines of the 1947 original with multiple driving slots. A new design with shock absorber centre went into

ABOVE The unit construction A65 in 1964 with gearbox driven speedometer. Note excess brake rod length

the unit models from 1962 and was changed from a four- to three-spring layout for 1966 and further revised for 1970.

Clutch bearings

On all semi-unit models the clutch chainwheel ran on 18 rollers with a thrust washer behind them. From 1951 this latter part became available in a choice of three thicknesses to enable the chain alignment to be maintained.

The design changed for the pre-unit models to a ball bearing arrangement with inner and outer rings and two cages with 0.187 in. diameter ball bearings. This design was used up to 1961 but was joined in 1960 by a roller type similar to the 1947 one. The revised one had 20 rollers, which rotated on the centre hub and on which the chainwheel ran.

The same rollers but 21 in number were used in similar manner for the unit engine, four-spring clutch with the number decreasing to 20 from 1966 on. At the same time the 1962 design of thrust washers was altered to a single one on the lines of the late pre-unit style. This arrangement stayed in use to 1972.

Sprocket and housing

These two items are made as a single assembly with the bearing race at its centre. The part is prone to wear on the sprocket teeth and in the housing slots and in either case repair or replacement may be necessary.

The original assembly had a duplex sprocket with 54 teeth. Its outer cover was held by 12 nuts and bolts. For 1948 it was fitted with studs so the cover was retained by nuts. It underwent a further revision in 1951, when the bearing thrust washers altered, but otherwise continued as it was to 1957.

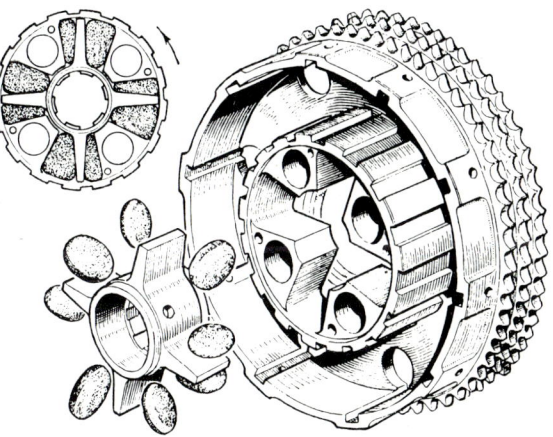

The clutch sprocket, housing, hub, centre and shock absorber rubbers for the 1962 unit models

For machines with pre-unit engines and pivoted-fork frames in 1954 there was a new chainwheel with a single row of 43 teeth, Ferodo inserts set in it and a simple band round the driving tongues. This was modified in 1958 and in 1960 joined by a similar design but without inserts and which ran on rollers.

The unit engine clutch had a triplex sprocket with 58 teeth. The 1962 design had the thrust washers bolted to it, but this went for 1966, when the arrangement was simplified and the three springs adopted. The design remained essentially the same from then on, but the chainwheel did alter twice more for 1969 and 1970, in the latter case to suit a revised thrust washer.

The 1960 A7 with transmission much as a decade earlier

Springs, cups, pins and nuts

These details all varied to some degree and all need checking over. Expect to change the springs unless you know how old they are and their condition. Over the years there was some variation but not for the semi-unit engines, which had just one type for all years. In the pre-units there was one for the six-spring clutch and another for the four.

The unit engines used their first spring to 1964, when it was joined by a stronger one for the A65R. These were both replaced by one type for 1966 and the three-spring clutch, and this was changed once more for 1968.

Spring cups were simple with one type for semi-units, one for six-spring pre-units, one for four-spring pre-units, another for four-spring units and a fifth type for three-spring units. Spring pins did not appear until 1960 for the pre-units. A different type went into the unit clutch for 1962, but from 1966 the pre-unit type was fitted.

Spring nuts began with domed heads and slots for turning them and this self-locking design went into all semi-unit clutches. For the pre-units from 1954 the design was changed to a pair of plain nuts locked together on each stud. This was changed for a Simmonds self-locking nut for each stud in the six-spring clutch for 1960, while the four-spring one used a dome-headed nut similar to the 1947 type.

This went into the early unit clutches but was soon changed for another similar version. It reappeared in the three-spring clutch in 1966 and was modified for 1971, when its thread changed from Cycle to BSF. Both being 26 tpi, BSA got away without changing the pin thread, which was naughty but not unexpected at the time.

Plates

These come as plain, bonded or inserted and pressure. Numbers of the first two vary from five to six and in the semi-unit clutch there were five plain plates of one type and one of another. Between them went five plates with inserts. The six-spring pre-unit clutch continued with five inserted plates, now with Ferodo inserts, and plain plates of three types. Four had angled slots in them as did a fifth of modified form. A sixth plain plate went behind the chainwheel on the hub.

For 1958 the inserted plates changed while the four plain plates were replaced by four more of the fifth plate to make five in all. The sixth plain plate remained. For the four-spring clutch introduced in 1960 there was a new pressure plate, five new plates with inserts and six new plain plates.

The unit engines had a new clutch but with five of the 1960 inserted plates. There were six plain plates and a new pressure one with a central adjusting screw and locknut. In 1964 new inserted plates were added for the A65R. For 1966 and the three-spring clutch there were six new inserted plates and six plain ones of the type fitted to the 1960 clutch. The pressure plate changed to suit the new spring layout and again for 1967, when the adjuster screw was altered. For 1968 the inserted plates were altered as were the plain ones in 1969.

The design of the clutch pushrod and pressure plate is rather crude and the first is poorly located to the second, which gives high pressures, wear and a poor feel. A conversion to add a needle roller thrust race will overcome the snags and is well worth carrying out as it gives considerable benefit for little outlay.

Clutch mechanism

This is the system that connects the clutch cable movement to the pressure plate and it goes under the outer gearbox cover and includes the clutch pushrod. Three designs were used but all come apart easily and should be checked over for wear or damage. The pushrod must be straight or the clutch will feel very heavy. Grease the load points of the mechanism on assembly so that the action is smooth and easy.

All non-unit machines had a simple lever system with the outer arm formed in one with its shaft and connected to the operating cable. At its lower end went a short arm with an adjuster screw with hardened tip. This design remained the same from 1947 to 1963 but the original pushrod was only used up to 1957. A new one went into the pre-unit clutch in 1954 and was joined by another for the Super Rocket in late 1960 from engine number DA10R-2443. The Rocket Gold Star had its own, which remained common for all years.

The unit engines had a simple lever to move the pushrod and relied on the screw in the pressure plate for adjustment. This design, with minor changes to the cable connection and abutment, remained in use up to 1969 with a small alteration to the lever for 1967. For 1970 a three-ball ramp mechanism was adopted and for 1972 both lever and ball ramp thrust plate were modified with the first losing its turned over cable attachment point.

Chaincase

Semi-unit engines only required an outer chaincase as the crankcase formed the inner and the same applied to unit engines. Pre-unit ones, however, had inner and outer cases and any distance pieces behind them must be in place and of the correct size. If omitted the castings may be cracked when the fixings are tightened.

In all cases the castings need to be cleaned and carefully inspected for cracks, damage, poor threads and irregular joint faces. Detail parts should also be cleaned, inspected and renovated as required.

One case outer and one filler cap did for all semi-unit models and the same cap continued on the pre-unit machines. They had one inner case plus sealing felt and plate for all years but the outer altered for 1960. Up to then it had the single filler cap but for that year gained two new items. One was a standpipe in the underside to set the oil level and the other a small cap whose removal enabled the clutch spring nuts to be turned. They had of course become lock nuts at the same time, but while this change allowed them to be adjusted without removing the outer case it did not allow the owner to check the plate lift for its visual squareness. Curiously the outer case part number did not alter, but the distinction between the cases is quite clear.

The unit outer case varied rather more. The first type had two caps side by side, one for clutch spring adjustment and the other for the pressure plate screw. The two caps were covered by an outer plate secured by two screws. For 1966 a new cover with a single access cap on the clutch centre line and a second one on the cover shoulder was fitted. The top cap gave access to the primary chain for checking the tension, a job done before by feeling through the hollow chain adjuster bolt.

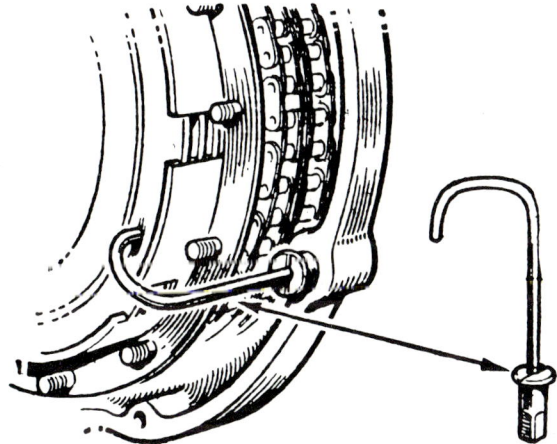

ABOVE *Using a spoke as a marker to check that the clutch plate is lifting square as it must for clean gear changes*

RIGHT *Unit engine chaincase in 1966 with access holes for lubricant, checking chain tension and clutch adjustment*

For 1967 another new cover was introduced which had the same two caps, still the 1962 part, and a small round cover at the front. This was retained by four screws and its removal exposed the rotor, which was marked for ignition timing by strobe. The fixed mark was a pin set in the cover recess and thus retained by it.

The cover, caps and the rotor cover all changed for 1969 with the last part gaining a winged BSA motif cast into it as on the points cover. The two parts were, however, not the same item. The other changes were due to the partial adoption of Unified threads and the cover itself changed again for 1970 with the addition of drain and level screws in its lower part.

Gearbox

All BSA twins had a four-speed gearbox with positive stop gearchange and right-side gear pedal and kickstart lever. The gearbox design was conventional English, with the sleeve gear carrying the output sprocket concentric with the clutch and mainshaft. Semi-unit models had the gearbox as a separate unit but bolted to the rear of the crankcase, while the pre-units just had the box mounted in engine plates. The unit construction engines had the gearbox built into a shell formed as part of the right crankcase half.

Dismantling is straightforward and with non-unit boxes is best done with the shell clamped in a vice by a lower lug. Check on the mesh between camplate and quadrant, where fitted, to confirm that all is as it should be, don't muddle the selector forks, which may be identical but prefer to remain with the gears they have run in with, and don't muddle the gears and associated thrust washers and circlips. During assembly the same points should be watched and the box operation and gear selection tried and checked out on the bench. This is easier with the unit engines as the whole assembly mounts to an inner cover plate.

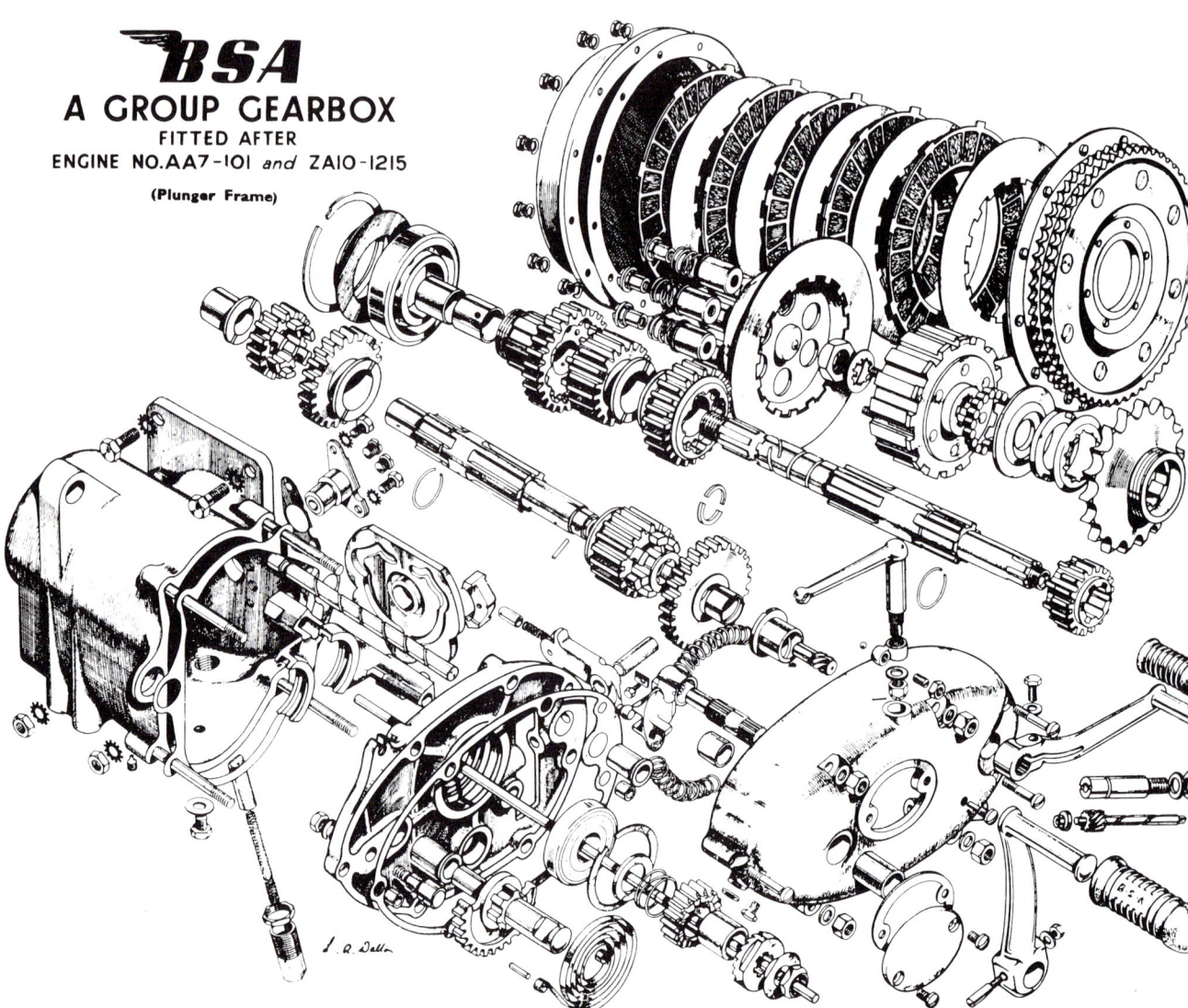

Gears

These must be carefully inspected for signs of wear or damage on the teeth and the driving dogs and splines. Replacement is usually the only answer if things are bad, although it is possible to build up and machine or grind back to original if the dogs are worn. Not easy to get right and very specialized.

There have been a number of changes to the gears over the years so if parts are needed care must be exercised to ensure they match. It is good practice to replace them in pairs as an old gear can easily wear out a new one. Before shopping consult the tables on the numbers of teeth on the gears and note the form of the gear to guide you to the correct part.

Except for the Spitfire and the Rocket Gold Star all non-unit models had the same standard gear ratio from 1947 to 1963. In addition a wide-ratio set was available from 1947 to 1950 and 1954 to 1957. For the pre-unit gearbox it was feasible to consider any of the options listed for the Gold Star single, although none were officially listed for the standard road twins. For the Spitfire the Scrambles gear set was fitted and for the RGS the Extra Close set.

While the standard ratios and numbers of gear teeth remained the same over those years the actual gears did not. The first change came in 1950 from engine number ZA10-1215 and 1951 from AA7-101 and brought in new gears and shafts to improve gear changing. The parts do not interchange with the earlier ones.

New shafts and layshaft top and second gears appeared in 1954 to suit the new gearbox shell used for the pivoted-fork models and all shafts need to be inspected for damaged splines, poor threads, bearing surfaces and the condition of the clutch pushrod bush.

Replacement is normally the only answer if there is a problem and the shaft type must be correct for both gears and shell. The only other pre-unit changes were to add the gears and shafts for the Spitfire and RGS.

For the unit engines there was a small change of ratios but a major change of gears in the first year of production. Two gears, both the same part, continued but the rest changed. They were joined by a close-ratio set in 1965 and this had its third gear ratio raised for 1967 by changing a further pair of gears.

Otherwise the layshaft sleeve gear changed for 1966 and the layshaft itself for 1967 having lost its speedometer gear the year before. The ratios for the standard box were unchanged after the early alteration.

Bushes and bearings

Ball and needle races need to be completely cleaned before they are checked and if there is any doubt as to their condition they should be renewed. Some play is normal for ball races but there must be no rough spots. Bushes were used for the earlier layshafts and in the layshaft first gear. If worn they can be renewed.

The ball race at the right end of the mainshaft was $\frac{3}{4} \times 1\frac{7}{8} \times \frac{9}{16}$ in for all BSA twins. The sleeve gear ball race was $35 \times 72 \times 17$ mm for non-unit gearboxes and $1\frac{1}{4} \times 2\frac{1}{2} \times \frac{5}{8}$ in. for units. Each was located by a circlip with one type common to all on the right while the sleeve gear one varied to suit non-unit and unit engines.

Up to 1950 an oil washer was fitted outside the sleeve gear race, but from 1951 an oil seal was used with one type common to 1963 and another for unit models. The layshaft turned in bushes up to 1963 apart from the RGS, which was fitted with the needle

LEFT *The semi-unit gearbox and clutch shown exploded. Used from 1951 on for 500 and 650 cc machines*

BELOW *The gears and shafts of the unit gearbox where the layshaft is positioned aft of the mainshaft. Round casting is the inner bearing plate*

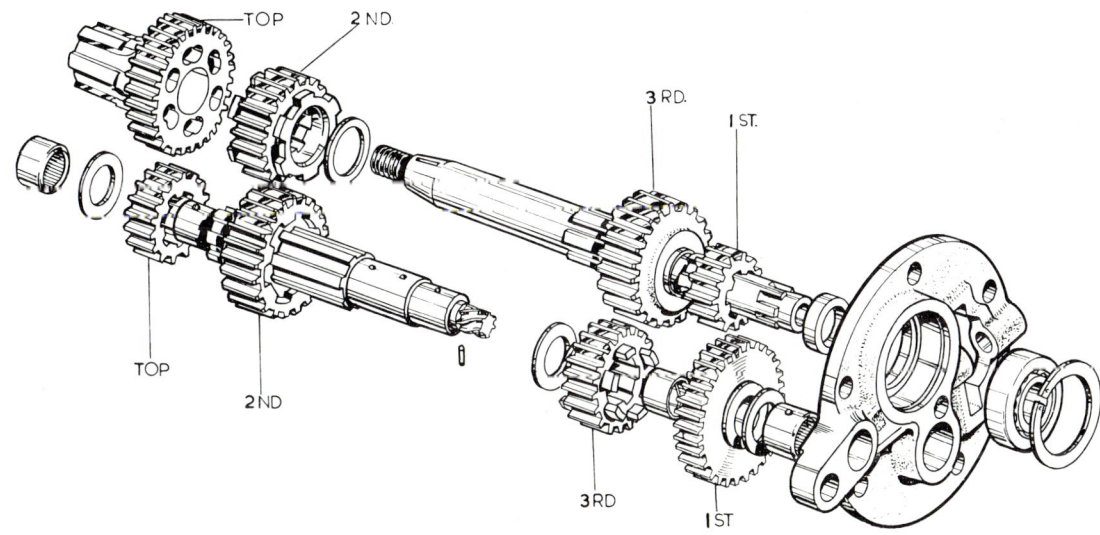

roller layshaft, while all unit engines had needle races for their layshafts. The one on the right was as used by the RGS. Only the RGS had a needle race in the sleeve gear as all other models had bushes of one or two types. The layshaft first gear was bushed and the part was common to all from 1947 to 1972.

Shell and covers

All models have an inner and outer cover and the non-unit ones have a separate shell and an inspection cover on the outer one. The pre-units also have an inspection plate in the rear of the shell, while the units have a bearing plate to support the right ends of the gearbox shafts. The parts need attention as for any other alloy casting to check for cracks, damage, threads and joint faces.

Just one shell was used for all semi-units along with a single inner but the outer changed for 1951, when the kickstarter details were revised. The inspection cover remained common to all non-unit models but the other items all changed for the pre-unit installation.

One shell covered all pre-units except the RGS and the single outer cover was used by that model as well as the rest. This outer can be recognized by the gear pedal boss, which stands out from the cover in contrast to the earlier version, which had a recess for the pedal. The inner cover was changed for 1960 in detail only, while the inspection plate was common to all pre-unit boxes.

The unit models had the first change to the bearing plate for 1966, when the gearchange and kickstart details were modified. It was altered again for 1970 during the change to Unified threads. The inner cover has been covered in the engine chapter but briefly went through eight versions as original 1962, plus one screw in 1964, rev-counter drive added for A65R in 1964, no speedometer drive in 1966, plus filler cap hole in 1967, change to idler bush in 1969, new clutch lift mechanism in 1970 and extra screws in 1971. Life was simpler for the outer, only changing in 1970 to suit the new clutch lift and in 1971 for the extra screws.

Gearbox filler cap with oil level dipstick. Note that it goes into the inner cover on this 1969 model and the original crankcase location further in

Gearchange mechanism

This starts with the rubber on the gear pedal and runs through to the selector forks which move the gears. There are a number of wear points that need to be checked, and the sides of forks are the areas most likely to be worn. The various springs need to be changed if tired and the whole mechanism must operate smoothly.

The non-unit gearboxes all used the same basic design, but the details changed to some extent, mainly when the separate box was introduced in 1954. The first detail alteration came earlier, for 1948, when the gear pedal was amended along with the camplate. The next change came in 1950 with a new pedal for the A10 and, during the year, new selector forks to suit the modified gears, which went in at engine numbers ZA10-1215 and AA7-101 in 1951.

For 1951 the A10 adopted the 1948 gear pedal to bring it in line with the others and the next change came for 1954 with the separate box. Details such as the camplate index plunger, selector forks and casting plugs remained unchanged, but the positive stop mechanism was new with its own camplate and gear pedal. At the same time the semi-unit boxes changed their gear pedal to the 1950 A10 type. From then on there was simply a return spring change for 1960, when the Spitfire adopted the 1948 gear pedal, and the special camplate and other details for the RGS in 1962. The gear pedal rubber remained the same for all years.

The unit engine gearchange had rather more changes, although the design remained the same for all years. The change quadrant and details were soon revised as was the gear pedal rubber, although this was not to change again. The selector forks also changed and for 1964 a grub screw was added to lock the return lever to its shaft.

1966 brought changes for the return spring, lever, quadrant and camplate and this last changed again early in the 1969 model run and once again for 1970. That latter year also brought in a new return lever and spring plus a cup added for this item. 1971 brought a new quadrant and change plunger, while the plunger retaining plate was again altered, having already done so in 1968.

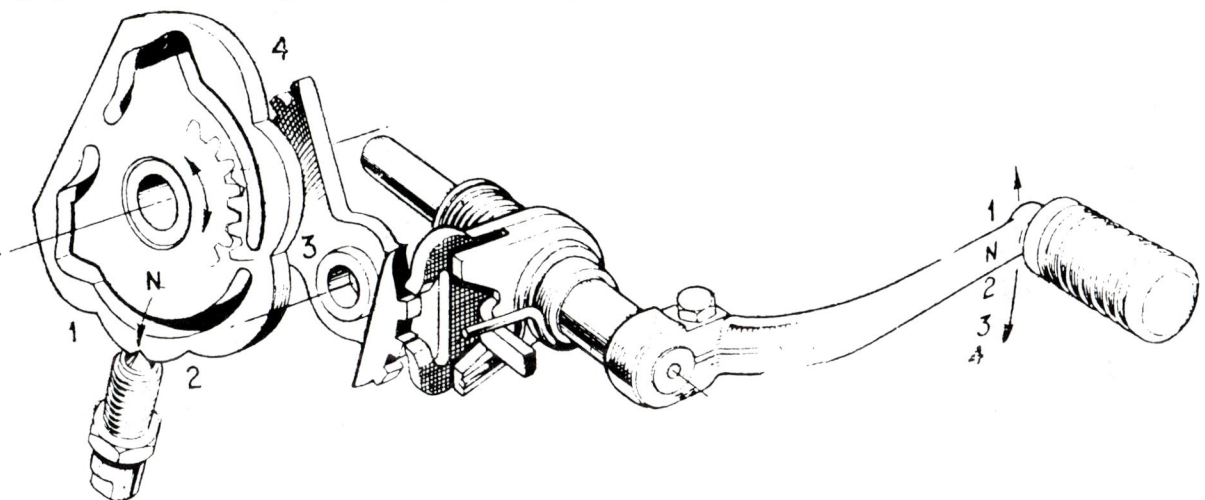

ABOVE *The complete gearchange mechanism from pedal rubber to camplate as used by the twins in the 1950s*

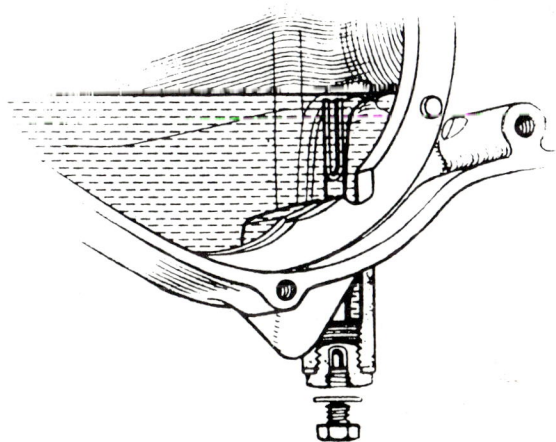

RIGHT *Standpipe to control oil level in the 1962 unit gearbox. Pipe also acts as drain plug*

A 1961 A10 with massive Carmobile sidecar which would call for well lowered gearing

Speedometer drive – gearbox

This was used from 1947 to 1965, at which point the range of gear pairs reached too high a level so the drive was moved to the rear wheel for 1966.

For the non-unit models a single gear pair was used with a six-tooth pinion in the layshaft meshed with an 11-tooth one connected to the cable. The only exception was for the RGS, which had different gearing and gearbox internals anyway.

With a fixed ratio, no change to the sleeve gear pair and just one tyre size the variations of gearbox and rear wheel sprockets affected the speedometer cable running speed. To cope with this the speedometer heads were changed to suit and care is needed to finish up with the correct part.

In the unit engines the problem was solved by changing the gear pair, but the single 1962 pair became four for 1963 and six for 1965, which was just too much. A further trouble arose in that several pairs used common numbers of teeth for one gear but not the other. As all had to run at the same fixed centre distance the tooth form had to be modified to suit. Despite letter marking it is all too easy to mix the wrong gears, which will result in rapid wear. Pairs exist with 6/11, 7/10, 7/11, 7/12, 8/11 and 8/12 tooth combinations, which highlights the potential trouble. Helix angles were changed and this is hard to detect, so be careful when buying a layshaft with fitted gear.

Kickstarter

All models had a similar system with a quadrant meshed with a ratchet gear on the end of the mainshaft. Some details were common throughout. Parts need to be cleaned and examined for wear with replacement the normal remedy.

The first change to the design came in 1949, when the ratchet sleeve was modified. It was altered again for 1951, after which it continued in use to 1972. 1951 also brought a new quadrant with spindle, return spring, spring peg, ratchet and pinion. 1953 saw a folding crank for the Super Flash. The next alterations were for 1954 and the separate gearbox with another new quadrant, a new pinion and the folding crank for the Road Rocket. For 1958 the standard crank was altered and for 1960 it was fitted with a revised pedal rubber. The folding crank was also fitted to the Spitfire and the RGS.

There were few changes on the unit models. The quadrant stop altered for 1966 and the mainshaft nut lockwasher lost its 1947 shape for 1967 and later. The quadrant changed for 1971 and that was it, with all other details retaining their 1962 form.

Sprocket cover plate

This item seals the back of the primary chaincase on the unit models and its removal gives access to the gearbox sprocket. It needs to be checked for damage in case the rear chain has attacked it at any time and cleaned up to remove the grease and road dirt that accumulates on it. Expect to change the oil seal, which has to work hard in that environment.

The cover and seal were both common to all models and years of the unit engine.

Gearbox sprocket

Expect to renew this. Check for worn or damaged teeth, tired splines that don't fit the sleeve gear well and a rough oil seal surface. Fit a new oil seal unless the existing one is perfect. There is one for all non-unit boxes from frame ZA7S-19337 built in 1951 and another for all unit boxes. Prior to the 1951 change an oil washer was fitted.

The non-unit models used an 18- or 19-tooth sprocket most of the time with the other an option, both being modified for the oil seal during 1951. In 1958 these two were joined by one with 17 teeth for use on the A7 models when pulling a sidecar and in 1960 came a 16-tooth sprocket for the Spitfire. All were retained by a common nut and lockwasher.

The unit twins had a new nut and washer with the first going on all models and the second being modified for 1966. Outboard of the sprocket a felt ring was fitted from 1966 to augment the sealing design.

The sprockets varied in number of teeth from 16 to 21 without the full range ever appearing in one year. As all interchange, the required gearing can usually be arrived at by suitable selection. On the A70 only a distance piece went with its 21-tooth sprocket.

Rear chain

Bound to need renewal on any rebuild. The size is the same for all models with 0.625 in. pitch × 0.400 in. roller diameter × 0.38 in. between inner plates and better known as $\frac{5}{8} \times \frac{3}{8}$ in. Non-unit chain lengths vary from 96 to 104 links and the units from 98 to 110.

Assembly

This is a straightforward job but the details need to be checked as you go along. Bearings should be held in place with Loctite as an added security and joint faces can be sealed with the traditional gasket or a silicone rubber compound. As always this should be used sparingly.

Work to the manual and check each stage for correct operation. Make certain you have the selector forks in the correct positions and engaged in the proper cam tracks. Double check the gear selection as a mistake can be traumatic on the road. If you leave the main nuts until you have the machine assembled (so you can use the brake to hold the shaft), make sure you cannot forget by some means or other.

Remember to fill the gearbox and primary chaincase with oil before using the machine. A tie-on label on the filler or the gear pedal may help.

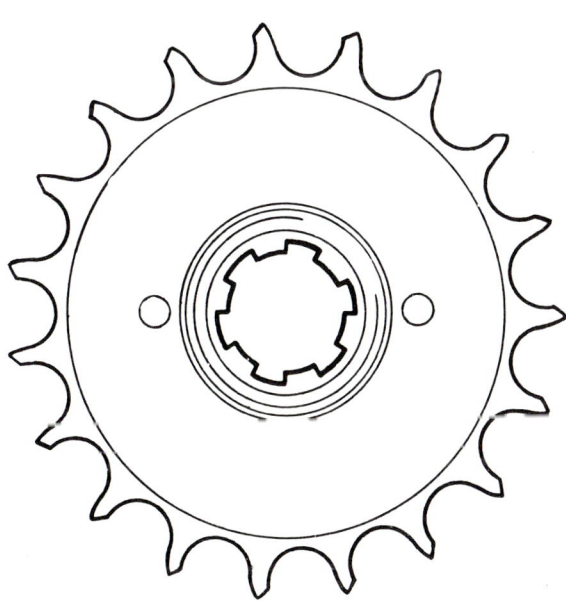

ABOVE *Any sprocket like this needs to be changed*

RIGHT *1956 A7 fitted with the optional full chaincase. Access hole is for hub fixings and other one for checking chain tension*

5 Carburettor and exhaust

These are two areas that can give the restorer considerable problems unless the parts are simply replaced. The difficulties arise as the first wears and the second corrodes all the time the machine is in use and so their condition changes continuously. Both affect the performance of the machine, especially the carburettor, and both are important to the final appearance of the model.

All BSA twins had Amal carburettors and the standard models used type 6 to 1954, Monoblocs from 1955 to 1967 and Concentrics from 1968. TT and GP carburettors were used by some Rocket and Spitfire models.

A variety of exhaust systems was fitted to the twins over the years with the most common being a separate exhaust pipe and silencer mounted low down on each side. In the early 1960s siamezed pipes were used for a year or two with the silencer low on the right while the mid-1960s brought more variety for the US market. From 1969 balance pipes were adopted.

The Amal number system

Amal stamp all carburettor bodies with a number sequence that is their method of stock control. This is the build standard and up to the late Concentrics is unique as to the internal settings of the instrument. Thus if *any* setting was changed the assembly received a new part number and was stored accordingly. In this manner they could easily check that they delivered the correct unit to their many customers and they in turn could readily check them into their stores and in time out again onto the correct machines.

The type six carburettors are stamped with the basic type number followed by two letters, an oblique line and a further three-digit mark. The type number is 275 for units up to $\frac{7}{8}$ in. bore, 276 for those of $\frac{15}{16}$ to $1\frac{1}{16}$ in. and 289 for $1\frac{1}{8}$ in. and above. The two letters give the build standard of the settings while the final series indicate the float chamber that goes with the unit.

Monobloc carburettors have no need for this last and are stamped with the type number followed by a two- or three-digit build standard number. The first can be 375, 376 or 389 with the same size limits as the type 6.

The Concentric carburettor uses the same system for the 600 and 900 series and the units are numbered R or L for right or left-hand, followed by a six or nine plus the bore in mm, to give 626 or 928 for example, with the build standard to finish.

The effect of this system can be seen in the carburettor settings list.

A perfectionist would seek to fit a carburettor with the correct number stamped on it but otherwise there is no obstacle to just changing the settings to the correct ones for the machine in question.

Amal restoration

The instrument has to be taken apart and checked over. New fibre washers, float needle and seating are normal practice and a new needle and jet may not come amiss. Checking the mounting flange for flatness, its holes for clearance and all the internal passages for obstructions is also usual with any rebuild. Pilot screw damage is common.

The earlier type 6 Amal with separate float and mixing chambers

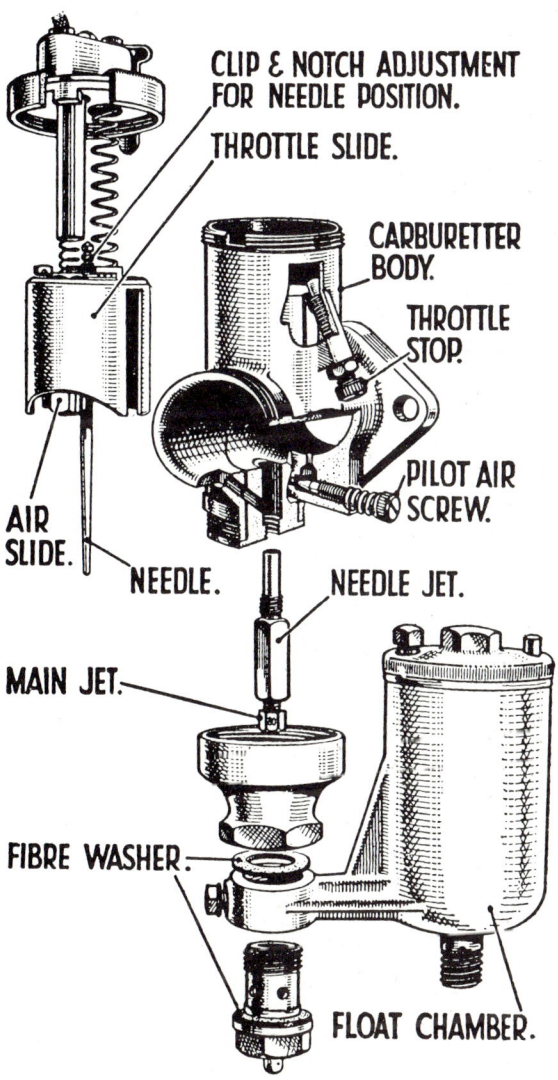

LEFT *Twin Amal Monoblocs on a 1966 Lightning. Handed for access to the air and throttle stop screws*

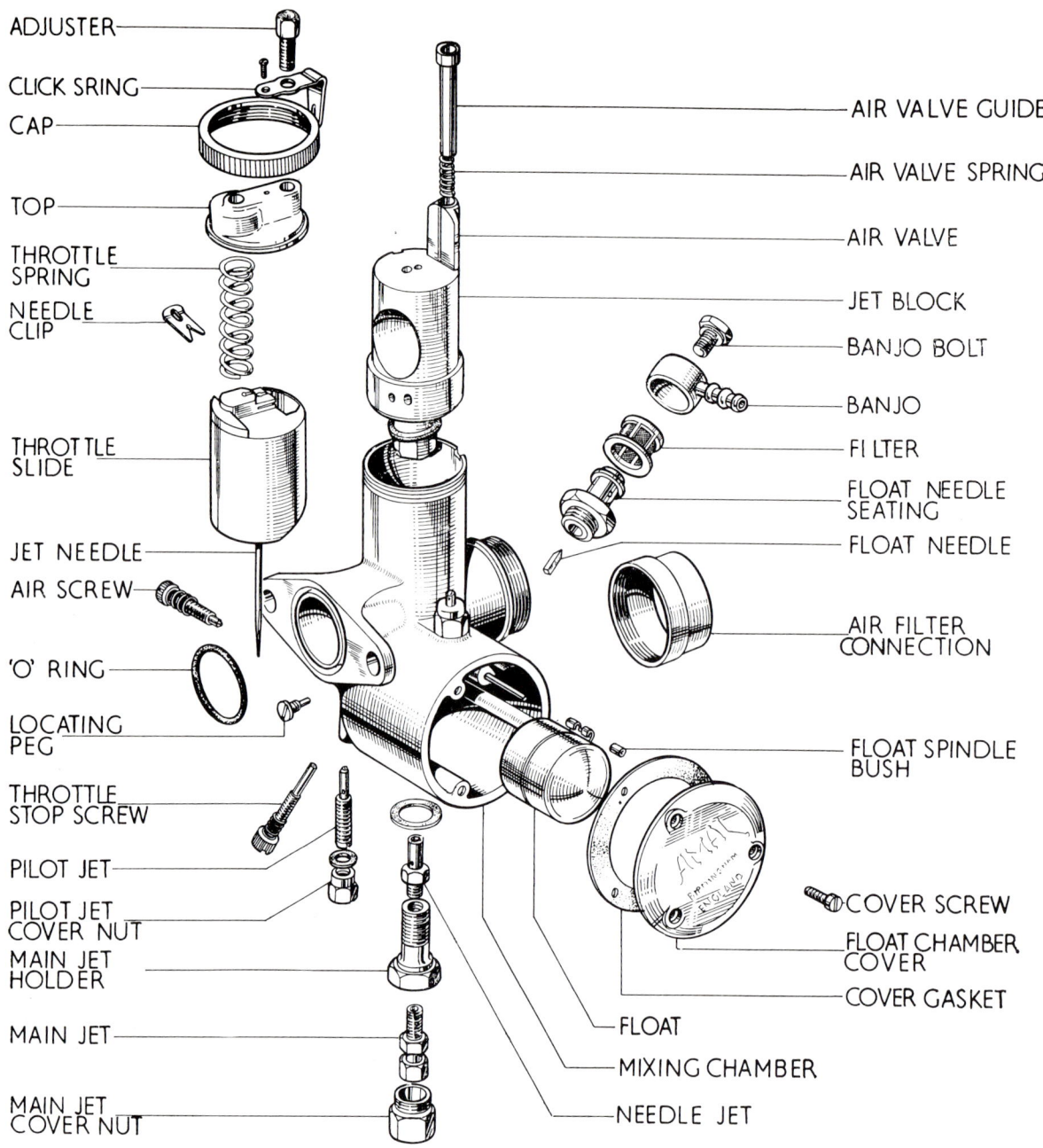

The problems arise from body and slide wear plus doubtful threads, especially the one for the top ring. Most of the other threads can be repaired or reclaimed with an insert, even in some cases by a thread change with a new mating part made from scratch. The top ring, or mixing chamber cap, is more tricky and often the chamber thread will be found to be damaged or worn away to a taper. It is possible to cut it deeper and make a new ring but it is a tricky engineering job needing good equipment.

The wear problem can be dealt with by sleeving the body. Again this is a tricky job which must be done to a high level of precision. As with all carburettor work it must be tackled with a delicate touch as the parts are fragile and easy to break.

If you can find replacement parts it will be easier than repairing an old carburettor and the notes about Amal numbering should help. The units were handed so you must check that you have the correct item for your model and also note the positions of throttle stop and air screw.

Chambers and their floats require normal inspection but usually it is only the needle and its seating that wears. Make sure the float in a Monobloc

CARBURETTOR AND EXHAUST

can move freely on its pivot as a tight spot can cause confusion. Check all floats for leaks.

Assemble the instrument with care and make sure the petrol feed area is as it should be. It is well worth connecting this up to a tank and checking that it holds a level and does not flood. Better to find out before it goes back onto the machine and drips all over the magneto.

The finish of the earlier Amal bodies was in a silver-grey paint specially developed to resist petrol. This is no longer available as no one is prepared to order the required large quantity, so a problem exists. Do not be tempted to use any other paint without a trial first as it may react with the fuel to produce a dreadful mess that is more a sludge than anything and a full clean-out will then be needed. Better to go for vapour blasting, which gives a very similar result, but do check every passage afterwards in case the job was not correctly masked.

Petrol pipes

The early twins used copper tube and brass end fittings for their petrol pipes, but from 1950 began to turn to the better flexible type. From then on they comprised the appropriate lengths of tubing held onto the required end fittings by crimps.

The early armoured hose and the transparent plastic that followed it should be treated with suspicion as both age and may then leak. Replacement is usually essential on safety grounds.

The pipe end fittings need inspection to make sure they seat and seal as they should and that the nut threads are in good order. Older pipes can take a set and are often very stiff, so they will pull on the tap or the carburettor, which is not a good idea.

If new pipes are needed and total originality is not required then modern black neoprene is to be recommended as it has a long life and holds onto the fittings well even without any clips. It also remains

LEFT *Exploded Monobloc. Note float needle assembly as this is often wrong which affects fuel level*

RIGHT *Bolting the float chamber onto a 1954 A10. Enough torque and no more is used or the threads distort*

BELOW *Cutaway drawing of Concentric Amal as used on the unit twins*

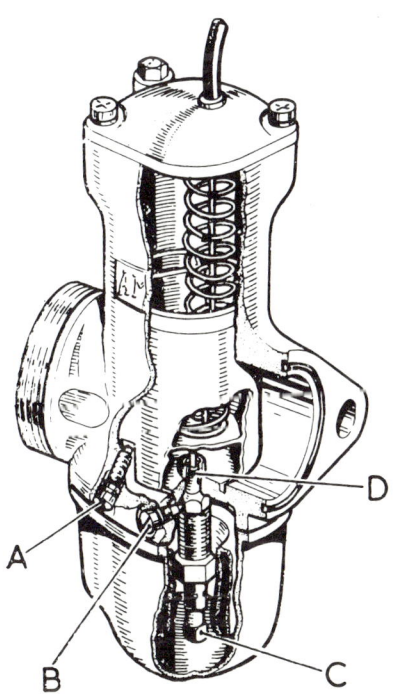

very flexible even in cold weather, which is a good point. When making up pipes ensure they are long enough not to pull at the ends or kink, that they lie naturally and avoid vertical loops, which can cause air locks.

For such a simple part BSA managed to use a great variety of them, with some 35 items being listed from 1947 to 1972. The seeker of originality thus needs to be careful. The first twin had two petrol taps and one carburettor connected by copper pipe and this was made up into one assembly. This joined the two taps and the cross-pipe included a T-junction from where a pipe ran down and then up to the float chamber base.

The 1949 A7 used the same idea but of different construction. In this, one pipe ran down and round to the float chamber with a tee in its length and this connected across to the second tap. For the Star Twin there were two pipes, each one connecting one tap to one chamber. These pipes had a flexible section in their length with this swaged to the tube ends.

The A7 arrangements continued for 1950, but for the A10 there was a flexible supply pipe and a copper cross-pipe to connect the two tank halves. With the revised A7 of 1951 came a simpler arrangement in armoured pipe with a run from each tap crimped to a single float chamber banjo and this went onto all models.

This position was revised in 1954 with two new armoured pipes, one used by the plunger A7 models for that year only and another by the plunger A10 to 1957. The A7 one continued in use on the pivoted-fork models for 1954, but was replaced by a version with plastic tubing for 1955 on. The Super Flash and Road Rocket had two flexible supply pipes. This continued for the Super Rocket while the rest of the range continued with its 1955 design. For the Rocket

BELOW *The GP carburettors with remote central float chamber on the 1966 Spitfire Mk II*

Gold Star there were three special assemblies made up to suit the three tanks available.

The advent of the unit twins brought a new pipe design. This had plastic pipe which connected to the horizontal outlet of each tap with a tee at the centre of the run. This had a short branch with the end fitting to the carburettor. The assembly was joined in 1965 by another for twin carburettor models which had a cross-connection pipe between the petrol taps with each tap banjo having a second outlet with pipe feed to one float chamber.

The twin-feed design was revised for 1966 while the single one continued. They were joined by a new version of the 1951 design with twin pipes connected to a common float chamber banjo. All three types were renumbered for 1967 and changed for 1968. That year there was first another version of the 1951 design but to suit a Concentric carburettor. With it came two designs of similar H layout but alternative tap connections. In both one pipe joined the two taps and another the two carburettors. In the centre of each a tee was inserted and the final pipe joined the tees. Tap fittings for one were banjos and for the other nuts.

This last type continued for 1969, but in revised form, as did the single-feed type. They were joined by a new version comprising a simple loop from tap to first float banjo to second float banjo to second tap. The first two ran on to 1970 but the third was replaced by yet another design. In this the two feed pipes from the taps ran down to join the cross-pipe between the two float banjos which thus had two tees in it.

1971 and the new frame brought four versions of an arrangement with feeds from each tap to each banjo and a cross-pipe between banjos, each of which thus had two connections. Two of these four were revised for the final 1972 year.

BELOW *Twin Concentrics with air filters went onto the Mk III Spitfire in 1967*

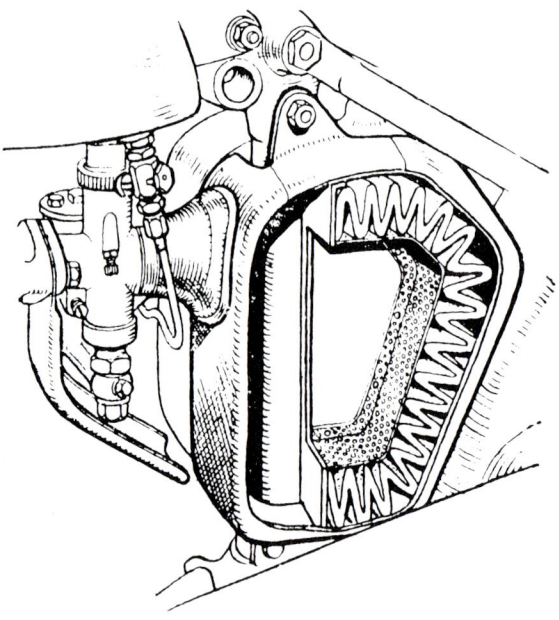

ABOVE *Early twins had a Vokes air filter sandwiched between the oil tank and the battery*

RIGHT *A 1956 Road Rocket with a water injection system added to its normal carburettor. A brief fad of the time*

Air filter

The element should be washed, dried and re-oiled or renewed according to type, while the body needs to be repaired and finished as any other sheet steel component. The hose connecting the filter to the carburettor must be carefully checked for cracks, which could cause air leaks.

The first A7 had its filter sandwiched between the oil tank and battery carrier, which was neat if inaccessible. This continued to 1949 up to frame ZA7-109, after which a revised housing and filter were used, the new element only needing three fixings to secure it. The twin carburettor Star Twin built for 1949 and 1950 dispensed with the filter but did have a gauze flame trap fitted to each bellmouth.

The A10 adopted the A7 system but with its own parts and these were used on all rigid- and plunger-frame models from 1951 to 1957. For the pivoted-fork models there was a new assembly that bolted in place ahead of the central battery on the tourers. The sports twins used either a circular filter attached to the carburettor or nothing at all. Some the parts were modified for 1960 and a filter devised for the Spitfire. In 1962 an air cleaner was listed for the Rocket Gold Star.

The unit twins began with a round filter screwed onto the carburettor and this had a water deflector clipped to it early on. In 1965 this type was joined by others of similar form for the sports models. For 1966 two more drum filters came which changed for 1967 and again for 1968, after which they stayed as they were to 1970. For 1971 the new frame meant a complete revision to the filtration system and two elements were used, each contained within a pair of die-castings attached to one side of the machine. There were rather a lot of these castings as the system had to supply either one or two carburettors, which meant two bodies and two covers for each side to total eight parts. For 1972 five of these were modified.

Induction bias

This was not a common occurrence on the twins and most cases that did occur were on the A10, with trouble on the A7 being very rare. The cure offered by BSA was a tapered spacer to fit between carburettor and intake flange, its part number being 67-359.

Exhaust system

This consists of the pipes and silencers plus the clips, brackets and stays that hold them to the machine. The parts are steel, chrome plated, and this finish often suffers from both heat and corrosion which detracts greatly from the machine's appearance.

Fortunately replacement with pattern parts is possible for these popular models and it is worth paying a sensible price for the items rather than looking for the cheapest. The pipes and silencers are an important facet of the looks of the model so well worth getting right for the sake of a little extra money. Quality parts will also fit better and last longer.

If the pipes, clips and brackets are in good order it may be feasible to clean and polish them for further use. Before the final polish they should be checked for their fit to the machine mounting points and to the cylinder head. All models have push-in pipes and finned collars. You may need to swell the pipe to ensure it is a snug fit in the port and heat plus a wooden wedge may be needed to do this. If any parts are distorted, real care may be needed to get everything back into line.

The brackets and clips should be easy to repair and re-finish, if this is needed, as most are simple parts. The correct, nuts, bolts and washers plus the D-section parts used with the clips should be checked and refurbished as necessary. On some models heat shields were fitted and these need similar treatment.

The silencer body is much more of a problem if you wish to re-use it and it is not in good condition. Often the thin outer shell will have corroded from the inside which makes repair a skilled metal-working job. A further problem is the plating, for firms that undertake such work will not want to put a dirty silencer in their tank and it is just about impossible to fully clean it.

Thus the existing silencer can only really be used if in good order and the practical alternative has to be a pattern part unless you are lucky enough to locate an unused original.

Waist level exhausts on a 1966 Hornet which also has twin carburettors, each with its round air filter

ABOVE *The Lightning Clubman of 1965 with its two into one exhaust system. Twin pipes were an option*

BELOW *How not to install. Left pipe joint is not home so the pipe touches the frame and its bracket fails to fit the mounting stud. It must sit in place without strain to avoid trouble*

Exhaust pipe types

These vary and it is important to get the right one or you can have problems. The first pair for the 1947 A7 went onto all rigid and plunger 500 cc models up to 1954 and was joined by a similar pair for the A10. A welded lug on each attached to a crankcase stud and the A10 plunger pair continued in use to 1957. The A10SF right pipe was a special.

In 1954 came two new pairs of pipes for the pivoted-fork models, one pair for the 500s and one for the 650s. All four changed for 1958 and the new ones continued in use to the end of the pre-unit models. There were also high-level pipes with leg protectors for the Spitfire and a siamezed pipe for the Super Rocket and RGS in 1962.

The unit twins shared a pair of low-level pipes for their first four years with the option of a siamezed pair for those who wanted that style. For the A65R in 1964 the arrangement was reversed, with the same siamezed pair fitted as standard and the twin pipes the option.

Also in 1964 a waist-level pair appeared for the off-road twins and these were revised for 1965, this latter pair going onto the Wasp in 1966. The original pair had a tie rod linking a lug welded to each pipe just below the exhaust port, but the revised one used a bolted-on strap. The same change went onto the standard models for 1966, so these too gained a tapped boss for the strap to fix to. These continued on the road models to

Exhaust balance pipe on a 1969 Lightning

1970 but for the off-road models there was a revised pipe pair and for the West Coast Hornet yet another pair.

1968 brought the Firebird Scrambler, which had its own pipes, while 1969 saw further changes. The 1966 pipes continued on the A50 only, while the Lightning and Thunderbird changed to a pair with a balance pipe close to the exhaust port. For the Firebird there was a new system with both pipes carried on the left side at waist level with the right one above the left. At their ends was a connector piece that joined each pipe to its silencer and also provided a balance link between the two. To protect the rider a wire mesh grille was attached to the pipes.

The pipes were all revised for 1971 but continued in the same style with the Firebird ones finished in matt black. The 1969 balance pipe remained in use for 1971 but was altered for 1972.

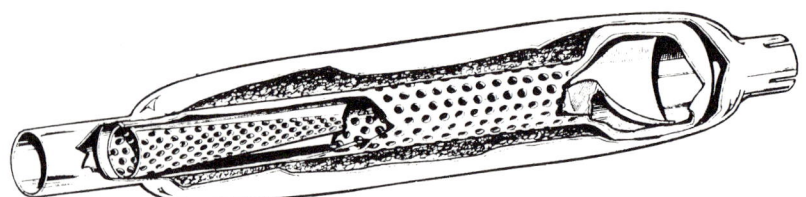

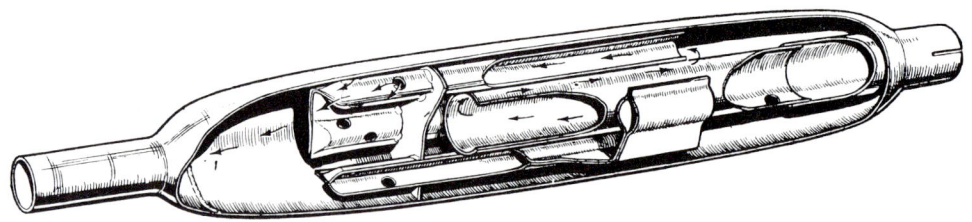

ABOVE *The silencer introduced for the Super Rocket and RGS in 1962 (above); unit twin silencer used from 1964 on the road models (below)*

BELOW *The silencers as fitted to a 1970 Lightning*

Exhaust pipe collar

This is finned and clamped to the pipe with no real contact with the cylinder head. One was used from 1947 to 1950, a second from 1951 to 1959 and a third from 1960 on. This last went onto the unit engines and continued in use to 1972.

Silencer types

The first A7 had a pair of tubular silencers held by a single bolt to the frame. As with all such systems the silencer should be pushed well onto the exhaust pipe before its clip is tightened to make sure it is not trying to push away from the engine. The reverse is better if it can be achieved.

The rigid-frame models all used these silencers, which were handed and were joined by one new one in 1949. This was not handed, had a recess in its underside for the centre stand feet and went on all the plunger-frame machines. A new part appeared in 1953 for the Super Flash and a pair in 1954 for the pivoted fork models, which were altered to a new form for 1958. These were changed again for 1960 and in 1962 came a final version for the Super Rocket and RGS, another for the Spitfire and a third labelled track silencer for RGS.

The unit twins begin with a silencer unit common to both sides of the machine, but it was soon revised. It was joined by a similar one for use with the off-road models in 1964 and this was used in 1966 for the tourers and sports models while a new one appeared for the Spitfire. In 1967 this last continued while the first became the USA general fitment and the revised original went back to being the stock home-market fit.

For 1968 these three were joined by another for the Firebird. This last was revised for 1969. That year only the revised original continued with it and both remained in use for 1970. 1971 brought megaphone silencers for road use and black ones for the Firebird.

The unit silencers were mounted to brackets and the original pair were made heavier in 1966. These were changed for 1971 from a triangular form to a similar one with curved top to suit the new frame and silencers. The Firebird had its own single plate for 1968 and welded assemblies of different forms for 1969, 1970 and 1971. The leg guard remained the same for all three years.

As a final reminder, remember that the whole system must fit the machine without stress or strain to avoid fractures or parts coming adrift.

Full café racer style with non-standard, swept back Dow pipes on a 1965 Lightning Clubman

6 Lubrication

All BSA twins have a dry sump system and most a separate oil tank mounted on the right side of the machine under the saddle or front of the dualseat. Exceptions were the 650 cc oil-in-frame models of 1971–72 which used the main frame beam as the tank. The oil was circulated by twin gear pumps mounted in a single body and driven by a skew gear on the crankshaft. It circulated through internal passages with a release valve to control the pressure. From 1969 a pressure switch was added to the timing case, but up to then neither gauge, indicator or warning light had been provided.

Filters were fitted on the feed line in the oil tank and in the base of the sump on the scavenge pipe. The earliest engines had no oil supply to the rockers, but this was soon introduced for the exhaust during 1947 and extended to the inlet for 1949. The supply was taken from the return line and the oil drained back down the pushrod tunnel.

The oil system was revised with the introduction of the A10 in 1950 to pass the excess oil from the release valve around the engine to do further work with bleeds and troughs. There was a further change in 1951 to revise and improve the flow to the big ends.

All pre-unit engines had a timed breather driven by the camshaft gear and working in the inner timing cover. This connected to a passage to the outside world. For the unit engines this was changed to a disc valve driven from the left end of the camshaft, which became hollow to let the gases out.

A 1950 A10 fitted with a two-way radio in Scotland. Oil tank in its traditional position

LUBRICATION

Oil pump

As this works in oil there should not be much wear, but if there is any doubt about this the pump should be dismounted and the parts inspected. More likely is distortion of the body, which can arise in different ways. On pre-unit engines the fibre washer on the third fixing stud is easily forgotten and without it tightening the nut will bend the body. On unit engines the gasket ran out to include the third fixing and the problem is more likely to arise due to over-tightening of the fixing nuts. Right at the end the body was changed to cast iron and this type is unlikely to bend and thus leak oil pressure away.

The original 1947 pump was first altered for 1956, when its four internal gears were changed; and of course these have to be used in complete sets although both used the same body. In 1960 this type was joined by one with an extended spindle for driving a rev-counter and was fitted to the Super Rocket only.

Rather the same thing happened with the unit engines, the original 1962 one being joined by a rev-counter-driving version in 1964 for the A65R model. This continued alone after 1965 until 1968, when a new body was wrapped around the existing gears and shafts. For 1970 the pump body was dowelled to the spindle housing and the drive from one pair of gears to the other modified. 1971 saw the cast-iron body appear and this part and the spindle were further modified for 1972.

The pump drive was by a skew gear threaded onto the crankshaft and just two were used, one for unit and one for pre-unit engines.

Release valve

This is the spring-loaded valve that controls the oil pressure reaching the engine. If this level is exceeded excess oil is returned to the sump and then to the oil tank. On pre-unit engines it screws into the front of the crankcase just inboard of the inner timing cover. On unit engines it goes into the right side of the crankcase beneath the timing chest. Nearly all can be dismantled, cleaned and inspected. They seldom give trouble, but look for poor seating of the ball valve and a tired pressure spring.

The 1947 type was only used on the early long-stroke A7 models and was joined by a similar design for the A10 in 1950. From 1951 this went on all pre-unit engines. It was also used by the early unit engines up to 1965. For 1966 the sealing washers became O rings and the mating parts were changed to suit, but for 1969 the latter changed again to Unified threads. This did not last for long as for 1970 a new design with piston plunger was introduced. This can be recognized by its domed outer cap. Several varieties exist, for a new type with new sealing washer appeared in 1971. The washer changed for 1972 and another release valve was used for the A70 model.

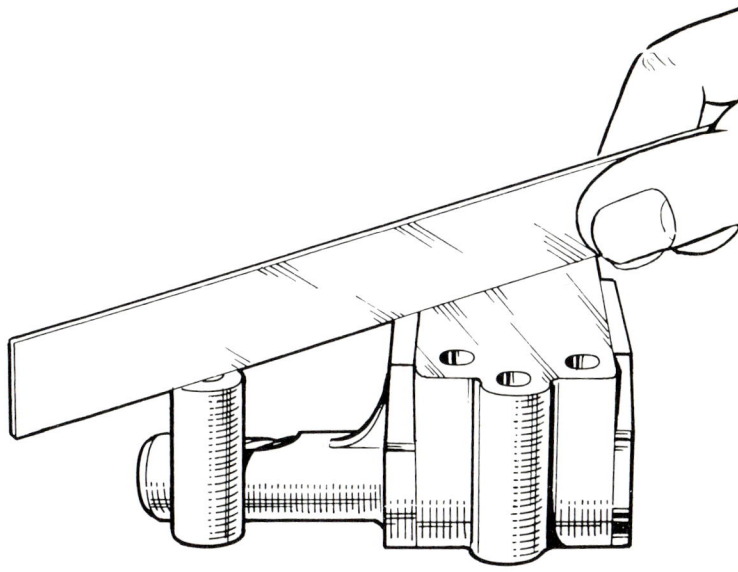

ABOVE *Checking the oil pump joint face. On non-units the pump can bend if the washer under the third bolt is left out*

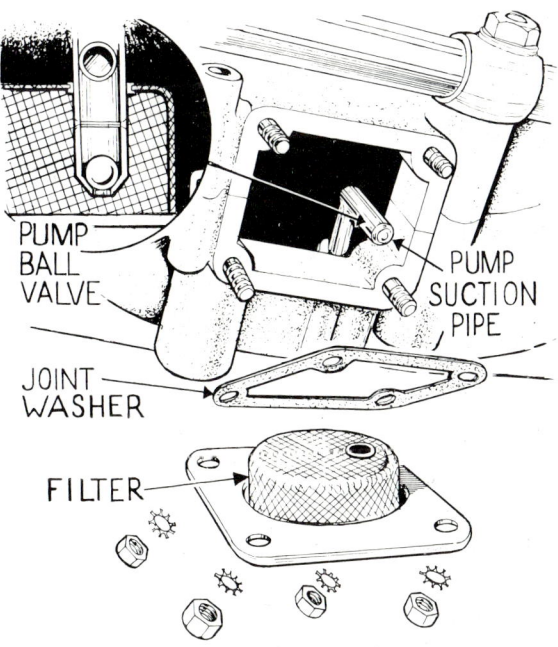

Beneath the sump plate lurks a filter and the suction pipe with its ball valve which must be free to move

Oil pressure switch

This was not fitted until 1969 as up to then the rider just had to believe there was oil pressure in the engine. The switch fits in the front of the crankcase next to the release valve and is a sealed unit that opens its contacts at the required low pressure. For 1969 this was 5 psi and the part carried /05 in its part number to signify this, but from 1970 this changed to 7 psi and /07.

Filters

There are two of these, one in the oil tank and the other in the engine sump, and both protect the intake lines to the oil pump. They are made from a metal gauze or mesh and need to be inspected for damage, which could cause the oil not to be strained. The mesh is either soldered or silver soldered in place so can be replaced or repaired with two provisos. The first is not to restrict the oil flow and the second is not to decrease the degree of filtration. Thus, do not replace a fine gauze with a wide mesh. Also check the parts for damage to the mechanical fixing and function.

All engines had a sump plate and filter through which the scavenge pipe passed, these parts being retained by four studs and nuts. The area is a natural for oil leaks, so check for these, and check the threads as they tend to get mangled. From 1947 to 1969 a cover and filter assembly was fitted, but for 1970 this became two parts with a gasket between them.

The tank filter used on plunger and rigid models remained the same for all years and secured the supply line banjo to the tank as well. A new type was introduced for the pivoted-fork oil tank and this was modified for 1958. The unit models were fitted with a side-mounted filter in similar style but differed in the method used to ensure the feed was taken from inside the mesh and thus was filtered. In 1971 the oil-in-frame model appeared and the filter was mounted on a plate at the base of the seat tube carrying the lubricant. This one-piece assembly of filter and plate was quickly changed to two separate parts in 1972.

Rocker box oiling

Initially none, this was introduced at engine number XA7-450 in 1947 as a feed just to the exhaust side. It was taken from the return line at a point next to the oil tank and went via a small-bore pipe to the left end of the spindle. From there internal drillways fed the oil to where it was wanted and these all need to be clean and unobstructed. The pipe in particular should be checked for kinks, which could restrict the oil flow.

In 1949, or rather from engine YA7-3402 late in 1948, the feed was taken to the inlet side as well, so a pipe with an extra banjo was fitted. This system continued on all pre-unit engines. The pipe itself changed to suit the other alterations, first in 1951, then for the pivoted-fork frame and again in 1960.

The unit engines had a different design to produce the same result, with an oil union in the rear of the cylinder head just below the rocker cover face. From this drillways ran forwards and up to the inlet spindle and then on via a cast rib between the left-side inlet and exhaust spindle supports. The oil supply continued to come from a take-off in the return line at the oil tank until 1968. The feed and return assembly at the engine was then altered to provide an additional return-side outlet and the rocker supply was taken from that.

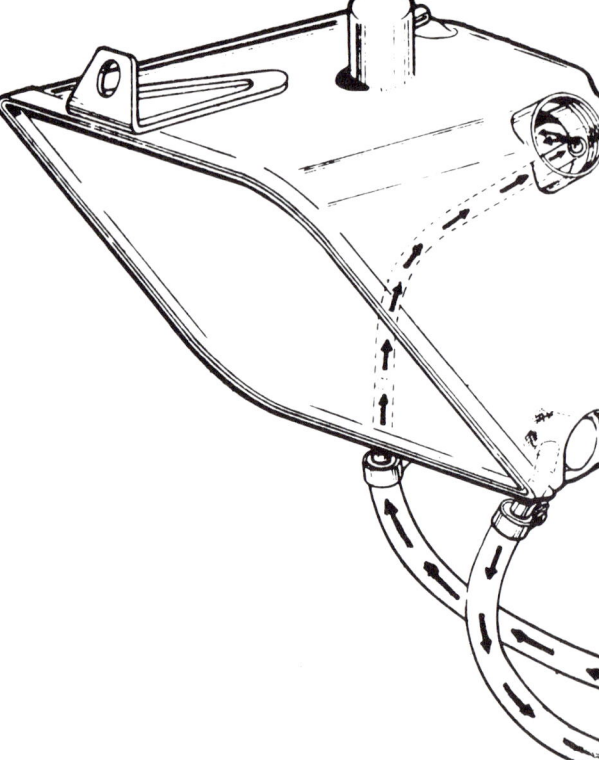

Unit engine lubrication system including rocker box take off from the return line close to the engine

Pipes

The main ones are the feed and return that connect the oil tank to the engine, plus the rocker box feed pipe and vent pipes. All need to be inspected for any signs of cracks or leaks. Check carefully any flexible pipes as their material may deteriorate and either swell or break away; either fault could block the pipe. Also check for any loose area that could flap about and stop the flow once this begins but which would leave the pipe clear when inspected. A rare fault maybe but confusing and expensive if it happens.

An important internal pipe is the scavenge that runs from the sump to the oil pump mounting wall of the crankcase. This must be secure and without leaks or cracks otherwise the pump will not empty the sump. Inspect closely in case there is a hairline crack, which may widen under heat so that the pump will scavenge at first and then begins to fail to clear the accumulation of oil. Check that its ball valve is free to move and clear of sludge.

LEFT *The oil pressure switch fitted from 1969 and seen on a Lightning of that year. Early 5 psi type which was changed to 7 psi for 1970*

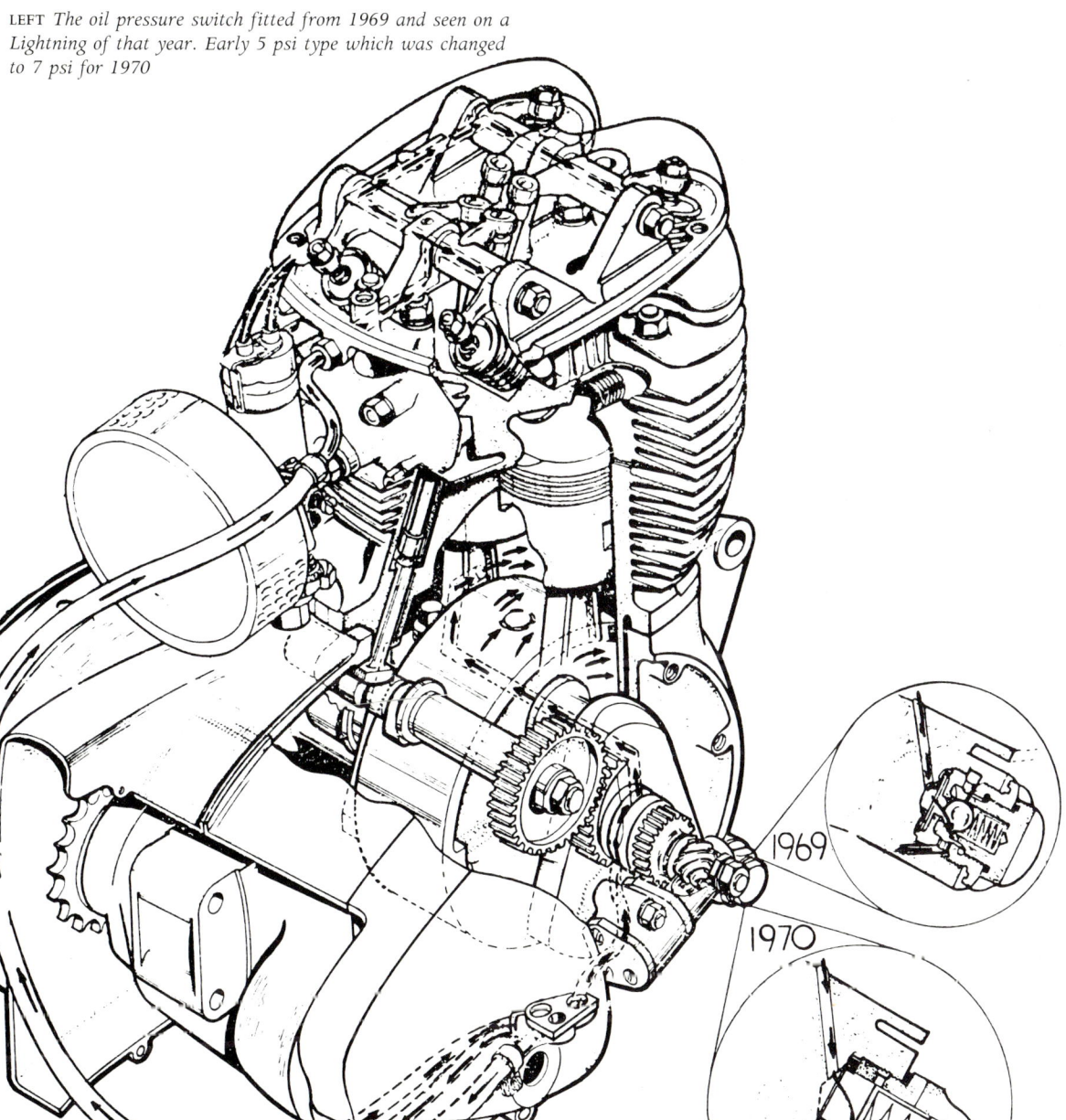

Under seat area of a 1955 A7SS showing the breather tower of the oil tank

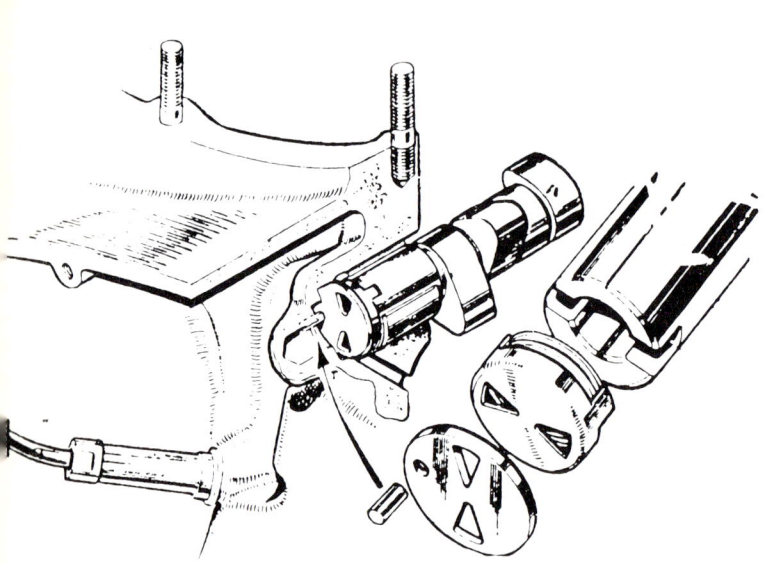

Timed disc breather introduced for the unit twins and driven from the left end of the camshaft

Breather system

This is an area that seems to give owners a headache if it has any problems. Perhaps the snag is that it consists largely of holes and as such cannot appear on a parts list.

Two designs were used on BSA twins, one for all pre-unit and the second for all unit engines. The first had a ported bush driven by a screw fitted to the camshaft gear, so its timing has little chance to be wrong. It is backed by a cork washer and this has to be selected from the several thicknesses listed to give a seal. The breather passage is through a drillway in the timing cover and then across the crankcase to an outlet pipe set in the left crankcase. The breather bush was changed in 1954 but otherwise the system continued for all pre-unit engines.

The unit models had a ported disc at the left end of the camshaft, which was hollow to let the pressure through and drove the disc. To remove the fixed disc the camshaft bush has to come out and it is important to engage disc with camshaft on assembly. A spring holds the two discs together.

If either system jams or breaks its drive then either the engine can breathe all the time and loses oil rapidly or it cannot breathe at all and the pressures generated will force their way out elsewhere and cause leaks. The latter trouble will also occur if the breather pipe is blocked in any way.

Good breathing is as important as good joints in cutting out oil leaks so it is vital that all the parts do their job correctly including all the holes that contribute to the system.

Oil tank

This container always sits in the same place, except where built as part of the frame, but comes in various shapes and sizes. Two basic forms were used to suit rigid and swinging-fork frames but each can be found in several varieties.

Leaving aside the finish, which is covered later, the tank needs to be cleaned and inspected. On a running model the first part is, or should be, no problem, but an unknown tank can be full of horrors. Oil tanks seem able to harbour more dirt, sludge, spiders and unknown substances than even the underside of mudguards; maybe it's the confined atmosphere. Whatever it is, you have to get it all out. It may take every solvent and detergent you have but clean it must be both inside and out. Only then can it be checked over.

Look for cracks and split seams which will need to be welded up. Oil tanks are prone to this due to the combination of heat and vibration. Thus the mounting system and the actual fastenings need to be inspected to ensure they are not straining the tank or themselves. Correct as necessary. Also inspect all the pipe or union threads and any washer seating faces that may need cleaning up. If this has to be done it is

ABOVE *On pivoted-fork models such as this 1955 Road Rocket the oil filter acts as the drain plug and fits to the supply pipe within the tank*

LEFT *The breather pipe of an early type oil tank being checked for obstruction. The frame joint at the base of the seat tube can also be seen*

worth fitting the parts and checking that paraffin won't seep through the joint even if you have to clean it out again. Better than finding an oil leak later.

Check the fit of the tank cap and its washer. Examine the breather, froth tower or any other ancillary feature. For oil-in-frame 650s make sure the oil filter plate fits and seals to the bottom of the seat tube. After all it is effectively the bottom of the oil tank and a leak will not be easy to spot unless it becomes dramatic. Then it's Hobson's choice between a seized engine and an oily rear tyre.

Oil tank types

The first oil tank was for the rigid frame only and was joined by another version in 1949 for the plunger frame. These two remained in use to 1951 and 1957 respectively, with a third for the Super Flash. They differed in that the first had an angled filler and the second a vertical one, the top bracket moved from the front to the centre and the shape was changed.

In 1954 the second one was joined by a slim tank which went on all pre-unit pivoted-fork models, although the side was more domed for 1958 onwards. The unit machines had a more angular tank as it was behind panels and it first changed for 1965 with new pipes and clips. In 1966 its top rear mounting was altered and in 1967 it was joined by a special tank used by the USA West Coast Hornet only. This had a greater capacity achieved by extending the right side to the rear and this section carried a bracket for a side-

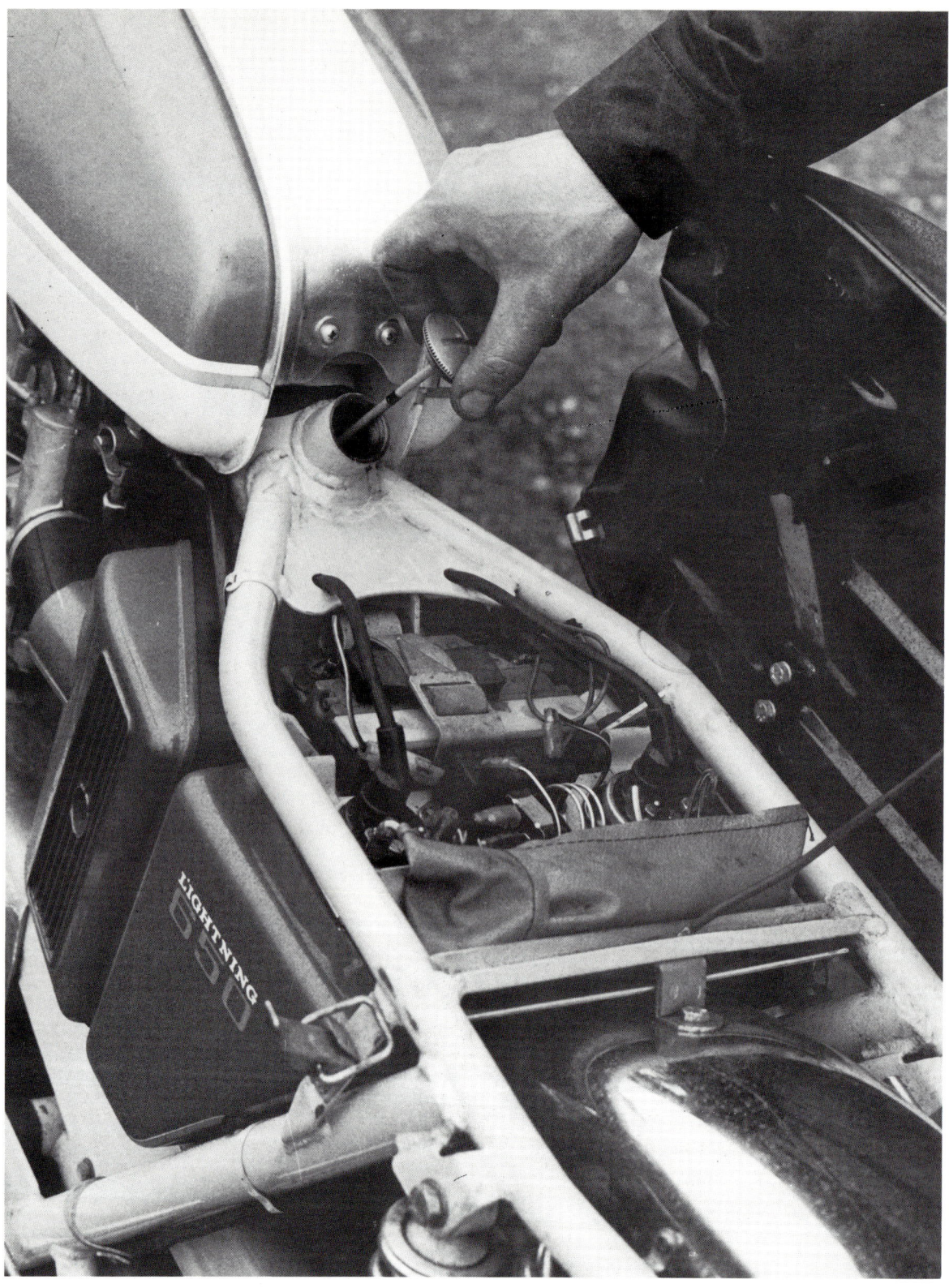

Checking the level of the oil-in-frame Lightning of 1971. Note routing of HT leads via unprotected holes

panel fixing clip. For 1968 the rocker oil feed line went but the general tank shape remained.

The tank cap also changed over the years. The 1947 screw in cap was modified for 1948 and again in 1951. This cap also went onto the unit tanks until 1966, when it gained a dipstick. This continued until the new frame in 1971, which had its own cap which was modified for 1972. The Super Flash tank had a hinged cap with wing nut fastener.

Engine oil grade

An area of myths and folklore over which owners argue well into the night.

In the beginning there were straight oils that were thick or thin. They had no additives and did not last over long. The grade of oil was classed by an SAE number, usually 20, 30, 40, or 50 and the rider changed to a thinner one for the winter and back again in the summer.

The additives were put in the oil to prevent oxidation, inhibit rust, improve the load level, etc., and many more to give monogrades. These still needed to be changed to suit the season but lasted longer and were especially suited to all ball and roller engines which many motorcycle engines are.

Finally there came multigrades, which combined the merits of thick oil for hot running with thin oil for easy starting, even in winter. These had an unfortunate time when first introduced, but those days are long gone and modern quality multigrades are excellent for engines with plain bearings. Without them cold starting would be very difficult indeed.

At first BSA recommended SAE50 in summer and SAE40 in winter, but by the 1950s had thinned these down one grade to SAE40 and SAE30. This continued long into unit construction and it was not until 1968 that they changed to list SAE20W/50 for the engine. All this leaves the BSA twin owner well astride the fence as he has two recommendations and an engine with plain and roller bearings.

In fact most BSA specialists suggest SAE40 monograde for the twin engines, which does seem to keep the bearings happy. With an end-feed crankshaft modification and proper location with better mains the engine reliability is much improved and this is the way to go for long life. However the choice is always the owner's.

Transmission oil grades

Pre-unit models simply used engine oil in both gearbox and primary chaincase while they relied on the rider to look after the final drive chain. This situation changed with the advent of the unit engines, with the gearbox using SAE50 oil and the chaincase SAE20. From 1967 the box changed to EP90 gear oil, which had a similar viscosity to the engine grade used before but was better able to cope with the increased stress levels. Thus EP90 would be a good choice for all gearboxes.

The final drive chain on the unit models was oiled from a catchment in the primary chaincase, but this is unlikely to be sufficient. The supply is not adjustable but could be cut off if it is wished to avoid this loss from the chaincase, but in either case normal chain lubrication will be required.

Typical unit model with oil tank hidden under side covers. This is a 1969 model A65T Thunderbolt

7 Electrics

This is an area which gives many owners considerable difficulties and even some very skilled engine fitters will own that it is all a big mystery. The problem stems in part because you never see the substance, only the effects. Also, like an oil leak, it can spread all over the place so easily without any obvious evidence as to where it comes from.

If you intend to do a restoration you have to accept that you must wrestle with the subject or it could defeat you. Fortunately real electrical faults are rare despite what you may think, as nearly all troubles are caused by mechanical failures in some way or other. Most can be cured by correct assembly and settings. Remember the need to comply with current local legislation.

Things to remember that help are as follows. The system has two sides, one dealing with charging and the other with use. Although they may connect in operation and control they can be thought of as two distinct areas and dealt with accordingly. The most common fault is a poor earth, which is simply a poor connection for the return of the current rather than its supply. Also very common is a poor connection in the supply lead. Finally buy the tools for the job. This means lighter spanners or wrenches, smaller screwdrivers, pliers, cutters, electrician's soldering iron and a small multimeter. The last does not have to be anything special as continuity checks will be its main job, but it will help a great deal. An old ammeter, preferably with centre zero, and reading 15 amps or so, is also worth having to check current flow in and out of the battery. Even if the machine has one it is not always convenient to use so a meter with leads can be better.

BSA electric systems
The twins ran the full range of post-war possibilities with their electrics, from magneto to coil and dynamo to zener diode control. They began with magneto ignition and dynamo charging with a separate control box containing regulator and cut-out.

The magneto was always mounted behind the cylinders and the dynamo clamped to the top front of the crankcase.

All standard pre-unit twins were built in this form, but in addition there were A7 and A10 models offered to the police that were fitted with an alternator while retaining both dynamo and magneto. These were available as early as 1957 and were built with special chaincase and other revised details, some to suit the altered design and others to provide police facilities.

All unit engines were fitted with an alternator and most had coil ignition, the exceptions being a couple of off-road models built in 1966–67 which had energy transfer ignition. In addition, for 1969 and 1970 capacitor discharge ignition powered from the alternator was available as an option. Initially the electric system was six-volt but in 1964 a 12-volt option with zener diode generator control was offered for the A65 only and fitted as standard to all road models from 1966. From 1969 an RM21 alternator was used in place of the original RM19.

The heart of the electric system is the battery seen here installed on a 1969 Lightning. Also visible are the ignition coils and stop light switch

Magneto type

Although BTH was mentioned in the 1946 machine description only Lucas magnetos were ever listed. Up to 1950 all models had automatic advance using a mechanism built into the drive gear, but in 1951 a manual advance magneto was fitted to the Star Twin. From then on the tourers retained the auto mechanism and the sports versions had the manual lever. All magnetos were bolted to the back of the timing chest using two ordinary nuts and one special long one. All were of the anticlockwise rotation type as viewed from the driven end.

Magneto service

This concerns itself with the points gap, which is 0.012 in., and the brushes. There are several of the latter, for in addition to the high-tension lead pick-ups in each side of the body there is a brush in the rear of the points plate on the later magnetos and an earth brush. In many cases there is also one in the cap for the earthing lead. If the magneto fails to work this is one time when a connection to earth is not wanted so disconnect it. In use it takes the low-tension side to earth to kill the magneto and an intermittent fault in the line or the button can be a trial to deal with.

Lucas magnetos have safety gap screws and these *must* be removed before any real dismantling is done as otherwise the slip ring will be damaged. All brushes need to be examined for cracks and checked for free movement in their holders and general good condition. If worn they should be replaced.

Note that on occasion a brush or gap screw may be masked by a label so care must always be exercised.

Magneto renovation

There is not a great deal more that can be done with a magneto other than to clean it and maybe replace the bearings. Dismantling is straightforward, but mark parts first as often they could be reversed. Once apart the details can be cleaned and inspected, especially for any cracks, which could leak the high tension to earth.

It is a fairly skilled job to replace and set up magneto bearings and even more tricky to change a condenser or rewind an armature. Unless you are really competent in this work it should be sent to a specialist. This is especially true if the magneto has lost some of its magnetism and is therefore sparking poorly, if at all. Magnetizing equipment is complex and expensive so not really a practical proposition for any other than the professional.

Grease the bearings on assembly which should give no problems. Do make sure all the little insulating washers and bushes are in the right places. More ignition systems fail to work after a rebuild for this reason than any other. Fit the leads, clamp the magneto in the vice, earth the plugs to it and give it a spin – anticlockwise of course. Check that the earthing connection does its job.

The magneto as used on the BSA twins and shown in exploded form

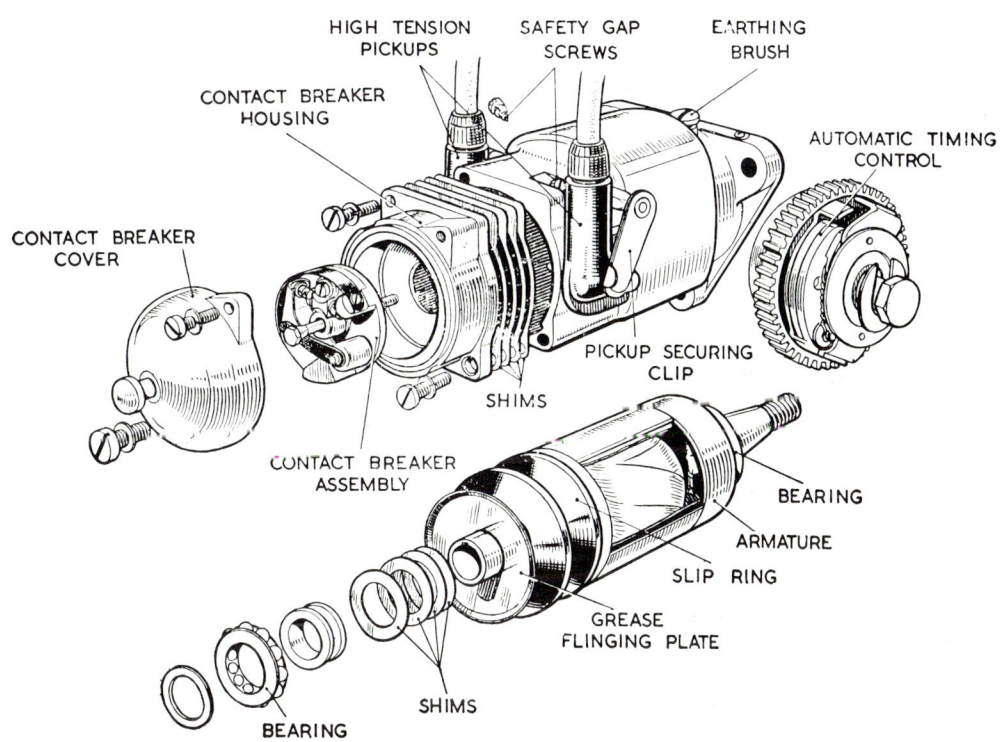

Dynamo types

All non-unit models had a Lucas dynamo clamped to the front of the crankcase and running anticlockwise. For 1947–48 the type E3H was fitted, but from 1949 the longer and more powerful E3L was used. For 1951 the electrical system changed from negative to positive earth and remained that way to the end of dynamos for BSA twins in 1963.

Dynamo drive

This was by an 8 mm chain from a sprocket fixed on the tapered end of the timing idler gear shaft. This end lay outside the inner timing cover so that when the outer one was attached a separate drive compartment was formed. Within this the drive chain was grease lubricated and this kept oil away from the dynamo.

The dynamo was clamped by a band and its rotation set the chain tension. On most engines it can be removed when the chain is fully slackened and the clamp and outer cover removed. For Spitfire owners a blanking plate assembly was offered to allow them to fill the resulting hole as these machines ran without any electrical system except the magneto.

Dynamo testing

This can begin on the machine by disconnecting the leads to the dynamo. Then join the two terminals, D and F, and connect a voltmeter from the join to the dynamo body. Run the machine so the dynamo speed is up to 1000 rpm and look for the voltage reading to rise smoothly and quickly to 10 volts. Don't run the dynamo faster in an attempt to push the volts value up. If there is no reading at all look to the brush gear, if it is about 0.5 volt the field winding is suspect and if between 1.5 and 2 volts then the armature winding is the likely culprit.

For any further work the dynamo will need to be dismantled.

Dynamo service

Mark parts before taking them apart and proceed with some delicacy as some items are rather brittle. Clean all the connections to reduce contact resistance and check that all wires are in good order and not frayed in any way. Examine the brushes and replace if worn down to about $\frac{5}{16}$ in. Make sure the brushes, whether old or renewed, can move freely in their boxes and that the brush springs are strong enough to hold them in contact with the commutator.

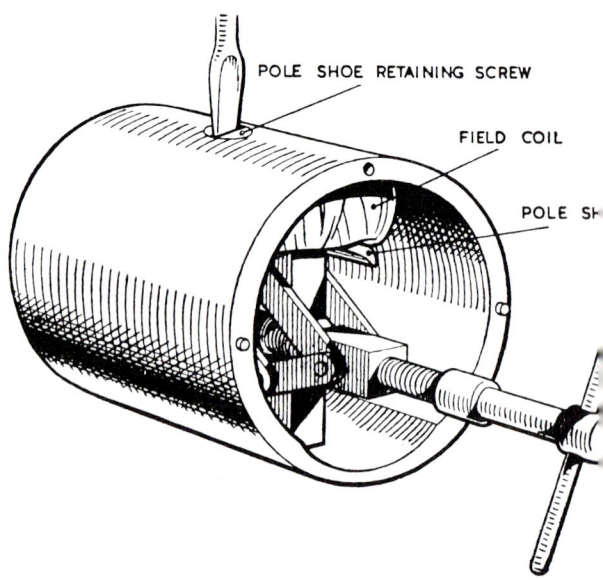

ABOVE *Using a pole shoe expanding tool while replacing the dynamo field coil. That retaining screw must be very, very tight*

BELOW *The general construction of the Lucas E3H dynamo used by many post-war British machines*

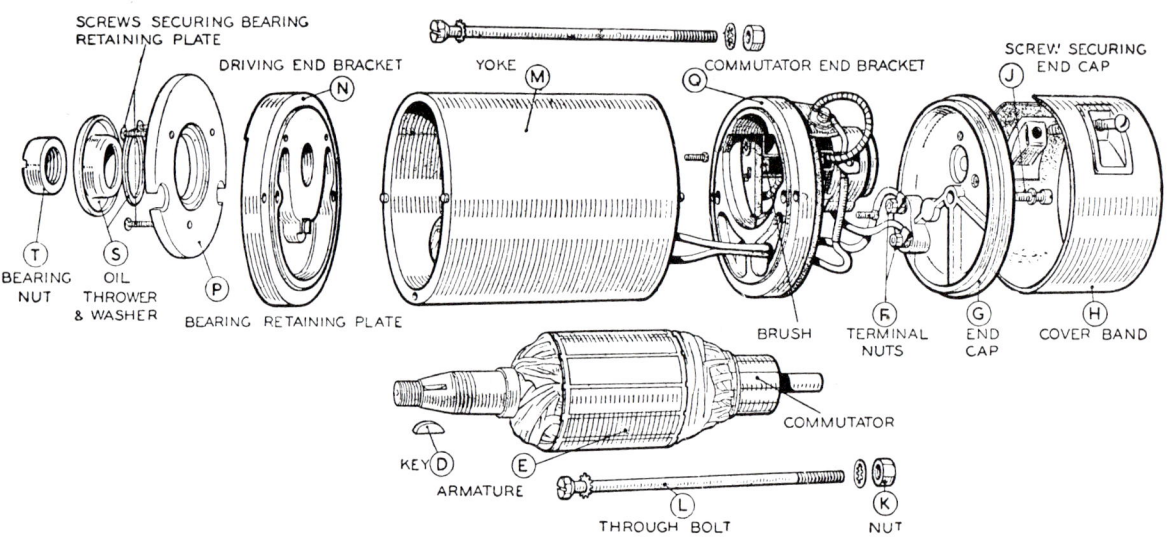

This last will need cleaning, and if burnt may need machining to restore it to true round. Should this be needed, remove the minimum of material and be prepared to undercut the commutator segments. Also examine the wire connections to the segments for any signs of overheating, which may indicate problems in the armature. Clean out all the carbon dust as it can short out the insulated wires.

Armature rewinds and field coil replacement are best left to specialists. The first requires special equipment but the second can be attempted with fewer facilities. There are two problems to overcome. First is the single fixing screw, which must be tight, and second is ensuring the new coil is really home in the body. Service departments used a special driver for the first and an expander for the second problem but both can be overcome in the home workshop.

Grease the two ball races of the longer unit and the single one of the shorter. Lubricate the bush of the latter with thin machine oil, but not too much or it will be all over the commutator. Reassemble with care to ensure everything goes back where it came from.

The finished result can be tested off the engine by connecting it to a battery so that it becomes an electric motor. This is done by joining the F and D terminals and connecting the join and the dynamo body to a six-volt battery. The body connection is to the normally earthed terminal. If all is well the armature will revolve. This is not as good a test as that with a voltmeter but is useful if the engine is by now apart and not to be available for some while.

Regulator unit

This is also known as the compensated voltage control unit or cvc and may be referred to as the automatic voltage control or avc. Not to be confused with the later cvc used for cars where the initials stand for current voltage control and the unit has three coils in its assembly under the cover.

The motorcycle cvc is simpler with just one control coil plus the cut-out under the lid. It has fewer connections than most cars with just four terminals in a row and these are usually connected to wires that plug in and are held by a strip secured by two screws. The wires are positioned by this strip and the screws are of different sizes to prevent a reversal of the connections.

The early twins used the MCR1 regulator, but from 1949 the MCR2 was introduced. This differed in that the control resistor became a carbon disc fitted to the main frame behind the coils and can be recognized by a swelling in the back of the cover put there to clear it. On these two models the terminals were labelled FADE, but for 1958 the unit was changed to a RB107, which had its connections in the order FAED. During 1960 the RB108 superseded this with a connection order of DEAF. This came in for frame GA7-8124 on A7 and A7SS machines, frame GA7-8324 for A10 models and frame GA7-8319 for the A10SR.

The cvc is a delicate electro-mechanical assembly and must be treated as such. It can be set up and adjusted by the owner but this must be done precisely or the system will not work as it should. Really no different to valve clearances or ignition timing.

Regulator function

Two jobs are done inside the cvc unit. The regulator side switches a resistor into series with the field coil to reduce the field current and thus the generated output. It is in a state of vibration while doing this. The cut-out is simply a switch that disconnects the dynamo from the battery when needed to prevent it trying to motor it, which would discharge the battery.

The confusion with the unit usually arises because the theoretical circuit diagram, practical wiring diagram and the unit all look completely different. Further confusion arises in that the internal frame is used as part of the electric circuit but is not an earth. In truth it connects via the cut-out points to the battery supply line so is insulated from the mounting frame.

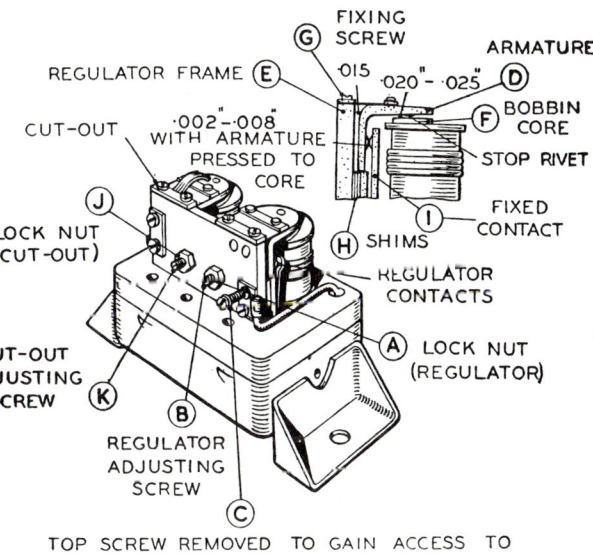

TOP SCREW REMOVED TO GAIN ACCESS TO CONTACTS FOR CLEANING

The Lucas MCR1 regulator used up to 1948 on BSA twins

Regulator service

If you decide to work in the cvc trace out the electrical circuit first so you know where each part fits into the scheme of things. It will then be much easier to check each item for continuity or open circuit using your meter. In most cases the only problem will be the mechanical aspects of the contacts, their cleanliness and their adjustment. With these dealt with the circuits are most likely to all function as they should.

Looking at the coils, the one on the left is the regulator with a few turns of heavy-gauge wire about its middle. The adjustments are made first by moving the armature, which is the bent steel part pulled by the coil magnetism and carrying one of the contacts. Next by bending the fixed contact on the MCR units and finally with an adjuster screw at the rear.

Air gaps are required between the vertical leg of the armature that carries the contact and the frame, also between the horizontal leg and the bobbin core on the MCR. The first should be 0.015 in. on the MCR1 and 0.020 in. on the MCR2. The second figure is 0.020 in. for both, but with a tolerance of plus 0.005 in on the MCR1 and minus 0.008 in. on the MCR2. On the MCR2, with the armature held against the bobbin core, the points gap should be between 0.006 and 0.017 in.

The RB107 and RB108 have a different method of adjustment. The armature screws are undone, a feeler gauge 0.021 in. put between the armature and the bobbin and the screws done up. The contacts are then adjusted so they just touch with the feeler gauge still in place.

The remaining adjustments are made with the cvc wired to the machine. Put card between the cut-out points and disconnect the lead from terminal A. Insert voltmeter between D and E and run the dynamo at about 3000 rpm. At 20 degrees Celsius the reading should be 8.0 to 8.4 volts and can be adjusted with the screw at the rear. If the temperature rises deduct 0.2 volt for every 10 degrees Celsius and if it falls add it. Then run the dynamo at about 4500 rpm, when the reading should not exceed 8.9 volts. Do all this quickly or errors will occur. If in doubt do it in steps.

Cut-out setting

For the MCR2 the armature to frame air gap should be 0.014 in. and to the bobbin core 0.011 to 0.015 in. With these two gaps held correct by gauges, press the armature down on them and check that the gap between armature and stop plate arm is 0.030 to 0.034 in. Bend the arm to adjust. Then place a 0.025 in. gauge between armature shim and core face and check that the contact gap is between 0.002 to 0.006 in. Bend the fixed contact bracket to adjust.

The RB107 and RB108 are set by pressing the armature down to the core face and checking the gap between its stop arm and its tongue, which should be 0.025 to 0.040 in. Bend the stop arm to adjust. Then adjust the fixed contact blade to give a blade deflection of 0.010 to 0.020 in. when the armature is pressed firmly down on the core face.

Cut-out checking

This is done on the machine and a full test covers both cut-in and cut-out. For the first connect an ammeter in the lead from dynamo D to cvc D and a voltmeter between there and E. Gradually bring the engine speed up and watch for the voltmeter pointer to flick back as the points close. This should occur at 6.3 to 6.7 volts and is adjusted by the screw, which increases the setting when turned clockwise. The ammeter should show a charge when the points close. When the engine stops the ammeter discharge reading is taken and should be between three and five amps when the contacts open.

The cut-out check is done by detaching lead A from the cvc and connecting a voltmeter between terminals A and E. Run the dynamo up to 3000 rpm and then let its speed die slowly away. The voltage should be between 4.8 and 5.5 volts when the contacts open and the reading drops to zero.

Regulator oddments

The resistance used in the cvc, which is placed in the field circuit, can be measured if you have a good meter. The value for a carbon one is 36 to 45 ohms while the wire wound type is 27 to 33 ohms.

If your machine has the short E3 dynamo fitted it would normally have an MCR1 cvc. If this is not available the MCR2 listed under part number 37144A should be used.

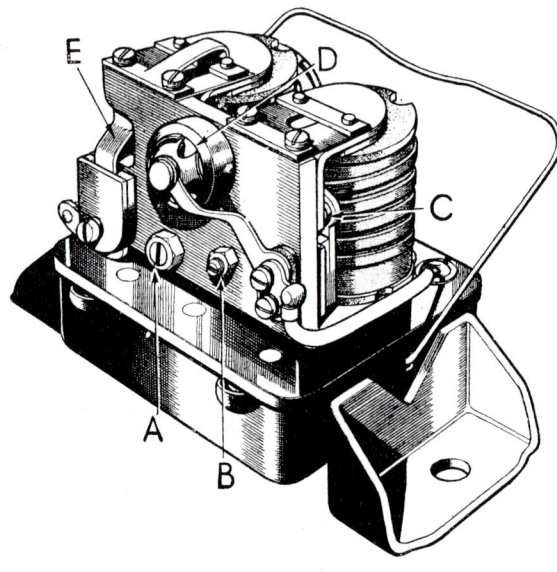

The later MCR2 cvc used from 1949 to 1957. It had a carbon disc resistor to control the dynamo output

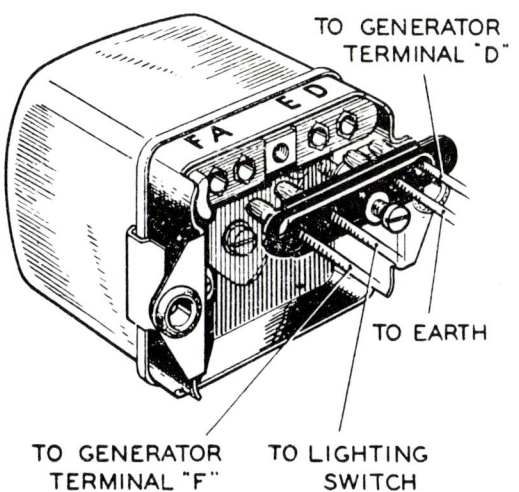 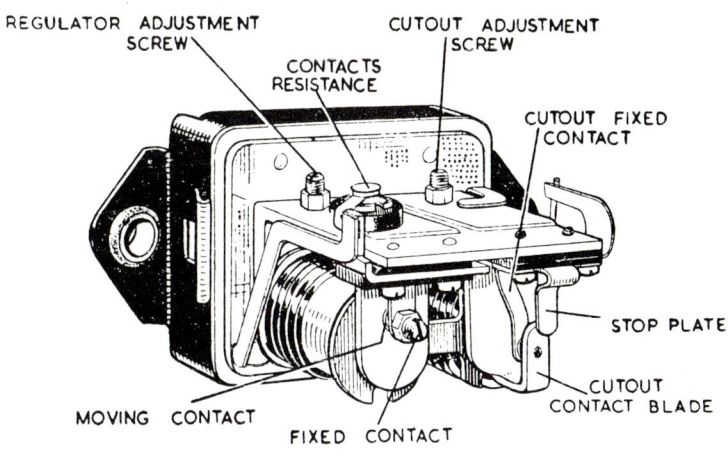

The later RB107 regulator with revised terminal order shown left with internals to the right

You can use the machine without a battery as long as the cvc is working correctly. This may not be fully legal in some way but can be useful in an emergency. However, if the battery is in circuit it must be topped up or the control is fooled into providing excess current, which can ruin battery, dynamo and cvc.

The contact points do get dirty and may need cleaning. If they do they will need re-setting for sure.

Should the dynamo polarity have reversed itself, which does happen, just hold the cut-out points together for a second or two and then pull them apart.

Do make sure that dynamo D is connected to cvc D and F to F. Although the dynamo leads are held by a kidney-shaped plate and the cvc one is non-reversible they could have been switched at some time. Detach and check by meter as they often run out of sight on the machine.

Modern regulators

By using modern electronic components the problems of the electro-mechanical cvc can be removed with solid state devices. This is electronic engineering quite outside most people's knowledge but specialist suppliers make it easy for the rest of us.

A unit is available to replace the cvc and is one waterproof box that does the same job and enables the machine to convert to 12 volts. Battery and bulbs also need changing, but not the horn. The change boosts output so better lights can be fitted. The new assembly is small enough to tuck out of sight so the alteration is not at all obvious for owners who wish to keep up appearances.

While this change departs from total originality it is to be recommended for any machine used on a regular basis in modern traffic, where good lights are essential. The move to 12 volts not only greatly improves the electrical efficiency of the system but also allows halogen lights to be used to give a further bonus.

Battery area and coils of a 1968 Royal Star

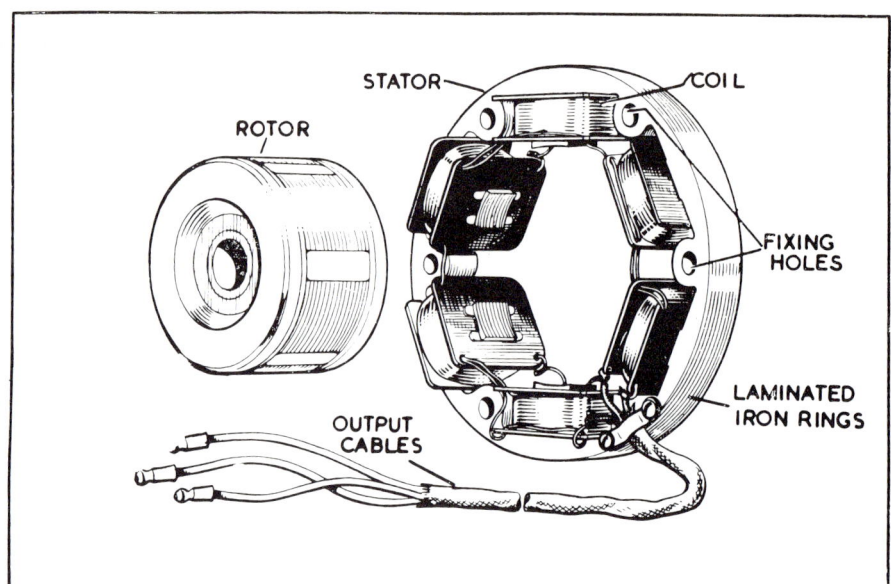

RIGHT *Typical Lucas alternator prior to the RM21 which was encapsulated*

1966 Royal Star under whose chaincase is fitted the alternator

Alternator

BSA were among the first of the major firms to adopt the crankshaft-mounted alternator, but it was 1962 before they fitted it to the twins. With it came the advantages of no touching parts to wear and other delights, but these included control problems and boiled batteries so all was not quite as good as it might have been. In time the zener diode came along and with it arrived better control and 12-volt systems.

The first models to use an alternator were the A50 and A65 in 1962 which were fitted with the Lucas RM19. In 1969 all models changed to the RM21 unit with encapsulated windings.

In addition to the standard systems there is the energy transfer set-up used by the A50W and A65H in 1966–67 with five leads from the stator. These models may be run minus lights and battery and require that the rotor is accurately timed to the engine.

Alternator checking

There is not a great deal that can be done other than cleaning and inspection. Check that the rotor has been running clear of the coil poles and look at the wiring for any damage. Use a meter to check continuity and insulation and establish which coils are connected together and how the wires are attached to them. Compare this with your wiring diagram and keep notes on this aspect. This may help a good deal when sorting out the connections to the rectifier.

Make sure the rotor is a good fit on the crankshaft. If it is not it is possible to machine it to locate on a made-up spacer against the engine sprocket, and with care and ingenuity to achieve a better design than the original. This will also allow a damaged crankshaft end to be overcome by using other means to hold the rotor true.

It is possible for the rotor centre to become loose

within the assembly and this can give rise to a nasty knocking noise in the engine. A cure is to machine away the alloy side enough to allow the core to come out and then to refit it using a Loctite gap filler.

Rectifier

Early alternators had their output turned into direct current by massive selenium plate rectifiers. The original boxes soon became a smaller set of four plates on a single central bolt and in time this assembly was replaced by a similar silicon diode rectifier.

All the four plate types give full wave rectification and the centre stud is one of the direct current connections and must be treated as such. It connects to the earthed side of the battery. The three plate connections have the other direct current line in the middle flanked by the two alternating current ones. These last two may connect either way round as reversal at that point will not affect the rectifier operation at all.

The rectifier can be cleaned and its electrical function checked for the correct working of each diode. These must pass current one way but not the other and a meter or battery and bulb will act as a tester. Do not move the central clamping nut or the device will fail. The nut tension controls the efficiency of the unit and must be left alone. Care is therefore needed when fixing the device to the machine.

Alternator control

On the face of it the stator coils connect to the rectifier, which connects to the battery to complete the circuit. Unfortunately there are complications. First the output needs to be controlled to suit the load and second it would be nice to be able to start even with a flat battery. To cope with these problems introduces complications in the switches and wiring and the result can be confusion.

The control is done for 6-volt systems by stator coil switching. The basic control is that two coils are permanently connected and with the lights off the remaining four are short circuited to reduce the output of the two in use. With the pilot light on the four are open circuit, so they don't affect the two and with headlight on all six are connected. This means that the light switch has to be joined electrically to the charging circuit.

Problem two is overcome by switching four coils to supply the ignition circuit direct to leave two to assist the battery on an emergency basis.

Where a 12-volt system is in use a zener diode is used for control. At first this was in conjunction with the light switch so that either four or six coils were in circuit, but this soon changed so that all six were permanently connected and the zener diode did the work. The same type of zener diode was fitted from 1964 to 1972 and up to 1967 was mounted on a flat plate. From 1968 to 1970 a finned heat sink was listed, but in practice it appeared on 1967 models. For 1971–1972 the zener used a mounting bracket as its heat sink.

If the connections are not as they should be or the switch contacts are dirty then all manner of charging problems will arise. The situation is further confused by variations that were available over the years and which may have been incorporated in a system. The mechanical components are generally interchangeable and on the electric side it is just a question of joining wires so anything is possible.

To add to the problems Lucas also changed the wire colours on the early alternators as the originals tended to become indistinguishable. First they were light, mid- and dark green. Then light green, green and yellow, dark green. Finally green and white, green and yellow, and green and black. If you don't have an original stator, rectifier and harness you could have variations.

ABOVE *The finned heat sink for the zener diode which was not listed until 1968 but was fitted to the 1967 models*

BELOW *The heat sink with the zener diode which must make good contact with the alloy but whose stud is easy to break*

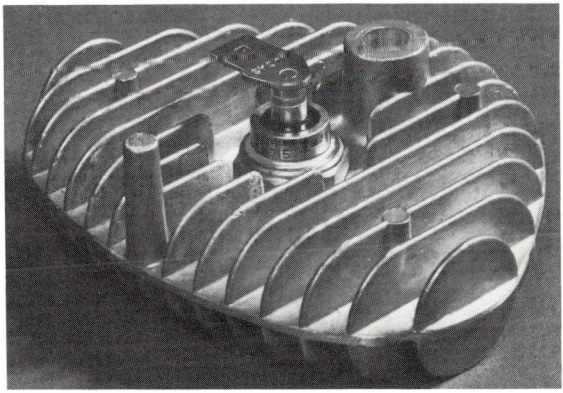

Further complications arise in that where the machine has magneto ignition the above applies with two coils always in circuit. For models with coil ignition it was common to have four in use and the mid- and dark green connections reversed. Another version had them all joined together to put all six coils in circuit all the time. The lead from rectifier to light switch, usually light green, may be simply disconnected and taped up as this has a further trimming effect on the output.

To sort out what you have and how to connect it you need to work out the alternator leads and circuit, the rectifier leads and the switch circuits. Then use the wiring diagram for the model and trace out what happens in each switch position. Not easy, I know, as the diagrams don't normally give the switch circuits and without those it is hard, hence the need to check the switch itself with a meter and write it all down.

Alternator voltage conversion

This is a popular way of getting more out of the system and can easily be carried out. It simplifies the wiring as all six alternator coils are permanently connected to the rectifier, which has the zener diode fitted between its supply terminal and earth. The actual details vary according to to the machine circuit, but can be sorted out using the wiring diagram and the information already established for the switches.

When first introduced the then available zeners could not cope with controlling the full output when there was no headlight load, so the switched connection was still needed. This had two coils permanently on for machines fitted with a magneto and four where coil ignition was used. Modern zeners can cope.

Battery, ignition coils, bulbs, possibly rectifier and maybe ignition condenser will need changing. The horn is not essential and any ancillaries need to be remembered.

Coil ignition

This was first used on the unit models in 1962 and all engines have the points in the timing chest with two sets provided to fire the coils.

Timing cover points

Essentially you clean and inspect. Replace the points, oil the advance mechanism and make sure the bearings are in good order and that the spindle turns freely. Attend to anything in trouble and rebuild.

Do make sure the points wire connection is the correct side of its insulation washers and check it with the meter.

Inspect the small pivot points in the advance mechanism and repair or replace as necessary. Replace the advance springs if these are tired, and check you have the correct type of advance unit installed.

The early points assembly seen here on a 1964 A65R

Two types of points assembly were used, these being the 4CA up to 1967 and the 6CA from 1968.

Energy transfer ignition
In this design some of the alternator windings are connected directly to a special ignition coil. This allows the machine to run without a battery on the lines of one fitted with a magneto, but the ignition timing is critical. Points cam and advance unit are specially designed for the job and must be used for it to operate effectively. The distributor range is limited and essential to the workings. Otherwise it is checked over as the others.

Ignition timing
This is often a source of great concern to owners and in one sense it is important. On the other hand the actual figure used may be less so. What is often forgotten is that the engine may be 20 or more years old, worn in various ways and running on a different blend of fuel to that available to it when new.

So while the original figure makes a good starting point it is not sacrosanct. The old-fashioned technique of advancing the setting until the engine pinks on a rising road and then backing it off a little, still works well even if it is awkward to carry out on some models.

Check the timing you decide to use on full advance and on both cylinders. The retard figure is much less important so may be ignored, although the particular will check it also to be sure. It is not uncommon for a variation to arise between the cylinders and this should be removed if possible as the engine will run much better. Beware of slack in the drive when checking and for slack in the advance mechanism bearings which can give a false reading. Recheck if in any doubt.

Electronic ignition
A worthwhile modification for late-type machines and available in various forms to replace magneto or coil ignition. It is also possible to adapt them to existing parts to retain the original drive system.

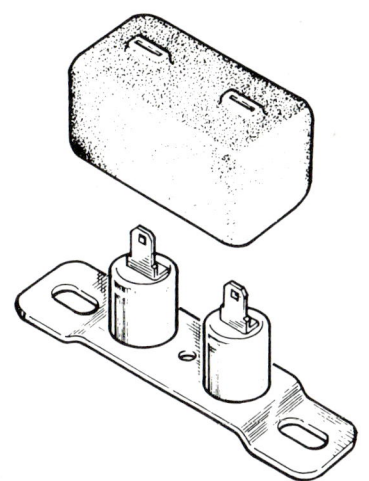

RIGHT *The two ignition condensers moved to a common plate and were protected by a moulded cover*

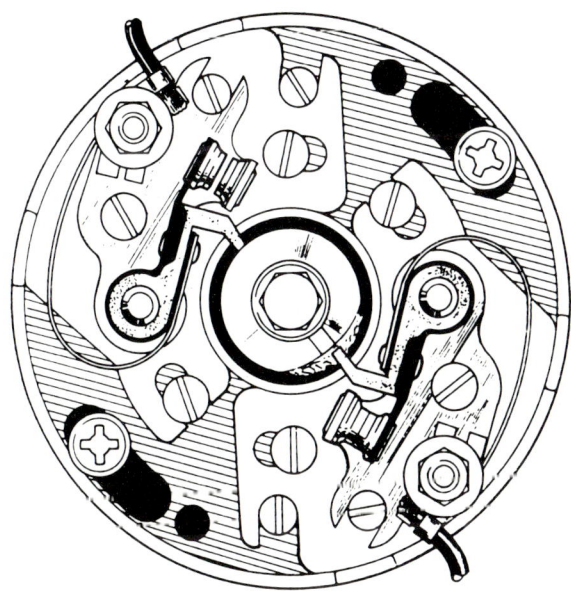

ABOVE *The later points set with each pair moveable on the baseplate and no condensers which have moved elsewhere*

RIGHT *The rotor mark and fixed pointer introduced in 1967 to enable the ignition timing to be checked with a strobe light*

The installation instructions supplied with the kit should be carefully followed especially regarding the timing. Electronic advance is normal, so the mechanical device must be discarded or locked up and the timing will have to be checked with a strobe. A timing mark will be needed for this and must be checked with a timing disc before the ignition is set up.

In addition to the electronic ignition kits a further option is open in the form of capacitor ignition using the alternator as a power source, a 12-volt zener diode control, a storage capacitor and the original points and advance mechanism. Effectively a variation of the earlier energy transfer system but much better in use.

Spark plug, cap and lead

The plugs should be replaced by a modern equivalent, although many owners do like to keep the originals if they are to hand. Some refit them for a concours, but for normal use a new pair of plugs should be fitted. Grades are listed in an appendix.

The caps should be the type that contains a suppressor and the leads must be in good condition. Make sure the ends are clean and make a good connection or an odd misfire may appear.

Lighting

Renovation of the lights is mainly by replacement as most of the parts are fragile and are either complete and working or in pieces. The bulb containers may need repair work carried out and finishing, which should be done in the same way as any other item.

For any machine being used on the road the current legal requirements need to be considered as some of the earlier fittings do not comply with them. In particular rear lamps have increased in size and needed to for modern traffic.

BSA used a variety of lighting systems over the years but essentially most changes were brought about by alterations to the electrical system or by styling. Early models had a separate headlamp, then came the cowl and later the nacelle and then separate headlamp shells for the more sporting modes. To suit these changes the switches also moved about.

Headlamp and switch types

The A7 was first built with a traditional English-style headlamp fitted with a small panel carrying an ammeter and the lighting switch. This had three positions comprising off, pilot and head, and was supplemented by a dip switch on the left side of the handlebars. This was fitted to the back of the clutch lever body and was matched by the horn button on the right fixed to the front brake body. For 1947 only the speedometer was mounted in the petrol tank, but the following year moved to the top fork crown.

The magneto cut-out was built into its end cap on the early models, but for 1951 a button was provided

ABOVE *The Lucas F700 pre-focus headlamp unit with inset pilot bulb as used from 1955*

BELOW *A curious home for an ignition switch shown here on a 1966 Lightning. Rain, headrace grease, steering damper debris could all reach it easily and access is not the best and becomes poor if a fairing is fitted*

on the handlebars and is sometimes found on older machines. Its connection can be by a screw terminal much as those used for the HT leads, while the button was located either on the left or the centre of the bars.

In 1952 the headlamp unit changed from the old pattern with a bulb that could be adjusted for focus and with a pilot light set in the main reflector to a light unit that took a pre-focus bulb that dropped in from the rear. This greatly improved the light output. Less popular was the change to the pilot lamp, which had to become a separate unit. It was fitted below the main lamp with a rectangular lens nearly invisible on the road.

The layout changed for 1953, when the headlamp was fitted with a cowl to style it to the forks. This carried the speedometer in the centre with the ammeter on the right and the light switch on the left. The angle was such that the ammeter could not be read while riding the machine. The dipswitch and horn button continued as they were, as did the underslung pilot lamp.

The export-only Super Flash did not have a cowl so continued in the 1952 style. This arrangement also went on the Road Rocket when it appeared in 1954.

By 1955 the technical problems of mounting the pilot bulb in the pre-focus light unit had been solved so the underslung pilot went. At the same time a steering lock appeared with keyhole in the cowl. For 1956 the horn and dipswitch became one item on the left, hence the central position for the cut-out button.

The 1958 models had a nacelle in place of the 1953 cowl and while the speedometer remained in the middle, the ammeter was moved to the left and the lights switch to the right. For export the Super Rocket was built in the style of the 1953 Super Flash, with separate headlamp with ammeter and switch in a small panel, but for the home market it had the nacelle like the other models.

In 1960 a ring-type fitting went on the left bar to provide dipswitch, horn button and cut-out and in 1962 the Rocket Gold Star appeared with fittings as for the export Super Rocket. The latter model continued with its nacelle on the home market except when the optional rev-counter was fitted. In this case the separate headlamp and RGS style was adopted.

The unit models also had a nacelle with central speedometer when introduced in 1962. For them the ammeter was mounted on the right side of the shell and two switches went on the left. The front one was for ignition and the rear for lights. The ignition switch was operated by a detachable key and had three positions for off, on and emergency, for which the key was depressed and turned to the left. The lights switch also had three positions for off, park and head and this last was supplemented by a ring-type combined hornpush and dipswitch on the left handlebar.

For the A65R in 1964 there was a separate headlamp shell with brackets for the speed instruments. The shell carried a central ammeter flanked by the ignition switch on the right and the lights one on the left. The A65T/R and A65L/R used the same arrangement, while the off road A50CC offered for the USA had a small headlamp with the light switch and dipswitch mounted in the shell. The Spitfire Hornet had no lights so no fittings.

This arrangement continued without change for most of these models for 1965, while the A50C, A50CC, A50C road US model, A65L and A65LC all copied the A65R with its separate headlamp shell. For 1966 there was no nacelle so the separate shell with central ammeter became the norm and had the light switch fitted aft of it in the manner of the 1947 model. The ignition switch moved to a location in the left steering head gusset plate.

1968 brought a toggle light switch, still fitted aft of the ammeter in the headlamp shell but with a red warning light for low oil pressure on its left. For the Firebird the standard ring horn push and dipswitch was replaced by a dipper mounted in the headlamp shell and a separate horn push on the handlebars. For 1969 the Firebird fell in line with the other models in this respect, all now having two warning lights, one on each side of the ammeter. To the right went the red oil pressure one and to the left a green for headlamp main beam.

The 1968 headlamp with toggle light switch and oil pressure warning light to the left of the ammeter

The Lucas rectangular type 564 stop and tail lamp with inbuilt reflector as used by much of the English industry

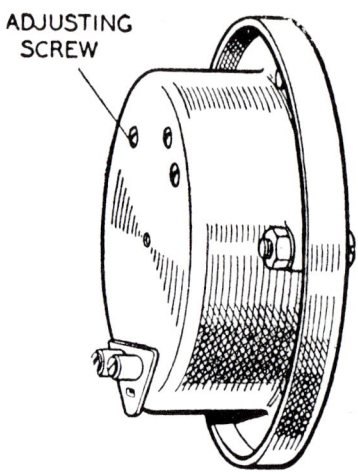

Typical Lucas horn with adjustment screw in rear. Wires should run through fibre plate around terminals

1970 was as 1969, but 1971 brought a new shallow headlamp shell without ammeter but carrying a turn switch for the lights and three warning lamps. These were red for oil pressure, green for main beam and amber for indicators. The clutch and brake levers both had built-in switches, but the ignition was key controlled with a switch in the right-side panel. 1972 models were as 1971.

Bulb types and ratings should be to the parts list if a standard build is sought, but for those riders seeking an improvement there are replacement light units available. If you have a 12-volt system a halogen lamp can be used. This is well worth fitting if you seek the best in lighting.

Stop and tail light

The A7 began with the same small round rear light as used by many English machines in 1947. In 1951 a stop facility was added and in 1953 the form changed to rectangular and the material to plastic. With this type there was a separate reflector fixed below the rear number plate and for 1955 another type was listed. In 1956 the reflector became part of the moulded rear lamp lens and this type remained in use to 1965. A year earlier it was joined by a 12-volt version and a revised shape for the US models. This last was itself modified for 1966, when it continued alone on to 1972. All bulbs should be as per list.

Horn

For most riders trouble with the horn comes in two forms. First it does not work, which turns out to be a fault in the horn button or wiring, and second is locating it on a basket job.

The first problem should be bypassed by checking with direct wiring between horn and battery. The second is dealt with below. If current is reaching the horn and nothing is happening then it may need adjustment. This may be by a screw in the back or a nut under a cover or there may be no adjustment at all. Where provided it should be moved not more than one or two notches at a time. On a scale of 24 notches this equals one full turn of the screw. Six notches from just not sounding should be about right, but the current flow should also be monitored and anything over five amps indicates a need for specialist attention.

Don't move the centre screw as this controls the basic points setting and needs special equipment to set. Given this and care the horn may be stripped and the case renovated in the same way as any other part.

Horn types and position

In the original design it was intended to use a small horn mounted on the seat tube behind the gearbox. With the supply problems that then existed BSA had to settle for the stock Lucas HF1234 (part 069239), which they hung from the left saddle spring lug just as on most of their other models. It was to stay there for all rigid and plunger-frame models.

By 1953 they were fitting the HF1235 horn, which for the pivoted-fork models went on the left side of the front engine mounting just above the fixing studs. For models without the fork cowl the HF180 horn was fitted in the same place. This practice continued for the Rocket series to 1963, but models with the nacelle from 1958 had a change. The horn type became the HF1441, which had no adjustment, and it went into the nacelle.

The mounting stayed in the nacelle for the unit models but the horn became the type 8H. In 1964 it was joined by the 6H, which went on the A65R only in front of the engine and just above the mounting studs. The horn went on to be used by all models without the nacelle up to 1968, while the 8H was fitted in the A50 and A65 to 1965.

For 1969 most models changed to the HF80 horn, which remained in the same position, but the Lightning had twin windtones fitted. These were the P101 and P102 and were fitted in the same area as the others, one on each side. With the advent of the new frame in 1971 a single 6H horn was fitted under the front of the fuel tank.

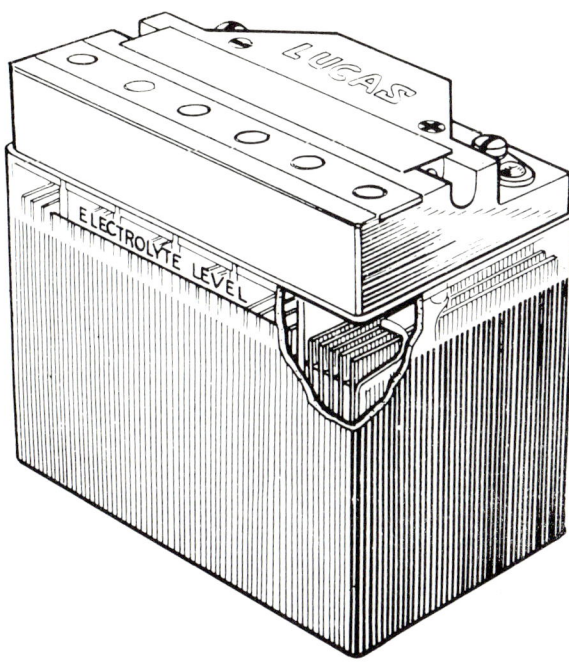

ABOVE *Lucas PUZ5A battery which took over from the early 6-volt type. Some models used twin 6-volt batteries as an interim measure*

RIGHT *Common problem for the restorer where corrosion caused by the battery electrolyte has damaged a good few items. Overcharging can do this and must be avoided*

Battery

The problem on some models is appearance as while the battery lived outside enclosing panels its looks were an important aspect of the left side of the machine. It is possible to obtain facsimiles of the early black-bodied 6-volt battery, which is one solution. Another is to adapt an old battery by cutting out the interior and fitting a modern one inside it.

For the rest, keep it clean, check the specific gravity and smear protective jelly on the terminals to keep corrosion at bay. Keep the battery working, so if off the machine run it down with a three-watt bulb and then recharge it. This will prevent it from collapsing when asked to do some real work.

Up to 1963 all models had a 6-volt system. For 1964–65 the A65 was offered with the option of 12 volts and twin batteries and from 1966 all road models had a single 12-volt battery.

Ammeter

There is not much one can do to repair one of these so either you have one working or it just acts as a dummy to keep the original appearance. In this case one terminal can be used as a junction point, but if the insulation of the case is in any doubt it is best to keep the wiring away from it altogether.

The ammeter did not change much over the years and at first came as part of the headlamp assembly. From 1951 it was listed as Lucas part 36084 and this also went on the early unit twins. It was soon changed to part 36296 and this was fitted until 1968, when part 36403 was adopted. After 1970 no ammeter was fitted.

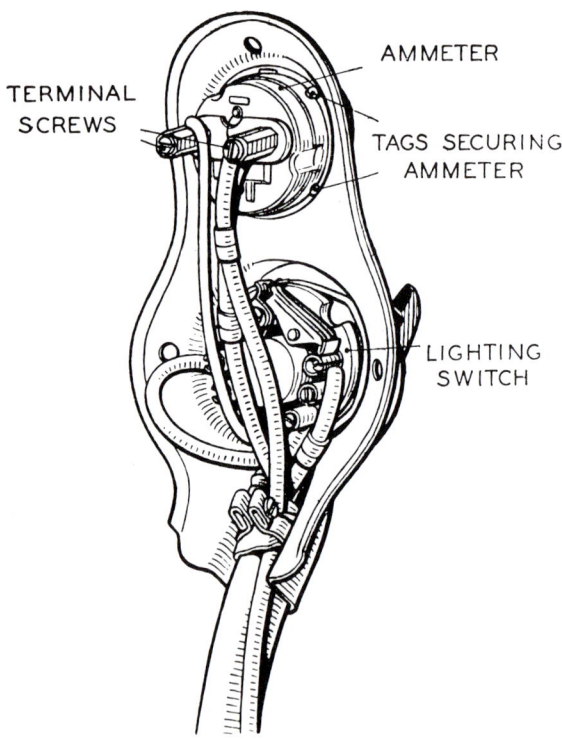

Wiring

The prime source of electrical troubles, with poor connections, poor earths and intermittent leaks to earth being the major problems. Switches can also cause many headaches if the contacts are not clean and making good connections.

If you intend to use the existing harness it must be checked over carefully for any signs of damage or chafing. These must be repaired. All wires must be checked for continuity and for this a wiring diagram is most useful. Most given in manuals are really circuits and very hard to use in practice so it is well worth drawing your own. While doing this you can lay it out as on the machine and add the switch internal connections so it becomes easy to see where the current is supposed to flow.

You will find that one section is to do with charging the battery and connects generator and control. The other is the consumption side and all flows from one point. The item using the current may be directly connected, as is the horn, via the ignition switch to the coil or via the lights switch. Total isolation of battery from system did not come until later. The horn current is not taken through the ammeter so the lead to this comes before the instrument. The same applies to some stop lamps.

If you have to rewire, first sort out the wiring diagram and then decide on the wire type and gauge you will use. Early models usually had black rubber-covered wire, possibly with a coloured or numbered sleeve at the end. This form of insulation perishes so is no longer used and wires are colour coded to ensure correct connections. The gauge depends on the current carried and it is as well to err on the fat side to keep voltage drop to a minimum.

A new harness is best built up on the machine as this will make sure it fits well. Tape it into place while doing this and then remove as one unit and bind the wires into one bundle to keep the weather at bay. Either tape or heat-shrink tubing can be used for this, as long as the final job will accept the movement it must get in the headstock area. Elsewhere it must be held firmly so it cannot fray away and is not trapped or pinched at any point.

Joints and connections need careful attention. Joins in the wires are best done with modern connectors with each wire crimped or soldered to its terminal. When doing this avoid nicking the wire when stripping the insulations, although this is hard to

LEFT *The small panel fitted to the rear of the early model headlamp. It carried ammeter and light switch with the wiring secured by screw terminals and held by a cable clamp*

BELOW *The stages in fitting a Lucas connector to a wire. The push-on design makes for easy connection; most common error is to leave the cover off*

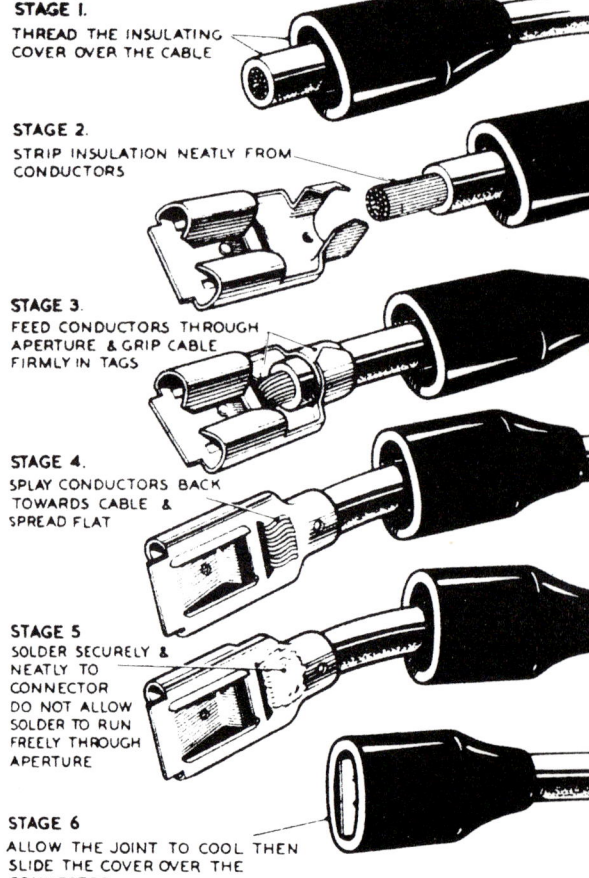

avoid, and don't use an excess of solder. In avionics, inspection count the strands to make sure none are missing, inspect each for a mark and expect to see each one just outlined by its solder shroud. Get halfway to that standard and you won't have any problems.

Crimp connectors normally call for special tools, but a serviceable job can be made using pliers of one sort or another plus common sense. Make sure the wire is firmly held and not slightly loose. If the wires are soldered in place don't let the solder run back into the wire or its rigidity will cause it to fracture under vibration. On the same lines, when dealing with older types of switches with terminal posts just roll the wire into a ball under the fixing screw. If you do use solder play safe by clamping the wire securely a short distance from the terminal. Electrical strapping will look neater than tape on the final assembly.

Switches

These must be checked using a meter for their correct operation. The older type can usually be taken apart for cleaning, but watch for rollers with springs behind them that can fly out and roll all over the floor. Re-check the operation after assembly. Draw the connections on your wiring diagram so you can see how the components connect up in each switch position.

In addition to the more complex lights and ignition switches also check out the dipswitch, horn button, stoplight switch and cut-out for correct operation in the same way. As you connect them into the circuit check each in turn to ensure correct operation without any errant connections.

Earthing

All the older machines rely on the cycle parts to do this job which is why they often have problems. Having carefully restored the protective paintwork of frame, forks, mudguards and panels it is rather a shame to damage this finish to complete the earth return.

The answer is to run an earth wire from each item back to the battery or to a suitable junction point. The wires must be of a gauge able to carry the current from all the items they are collecting for and at one point are best earthed both to the frame and the engine. Don't forget that the ignition system must have a complete circuit for both high- and low-tension loops.

Fuses

These were not fitted to early machines but are a good insurance for all. At worst a single 35-amp fuse in the main battery line can save the day in the event of a short circuit, while for more sophistication a modern fuse box with several fuses and spares can be wired into the circuit. Separate protection for the lights and ignition makes sense but this can be extended to one for each circuit.

8 The finish

This is the process that produces the final appearance, whether that is polished, plated or painted, and always the result depends on preparation. The final top coat is the easy stage, it is the work done to bring the surface for that coat to the required standard that takes time and effort.

The production finishes used by BSA were to either polish castings or leave them as cast, to plate certain major items and the details with either chromium or cadmium and to paint the steel parts that made up the bulk of the cycle side and also certain cast-iron items using the stove-enamelling process.

Petrol tanks and wheel rims were both chrome plated and painted on the earlier models, while the plastic and rubber items were as moulded. Transfers were added as a final touch at certain points.

Cleaning the parts

Right at the start you will have removed the outer dirt from the machine, but now each part needs attention. The process used depends on the part, its job, its material and the required finish. For internal items the cleaning process is likely all that is needed, but the visible ones take more.

Cleaning can be done mechanically or chemically depending on the surface smoothness desired and the shape and area in question. Some of the chemicals are not readily available in the small quantities needed by the amateur and all must be treated with caution and only used when protective clothing is worn. Read the instructions carefully including the warning notes and what to do if you splash yourself.

Detergents

Straight from the kitchen a household washing powder is most useful for cleaning castings. They are best done in a pan of hot water and before immersion all steel items must be removed. Don't leave the parts in for longer than is necessary as many of these products are acidic in nature and will attack the castings. When the cleaning process is complete wash all the detergent away with hot water and then dry the casting.

Often this is all that will be needed to restore an engine or gearbox casting that is simply dirty with ingrained oil, but do make sure all the detergent is removed.

The A7 in its 1951 form with revised engine and plunger frame

THE FINISH

Mechanical

At its simplest this involves scraping the finish, usually paint, away with a knife or some similar tool. This is slow, tiring and tedious but will get you down to the bare metal in time. It can also damage the surface if you are not careful enough to prevent the knife digging in.

More usually it means some form of blasting process where small particles are blown at the item to be cleaned so they knock the finish off. The speed, severity, substrate damage and visual finish depend on the abrasive material used.

For removing rust, paint and corrosion aluminous oxide grit blasting is suitable for motorcycle parts. Iron grit or shot are not and would badly damage castings and blow holes in sheet metal so avoid them. A less common and more delicate process is vapour blasting, which carries the abrasive medium in water, but the most popular method for smaller items is bead blasting.

This uses glass beads and so does not take material away. It is also used on castings that have been grit blasted as that process tends to open the metal pores. The beads close them up again, flatten the surface out and give it a polish that can range from matt to gloss.

All parts should be thoroughly cleaned and oil, grease and loose rust removed before they are taken for the blasting process. Threads, cylinder bores, tight tolerance holes, headstock bearings, oilways and tapped holes will all need protecting, not so much from damage as to make sure nothing is trapped that could cause damage later. It is all too easy to block an essential oilway with beads, which will wreck an engine in minutes.

Blanking off can be done using nuts, bolts, pieces of tube, several layers of masking tape or even Blu-tack. This last is excellent in recesses as it just absorbs the beads, which come away with it afterwards. Items such as headstocks in frames can be sealed using a length of studding, two metal discs and rubber discs cut from an old inner tube. Don't forget a screw for the grease nipple hole or your work will have been wasted.

A10 Golden Flash models being handed over to the Johannesburg Traffic Department in 1951

ABOVE *1956 model A7 in pivoted fork frame with light alloy hubs and full chaincase*

BELOW *The police version of the A10 in 1957 fitted with alternator as well as dynamo, radio, safety bars and special petrol tank*

THE FINISH

ABOVE *The A7 Shooting Star for 1958 with revised hubs and nacelle*

BELOW *The 1962 Rocket Gold Star with its special silencer, rear sets and other nice options*

The alternative to blasting is to remove paint, rust and, inevitably, some metal using emery. The manual method involves cloth strips, which can be useful on frame tubes, but for most items mechanization is essential. This takes the form of an electric drill and an emery flap wheel and is used more to remove deep scratches from the metal and to blend the damaged area into the rest. As with the blasters, for the best results you should let the tool do the work without forcing it. Don't use a sanding disc as it will take off too much and most likely score the surface.

The extension of this type of work is to finer and finer grades of abrasive so that you finish up with a polished surface. This was normally applied to the timing cover, gearbox end cover and outer primary chaincase but is often extended by owners to many more of the light-alloy castings. This will reduce the metal's heat dissipation and may not be as original but many owners like to have more polish than normal for their machine, which is their right.

Polishing can be done by hand, with mops or by a combination of the two. Industrial polishers use large mops driven at speed by a good-sized electric motor for they take a lot of power. They can also round off edges and draw out drilled holes in a very short time so if you do have access to such equipment practice on something that is scrap before beginning on your BSA parts.

Small mops can be used in an electric drill and must be kept charged with mop soap. Again proceed with care, especially where there are sharp edges you wish to keep. Before mopping the easy areas you should deal with the awkward crevices. Very tempting to do it the other way round but not advisable.

The manual way of polishing involves wet-and-dry emery cloth in paraffin. You need medium and then two grades of fine and it is a tedious and dirty job. The recesses can be done with an emery stick and this may be driven by a drill. The major areas can be done using a Loyblox, which is a block of rubber impregnated with emery grit, which can be used wet or dry.

The final touch is a polish with Solvol Autosol applied with a soft cloth.

Chemical

There are chemical cleaners available for light-alloy parts and as with the detergent mentioned above they must be well washed away after use. Most are acidic in nature so care is necessary when using them and the instructions must be followed.

More usually chemical cleaning means a paint stripper and this is another messy operation but one that is quick and effective. Wear protective clothing and avoid contact by wearing gloves and eyeshields. It is a nasty substance.

Spread plenty of newspaper out, put out the parts for stripping and paint the liquid on. After a while the paint will start to bubble up and often comes away in sheets. A scraper may be needed to help it along and all the old paint must come away. Then get rid of the old paint and paper remembering that it is now an industrial hazard. Burning is a good method if possible but will smell and must be done out of doors.

The parts will need to be cleaned with water if the stripper was so based or thinners and wire wool. You *must* make sure that all the old paint and stripper is removed or the new coat will lift within days of application.

At this point you may find that under the paint there were patches of filler from some long-distant repair. These will all have to come away so you can get down to bare metal and can check on the exact damage. Don't be tempted to leave it, as having been disturbed by what you have done so far it will be close to falling away anyway.

Rust

You now have the steel parts in an ideal state for them to rust. However they have been cleaned they will immediately begin to oxidize and any handling only makes matters worse due to the acids of the skin.

So proceed to the next stage quickly.

If there is a delay and surface rust forms then it will have to be removed again before the finishing process is continued. There are a number of products available to do this and most have a phosphoric acid base. Many will also act as a primer for painting, but if the part has to be plated, wax or oil would be a better protection as they can be removed by degreasing.

Parts that are due to be painted should be given one coat of etch primer as soon as possible after the blasting or stripping process. This will keep the rust at bay while you draw breath.

Restoring the surface

If the part is to be plated then a metallic surface is essential and defects cannot be resin filled as they can for painted items. Thus it may be necessary to weld or braze, depending on the material, in order to obtain the required surface in the right substance.

This technique will work for castings and the heavier steel parts, but sheet steel components in general and the petrol tank in particular need sheet metal skills. If you have these you will have the hammers and dollies to do the work and if you don't then you had best farm all but the simplest tasks out.

Even professional restorers often send petrol tanks to a specialist as a repair usually entails cutting the bottom out to give access for the panel beating and then welding it back in again. A skilled job and not one to be attempted unless you really know what you are doing.

Filling

Steel or iron parts that have been left for years are likely to have a pitted surface and it is not practical to

ABOVE *Little changed since its introduction, the 1964 A50*

BELOW *The A50 Cyclone Competition off-road model built for the USA 1964–5 with high bars and open waist-level exhausts*

ABOVE *The 1964 A65R Rocket model with separate headlamp shell and two-into-one exhaust system*

BELOW *A 1965 Lightning Clubman A65LC plus a good selection of Eddie Dow extras*

THE FINISH

ABOVE *For 1965 BSA built this A50 Cyclone road model for the USA and based it on the competition version*

BELOW *1966 Lightning A65L in English form*

fill these with braze or clean the surface down to remove them. The first would take forever and the second weaken the part far too much.

One answer is resin filler, which may come as a brushed-on liquid or a two-part resin and hardener kit. Several coats will be needed to give body to the surface and ensure all traces of pitting have gone. Once this is done the part will need to be left for several days to harden fully.

An alternative is lead filling as used for cars. The area to be treated has to be tinned first and this is done using a flux with powered lead in it. This is brushed on and warmed with a blowlamp. Do not use a welding torch as the heat will be too hot and too local.

Then continue with the lead, which comes as an alloy of lead and tin in sticks. The blowlamp will allow the lead to be kept movable without running about and a hardwood spatula will let you push it about. Wear a mask, try not to put too much on, remember you can always add more if needed, and finally dress down with file and flattening paper.

The surface then has to be rubbed down and this is done using 320 grade wet-and-dry emery used wet. It is a tedious job as the aim is a smooth, even surface that blends in with the rest of the part without bumps or hollows. This is not easy to get completely right first time, but hollows can always be given another coat of filler so you have another chance.

Pinholes in the surface are dealt with using stopper in a similar way.

Once you are quite certain the whole surface of the part is just right you can move on, but don't delude yourself. Any mark, any imperfection, will shine through no matter how many coats of paint you put on.

Painting

The traditional method of applying paint is by brush with a number of coats and the surface rubbed down between each. This was far too slow for mass-produced machines so the job was speeded up using spray or dip techniques and stove-enamelling paint. This gave a hard finish with deep gloss that stood up to knocks well.

In contrast a brush finish either took a great deal of time to apply or looked poor and was easily damaged. Fortunately not any longer, although time and care is needed if a really good finish is wanted. What is now easy to obtain is good coverage, a deep gloss and a hard surface that won't chip easily and even if it does it can be touched in without much trouble.

Most restorers therefore use a synthetic enamel. The most common make is Tekaloid, which is favoured by many professional men. Others simply shop at a high-street store and produce very good results using either the enamel as it comes or as a two-part product. The second item acts as a hardener, so the drying time is reduced, and it is also possible to low-temperature bake the finish.

A short drying time is characteristic of cellulose, which is normally used for spraying. It has to be mixed with thinners, is volatile and flammable, and must be handled with care as it can be medically dangerous.

A fast drying time is desirable as it helps to combat the home restorer's greatest enemies when painting – dust and midges. For this reason some do use cellulose, but in the end the finish depends far more on the preparation, clean atmosphere and operator care than the paint type.

To get this there are certain guide lines to follow. Paint after rain has washed dust from the atmosphere. Choose a warm still day and damp down the working area. Wear clothes that do not harbour dust, so avoid wool. Work in an area free from draughts and don't open the door once you have begun. But don't forget you do need air to breathe with. Don't breathe on the work and hang it from wire, not string, with the least important face pointing upwards. Use a tack rag on the surface immediately before you start and leave the working area as soon as the painting is finished.

The paint is applied by a brush and the name Hamilton is the one that comes up most often. 1 in. wide will cover most items, but a $\frac{1}{2}$ in. may be needed for details and a 2 in. for mudguards. Run the brushes in on something unimportant and wash out dirt with clean paraffin in several stages until it really is clean. Tap the handle against a piece of wood to shake the surplus out, do not finger the bristles or wipe them with a rag. After use clean in paraffin, wash in warm, soapy water, then clear water and leave to dry.

To do the actual painting pour some paint into a clean cup and load the brush from that. Do not put the brush in the paint tin. Apply with long flowing strokes with the brush running down the part under its own weight to avoid brush marks. A light touch will give a lovely finish.

Two or three coats are usual and between each the surface has to be rubbed down using 500 grade wet-and-dry, used wet. This gives a smooth surface and allows you to see where the next coat has to go, not always easy on a dark, glossy surface.

There are two areas where the above will not work so well. One is where there is heat, so brake drums and cylinder barrels are better stove enamelled. This means masking off and filling using materials that will cope with the baking temperature. The other is the petrol tank, where the problem is resistance to petrol and staining. Fine if you never spill anything when refuelling and the cap seal does its job, but otherwise consider going to an expert.

Some restorers give the tank a coat of polyurethane lacquer, but this is not advised as it will react with any spilt petrol and act as a paint stripper.

This 1967 Thunderbolt shows few changes and was the tourer of the range

Paint colour

Black is black for most of us but colours seem to come in so many shades and to suffer from fading which leads to matching problems.

Also remember that all paints are not the same and while you can spray synthetic onto cellulose it won't work the other way round. Using a sealer or isolator may work but don't expect too much. Better to get back to the basic surface.

For the paint you should keep to one type for all stages and colours including any lining you do.

Paint colours are given in an appendix and to more detail than in *BSA Twins & Triples* so should therefore take precedence over that volume with regard to the information given. Matching is another matter and an area of original paint that has been shielded from the light will act as the best guide. The inside of the toolbox or the underside of a clip are possible places, but of couse if your machine has been fully repainted at some time then this matching is lost.

It may be possible to judge what you are after from a brochure or a contemporary magazine advertisement, but otherwise you will have to find a machine to study. Museums, shows and meetings are all possible sources. Or you may be able, or lucky enough, to find a part in its wrapper in the right colour. Worth buying whether you need it or not just for the match.

Once you know what colour you need you then have to get the paint shop to mix it for you. Start from the British Standard Colour Chart as this should get you near, but expect to have to experiment a little. Persevere on odd parts until you are satisfied you have it correct or to the shade you want it to be.

Spraying

This takes more cash to get the equipment and tends to be expensive in paint as much goes past the work onto the walls. The technique has been much described but as with the brush, practice, preparation and no dust are the keys to success.

Investigate paint types as some give off a lethal vapour and are not for the amateur at all. Learn how to operate the spray gun, the effects of your techniques and changes to them and practice first.

ABOVE *Dreams in 1967 were this Mk III Spitfire but reality was usually something else*

RIGHT *By 1968 the Lightning had a new front brake, small US tank, more glitter and side reflectors*

Observe all safety precautions, which are more stringent for spraying due to the fire risk and the fumes. Keep a fire extinguisher of the correct type to hand. Make sure ventilation is good, don't have naked flames, gas heaters or open radiant fires and check on your electrics in case anything can spark. Wear a mask when working.

Coatings

An alternative to painting is plastic coating or powder coating. These will not give the gloss required by the perfectionist but the coats are tough. There are limitations on colour choice, filler cannot be used as it won't stand the process temperature and plastic coating can strip off if rust gets under the surface at any point.

So, again, preparation is important and will reflect in the final appearance. Dip coating can be done at home on items such as stands as the main requirements are a means to heat the part up to around 300 degrees C and a container for the powder the part is dipped into. An old, cleaned, oil can is a good starter.

Plating

Plating, like painting, depends on preparation for a good result. This means cleaning the surface and polishing it without damaging it. So once more the files, the emery and elbow grease are needed.

With some of the small parts the biggest problem is holding them. You can pay the plater to do this, but it is a labour-intensive job and costly, so the more you can do yourself the better. Some parts you cannot

replate as no one will touch them or allow them in their chroming bath because of contamination. The two common ones are silencers and wheel rims.

After preparation the trick is to find a good plater who is interested in your motorcycle work and for this recommendations should be sought. Whether you are aiming for a concours job or not expect to pay for good workmanship, which is always less expensive in the long run than a cheap job.

The major plated parts are finished with chromium but other plating processes are needed as well. Nuts and bolts that are not chromed are normally either cadmium or zinc plated. Bright nickle may be found on the spoke nipples.

Aluminium castings may be plated, although this does nothing for heat dispersion, or they can be anodized. This improves their corrosion resistance and the film formed on the surface can be dyed in a range of colours, with matt black helping the heat and looking smart. Note that the process acts as an insulator so don't forget that your electrics need a path for the current.

Lining and transfers

Signwriters do this freehand and this is one solution used by many restorers – they farm the job out. Alternatives are plastic tapes. These are simply laid on and either left at that or varnished. Masking using pvc tape may be used to give the outline required. An alternative for the straighter parts is car lining tape, which has a centre strip that is removed to leave two outers spaced parallel to each other. Tricky but not as much as trying to do it freehand. Don't forget that the lining paint must be the same type as that it is being applied to or you will have trouble. Remove the tape before the paint is fully dry so it can flow smooth. Gold lining will then need a clear coat to protect it and yacht varnish is often favoured.

Transfers are the final touch to a machine and should be applied with care according to their directions. Make sure they go in the correct place and when dry protect with a thin coat of clear varnish.

Stainless steel

An alternative for many steel parts that are normally chrome plate is stainless. Many owners refuse to use parts made in it, but in the right application and the correct grade it can say goodbye to a corrosion problem forever.

There are a good number of stainless steels, some magnetic and able to be hardened, some not fully corrosion resistant and so on as with other metals. With the correct specification all will be well as long as the part is correctly machined. And not if not.

Fibreglass

This material was used for the petrol tank and side covers of some models during the 1960s and poses its own set of problems for finishing. In addition the use of the material for petrol tanks was always suspect and was banned in the UK from around 1969. From that date tanks were legally required to be made in metal and some authorities think this always applied and was retrospective.

The change arose because many early tanks were made in fibreglass by home workers and in far too many cases their quality standards were not good enough. The result was leaks followed shortly by fires. There were also cases of tanks breaking up in accidents with the consequent fire hazard.

Modern EEC regulations allow the use of non-metal tanks, but at the time of writing this did not apply to the UK.

Which leaves certain BSA owners in a quandary if they want to use their machines on the road. There does not appear to be any easy answer if the original appearance is to be kept. Possible ones are to remake the tank in metal or to bond a metal tank into the original shell, but either is expensive. A change to another BSA tank in metal loses originality but is likely to be the easiest solution, but check clearance underneath to make sure all will be well.

The repair and finishing of fibreglass is different to parts made in metal. So different in fact that they are really not the same jobs at all. Metal is hard and unaffected by paint stripper or paint solvents. Fibreglass is a mixture of glass and resin and the latter can be attacked all too easily. Being soft it is easy to mark and scores can be produced without trouble.

When the material was first introduced we were told that repairs would be easy, which is true if you simply want to join up a crack or fill a hole. If you also want a good smooth surface for your final paint then the job takes much longer as tissue layers have to be used to build up the surface before it is shaped, smoothed and rubbed down.

Painting also takes much longer as each coat must be left for a week, sometimes two, to make sure any interaction is complete. If this is not done the result will be nice for a month and then all the repairs will show through.

Practice your technique on a scrap part and allow as much time as you can between steps to make sure all the chemicals have done their job and stopped reacting. This is golden rule one when dealing with any fibreglass part. Make sure you use the correct materials has to be rule two and read the instructions FIRST is number three.

The touring A50 Royal Star of 1968 had a little less chrome and the older type of front brake

9 Frame and stands

With these items you have something solid to work on so most minor repairs are easy to do. Bent brackets can be heated and returned to their correct position and cracks around them welded. Holes may need welding and re-drilling if elongated or tapping out if their threads are damaged at all.

All this is easy to do, but the real work on the frame is to check its alignment. This can be done with string and straight edges but does take a good eye to spot areas where there is a problem. A straightforward bend due to a crash is easy to see, but the twist that five years of sidecar work may induce is more subtle.

Getting the frame straight again is a specialized job and should be farmed out. Before this is done check it over for cracks, which will need welding, for the fit of the head races in the headstock and the rear fork pivot, as attention to these areas will involve heat which could cause distortion. Best to get all the minor work out of the way so that once straight the frame can be painted.

The stands need similar attention and are often distorted due to misuse. Expect to find damaged pivot holes needing attention and check that the spring attachment point is in good order and will hold the spring as the stand moves. Inspect the stand feet, as these do wear and may need to be built up again to ensure the machine stands correctly when parked.

Second year of the A7, still with original frame and front stand but with normal type centre stand

Rigid and plunger frames

The first models had a rigid frame with a curious centre stand that retracted up the seat tube and was held in place by springs and ratchets. It was not a total success as it required the rider to lift the machine bodily to get a wheel off the ground and its design was such that any failure would drop the stand into the ground like a sprag.

It was supplied on frames XA7-101 to XA7-1100, but from then on a conventional pivoted stand was fitted. At least with that a broken spring would just trail the stand on the ground and give the rider some warning to stop.

The frame was thus modified after the first 1000 to reflect this change and continued for 1948 as a brazed assembly. For 1949 it was changed again due to the addition of the plunger model, and to suit the two frames a two-part construction was evolved. The front section was common and comprised headstock, top tube, seat tube and twin front downtubes, which terminated under the front of the engine. The rear halves were either rigid or formed to carry the plunger suspension and attached to the front at three points. One was under the saddle with a sleeve to align the front section and the two chainstays that straddled it.

The duplex cradle frame introduced for the unit construction twins in 1962

A through bolt clamped the joint together. Two under the engine at the front where the lower chainstays ran forward to meet the downtubes. Three was with a forging brazed between the lower chainstays which included a socket for the lower end of the seat tube, which was retained by a cross-bolt.

The rigid rear part was modified for 1951, its final year, while the plunger one had the prop stand lug brazed in place from 1953. The front half was altered for 1953 with revised rubber tank mountings and continued with its plunger rear to 1957. 1953 also brought a new frame for the Super Flash, which thus differed from the other plunger models. It had its own marking with a BA10S- prefix to distinguish it.

Pivoted-fork frames

This type was introduced in 1954 and should be checked in the same manner as the rigid and plunger one. Its construction is straightforward, with the fork fitted with bushes and located on a spindle fixed across the main frame and held in place by a large nut and a location screw in the spindle head.

From 1956 the spindle was hollow with a brake cross-shaft contained within it. This continued on the unit models brought in for 1962. It continued in use to

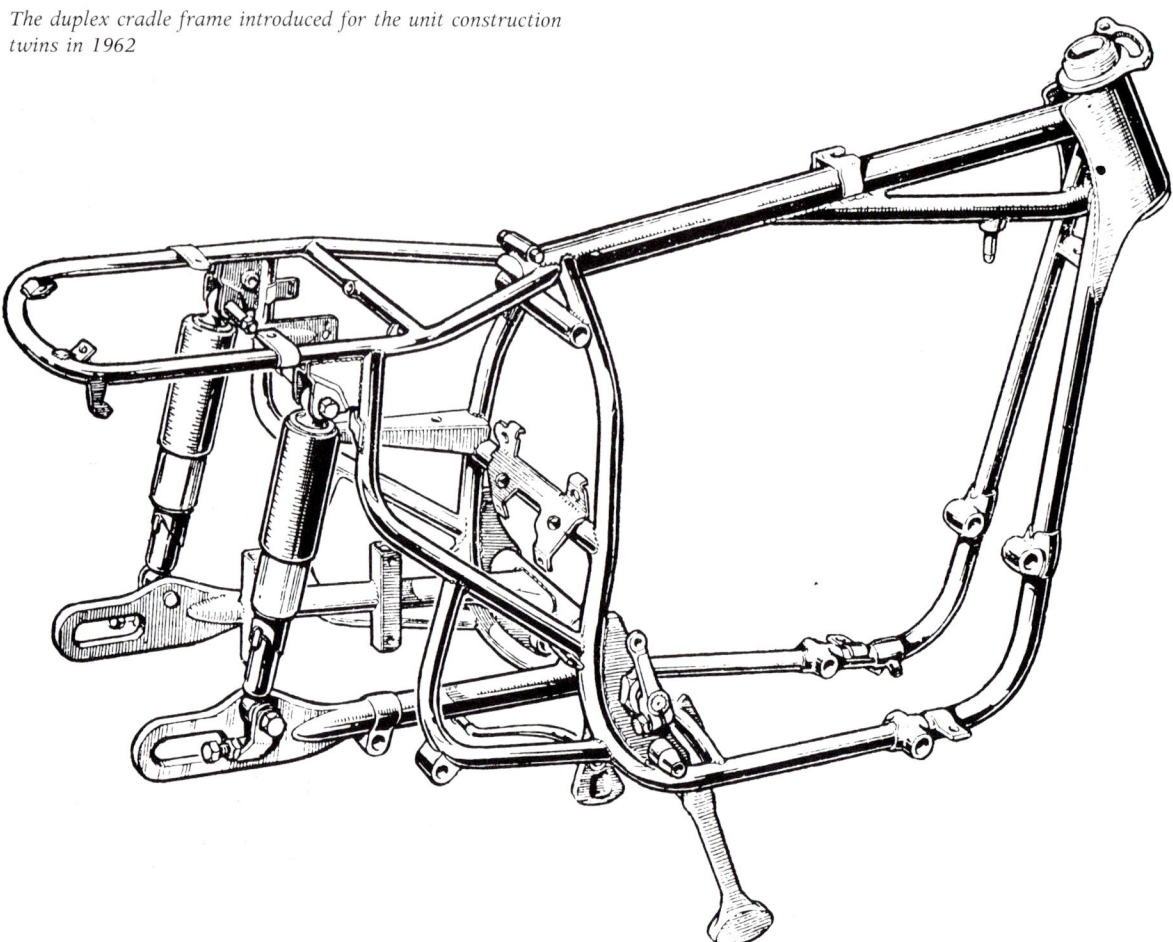

1965, but not on the more off-road models of that period, which had a single side brake on the left and thus no need of the crossover linkage. From 1966 all models were like this and this continued for the 1971 conical hub.

The main frame should be checked as for any of the earlier ones, the points mentioned also applying to the rear fork. The fork bushes may need changing and either Silentbloc rubber or, from 1969, steel-backed bushes were fitted. All parts should be inspected and renovated as required.

The original 1954 frame was altered by the addition of a steering-lock lug on the top front of the headstock for 1955 and sidecar fittings for 1958. In 1960 it was joined by the Spitfire frame, which was the standard one lightened down by the removal of all excess fittings. 1962 brought the Rocket Gold Star with its own frame modelled on the single-cylinder Gold Star but without the famous oil pump kink in the right under engine tube. Thus it was much as the stock twin frame but with extra gusset plates around the headstock area. A real one has a frame prefix of GA10- and is the only one so stamped. It thus follows the precedent set by the Super Flash in 1953.

The pre-unit frame had some changes for its pivoted fork; the first coming in 1956, when the rear brake changed sides and its torque arm lug had to do the same. In 1958 it changed again for a similar reason and to suit a variation of the chaincase fitting.

The unit main frame had a good few detail changes and for its first four years was built in two forms, one for the UK and the other to take a right-hand sidecar. It changed in detail in 1963 and was joined in 1965 by two more frames with open rear seat loops. These went on the off-road models and the Lightning and for all machines in 1966 there was a new frame in this style. It continued with small changes for 1967, 1968, 1969, when fairing brackets were fitted to the headstock, and 1970. For 1971 there was the all-new oil-in-frame and a modified version was listed for the A70 in 1972.

The infamous oil-in-frame of 1971, this one being the Thunderbolt

The rear fork used for the unit models was first altered early on to suit the change from cable to rod rear brake operation. It changed in detail for 1965 but then continued until 1969, when it changed to accept the new pivot bushes. A new fork was brought in with the new frame in 1971.

Head races

Expect to renew these on a restoration unless they are in perfect condition. Even if they are, change the ball bearings. Up to 1970 all BSA twins fitted cup and cone bearings with loose balls and all models used the same parts. The cups were common, but different top and bottom cones were fitted. 40 ball bearings of $\frac{1}{4}$ in. diameter kept them apart.

For 1971–72 taper roller bearings were used as standard and kits to fit this form of bearing to older machines are available and worth using. Follow the adjustment instructions carefully.

Centre stand

After the initial batch of machines with their curious sprung stand the A7 fitted one of conventional form. For 1952 it was modified to lift the machine higher, to retract further when not in use and gained a ball-ended extension on the left to assist the rider's boot to get a purchase on it. This stand continued in use on the plunger models and was held up by the spring first listed in 1947.

The pivoted-fork frame introduced in 1954 had its own form of centre stand with the feet shaped to assist lifting the machine, its own spring type fitted on the right and a toe peg on the left. Its feet were changed for 1958, when they took on a more oval form, and again for 1960, when the spring moved over to the left side. At the same time the toe peg was fitted with a rubber, a feature not used on BSA twins up to then, and a second stand appeared specifically for the Spitfire model. In 1962 this last went onto the Rocket Gold Star as it suited the siamezed exhaust pipes of that machine.

The Spitfire stand also went onto the unit models for the first four years and was fitted when siamezed exhaust pipes were used. The models with twin pipes had their own stand and a third was used for the off-road models. This last used the spring from the 1954–63 pivoted-fork frame stand but the others had their own. All shared one type of toe pedal rubber.

For 1966 a new stand was used which went on all models and this continued until the new 1971 frame brought a change. For this there was also a new toe rubber and spring, the latter changing for 1972.

Prop stand

A prop stand was listed from 1948–52 as fitting to a bolted-on lug, but after that pivoted from one built as part of the frame. It continued in this form on the plunger frame with a special leg for the Super Flash

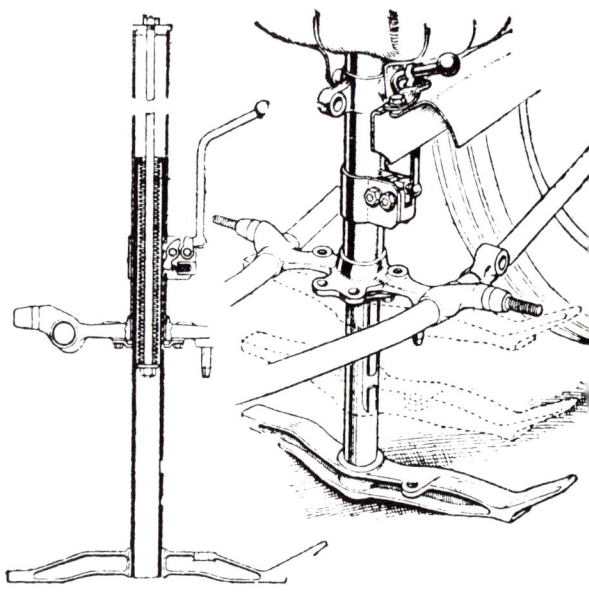

The curious centre stand of the first A7 with ratchet and spring in the seat tube, lever release and no real way of lifting the wheels clear

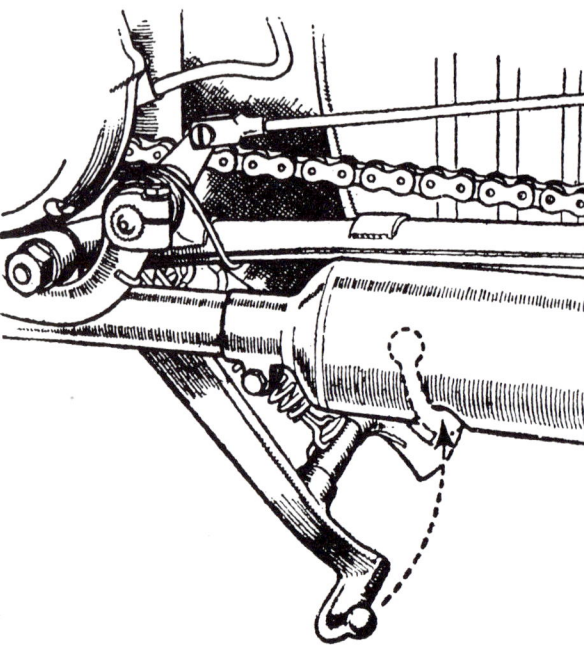

The centre stand extension and silencer cut-away for the 1952 twins

FRAME AND STANDS

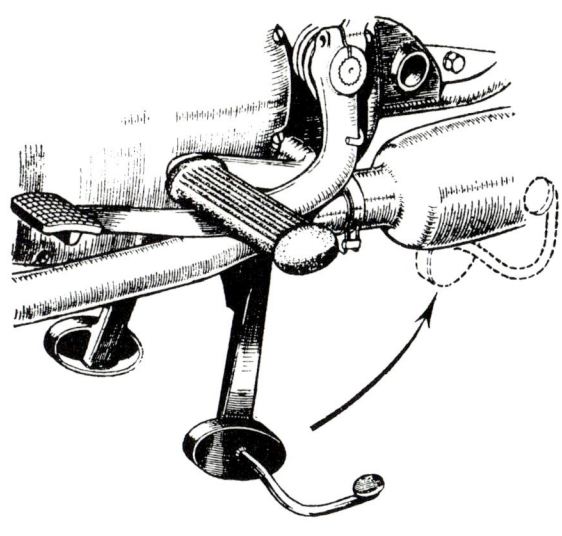

and was joined in 1954 by another leg for the pivoted-fork frame. This was modified in 1960 with a revised foot, the leg also going on the early unit machines.

It was soon changed and an alternative leg was listed for the US models. This became the standard fitting in 1966 and continued in use until the advent of the new frame in 1971. For this there was a new leg that simply terminated in a bent-out part without a foot.

One spring was used for all prop stands from 1948 until it was revised for 1968. This second type continued on to 1972.

For 1958 the stand gained roll-on feet and a new lifting pedal

10 Suspension

Front suspension of all models was by telescopic forks, whose appearance was changed for 1953 by the addition of a cowl. In 1958 this changed to a nacelle, but after 1965 this was phased out for a more sporting appearance. Machines then had a separate headlamp and fork gaiters but in the end the latter went in the name of styling.

At the rear the machine was rigid until the plunger frame was introduced in 1949. This continued in production to 1957 and was joined by a pivoted-fork frame in 1954. This system continued from then on.

Telescopic forks

Most of these are similar in nature and restoration follows common lines. Strip the forks following the procedure given in the manual and examine the parts for wear. Check each leg for worn bushes or sliders, which may call for repair or replacement.

It is common for fork legs to be bent and rolling them on a flat surface will reveal this. Wear can be overcome by hard chroming and grinding to size if new parts are not to be found. This will also deal with any pitting of the surface. Where this is minor, however, it can be filled with epoxy resin which is rubbed down when hard.

Expect to renew fork bushes and seals, but most of the other internal parts operate in oil and seldom wear. Check the springs for tiredness and shortening. If this has happened try to find new springs of the correct rate. Packing can be, and is, done but will affect the rate and may restrict fork movement. It can also give rise to clashing sounds if things have worked out against you.

All threads need to be carefully checked and repaired as required. As they hold the forks together or the front wheel in they do have a bearing on your well-being. Check the lower legs especially for any signs of damage.

If the fork tubes have been bent then it is most likely that the crowns will also be bent or distorted. Sometimes this manifests itself in the head races going tight at one point but slack at another. The crowns must be true to the forks and the frame and their threads checked.

The slimline front forks with four studs for each cap adopted for 1971 and shown on a Lightning

SUSPENSION

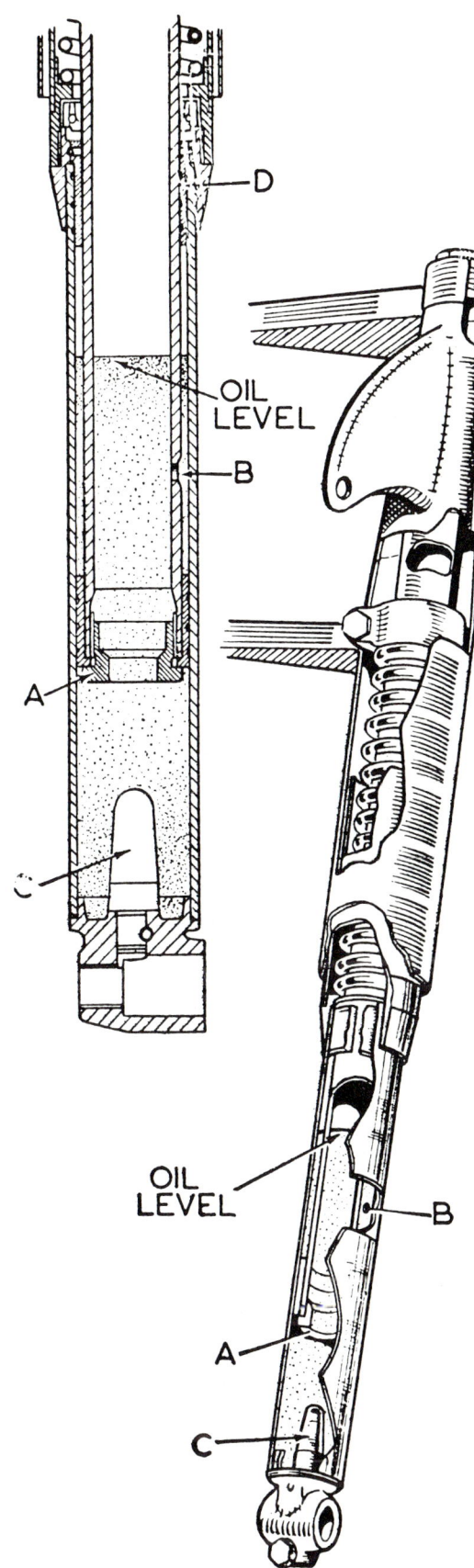

Assemble to the book, make sure the head races are correctly adjusted and that the fork legs are parallel so they can move freely without binding. Fill with the correct grade of oil and try to get the same amount in each leg.

Telescopic fork types

BSA kept to one basic type of fork for many years. For all that it had a good few changes, but mainly to suit other items. The first set came for 1948 and included new shrouds, bushes and solo springs. For 1949 the legs changed from a single mudguard stay behind the wheel spindle to two lugs, one forward and one aft. At the same time the bridge mounting changed from two studs to a lug to the rear of the leg with two bolt holes.

1950 brought the A10, which had its own legs to take the torque stay of the front brake and a new offside leg for the A7 plus a change to the sidecar spring. For 1951 the A10 legs became common, the solo springs changed, the stanchions gained extra holes for the damping oil and a new top bush was fitted. The next change was in 1953 when the cowl appeared and shrouds without headlamp lugs were used.

For 1954 there were new legs for the pivoted-fork frame models and another pair for the Road Rocket, which had shrouds with headlamp lugs. In 1956 the Rocket legs became standard. The appearance of the nacelle in 1958 also saw the arrival of fork legs with split ends and caps plus a stop peg to take the brake torque.

There were detail changes for the US models in 1960, a new sidecar fork spring, altered chrome ring behind the nacelle and legs with studs for the mudguard bridge. For the Spitfire there were short shrouds without headlamp lugs but fitted with gaiters and this model used the 1958-type legs. Finally, for the pre-units came the RGS in 1962 with legs to suit the 190 mm front brake, chromed shrouds and gaiters.

The unit models used many parts from the earlier models with some dating back to 1947. There were detail changes to the nacelle early on and in 1964 the A65R appeared with short shrouds with headlamp lugs and gaiters. In addition, where a single-sided brake was fitted, the old-type legs from 1954 were used with one end threaded and the other split to lock on the spindle.

The original simple but effective BSA front fork which remained in use for many years with only detail changes

BSA TWIN RESTORATION

The revised forks with two-way damping which went onto the 1966 models

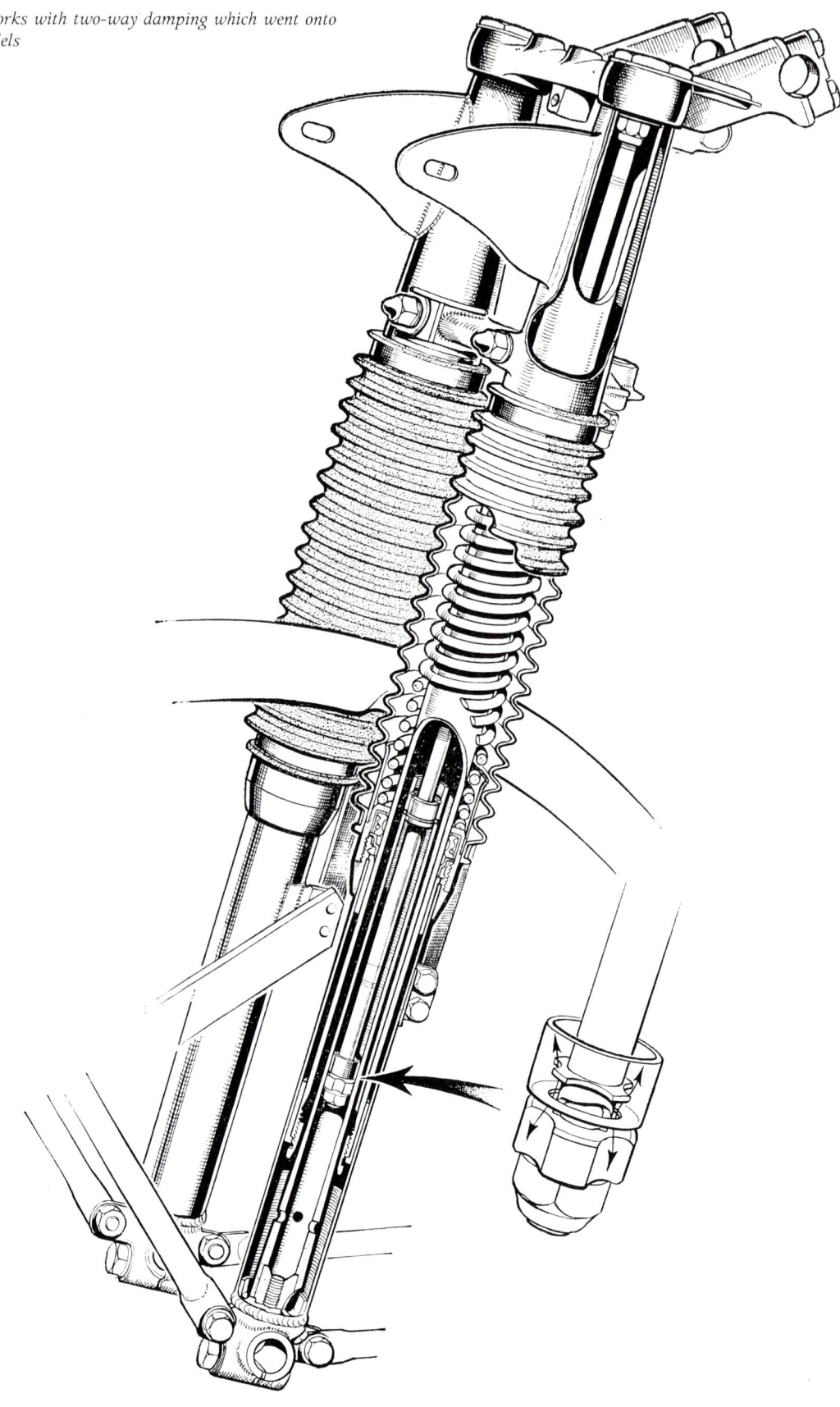

1966 brought revised forks with two-way damping and various new internal parts, although the exterior remained the same as did some of the insides. All models had the original form of leg to suit single-sided brakes and this continued for 1967 with revised shrouds and top nuts. For 1968 it was back to split fork ends and caps for the sporting models while the touring A50 and A65T kept to the 1967 parts.

It was all change in 1969 to fork internals with shuttle damping and new legs with split ends for all models. The shrouds were as for the 1968 road models, but the gaiters were new, as were the bushes, oil seals and stanchions. Even the adjuster for the headraces changed to a single item in place of the sleeve and cap used for so long, and the top nuts changed once more.

In 1970 the fork legs were modified with a change of drain plug screws and new stanchions with an improved finish. For 1971 the forks were all new to give a slimline look, gaiters no longer being fitted. Their internal design was changed and the fork end caps were held by four studs rather than two. The headlamp support became a piece of bent wire with a second type listed for the Firebird. For 1972 the springs, both solo and sidecar, top nuts and sleeve cap all changed.

Fork yoke types

These are also known as steering crowns and should be checked for damage or distortion. The first type were modified for 1949, the year plunger rear suspension first appeared, and the top one for 1953 to suit the fitting of the cowl. New yokes came in 1954 for the pivoted-fork frame and the Road Rocket with the Shooting Star using the Rocket lower yoke. The top yokes changed in 1955 to include the steering lock, and the lower yokes changed in 1958, when the nacelle came in.

The export models switched to the 1954 lower yoke in 1960, while the RGS kept to the one used by the Rocket and Shooting Star from that year.

For the unit models the original yokes were joined by a competition top yoke with extended bar holders and no lock recess. In 1966 all models changed to a top yoke of this type but with a lock, and this was joined by a revised lower yoke in the following year which changed once more for 1970. For 1971 there were new yokes with bushes to support the handlebars in the top one, and for 1972 the thread on the column of the lower one was made finer to make it easier to adjust the head races.

Handlebar fixings

From 1947 to 1970 all models used the same pair of caps. For 1971–72 only the bars were held in eyebolts, which were fixed into bushes with rubber insulation pressed into the top yoke.

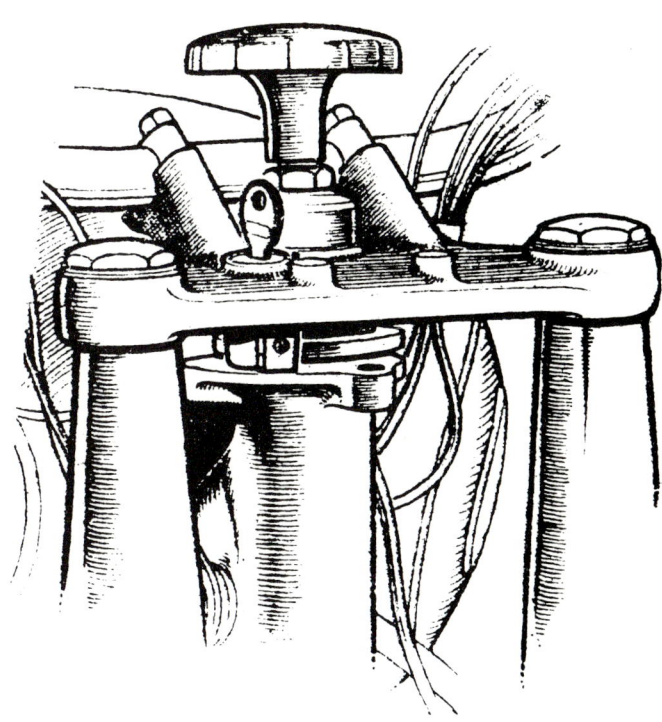

The 1955 top fork yoke with steering lock

Steering damper

This only needs checking as to the condition of screw threads and the friction disc plus its general good order. Many of the detail parts remained the same for some years. The first to change was the friction disc, which was amended for 1948. The next change came in 1954 with a joggled anchor plate for the pivoted-fork frame and a locking plate for the damper knob on the Road Rocket. A further locking plate appeared in 1960 for the Spitfire and also went on the RGS when it was without lights, while a third type was used on that model when with lighting. All these plates were held in place by two of the handlebar cap bolts and were one of the features of the sporting models.

The steering damper for the unit models was assembled from early A7 parts with the 1954 anchor plate and did not alter until 1966, when this part was modified. It changed again for 1968, when its tail was bent up to suit a new fixing to the frame. The damper knob changed for 1969 and again for 1970. This knob alone continued on the new frame and forks the next year, when all the other parts altered.

Plunger frames

These first appeared in 1949 and became standard for all models in 1952. They were joined by the pivoted-fork type in 1954 and remained available for all models that year alone. From then to 1957 the A10 only continued to be listed in the plunger frame, mainly for sidecar use.

ABOVE *Using a wood dowel to pull the fork tube up to the top yoke on a 1953 A10. Note screwdriver wedging bottom yoke to help the assembly*

RIGHT *Rear unit without protective covers on a 1969 Thunderbolt*

ABOVE *Plunger units of a 1949 Star Twin which can be a problem to keep clean and quiet*

The plunger units need to be checked and can be dismantled without tools if care is taken. A piece of screwed bar to thread into the top of the plunger column in place of the top plug is useful and may avoid thread damage. The units may need rebushing but often cleaning and greasing will be sufficient. Check that the covers can move up and down without scraping on one another and that all the collars are in place. Hand compression will get the assembly in and out of the frame so a compressing tool is not essential.

Only one part changed on the plunger units and this was the column plug, which was altered for 1954. All other parts were common for all years.

Rear suspension units

BSA fitted sealed rear units on their machines and these offer limited scope to the restorer. In all cases the outer covers and springs can be removed, but the actual damper unit is sealed. The rubber mounting bushes can be renewed, but repair of the unit requires that it is dismantled, which for most is not possible.

Given machining equipment it is feasible to strip, repair and rebuild units but it is a specialized business. If replacement units cannot be found then an alternative will have to be fitted. These are available and from the suppliers' lists it should be possible to find one with similar closed and open lengths, end fixings and spring. In many cases these new units have improved, and sometimes adjustable, damping and can be stripped for repair when this is needed.

In all cases check that the eyes at the ends of the unit and the frame attachments are in good order and will carry the loads they are called upon to support.

The original 1954 units had three load positions and were available with 110 or 130 lb/in. rate springs. In 1958 the mounting eye rubbers were changed but otherwise these units continued to 1963. The unit twins were also offered with solo or sidecar springs, and this practice did not cease until 1971 and the new frame. In 1968 the Spitfire and Lightning models were fitted with top spring covers only and chromed springs, while in 1969 all models did without any covers at all. There were new units, again without covers, for 1971.

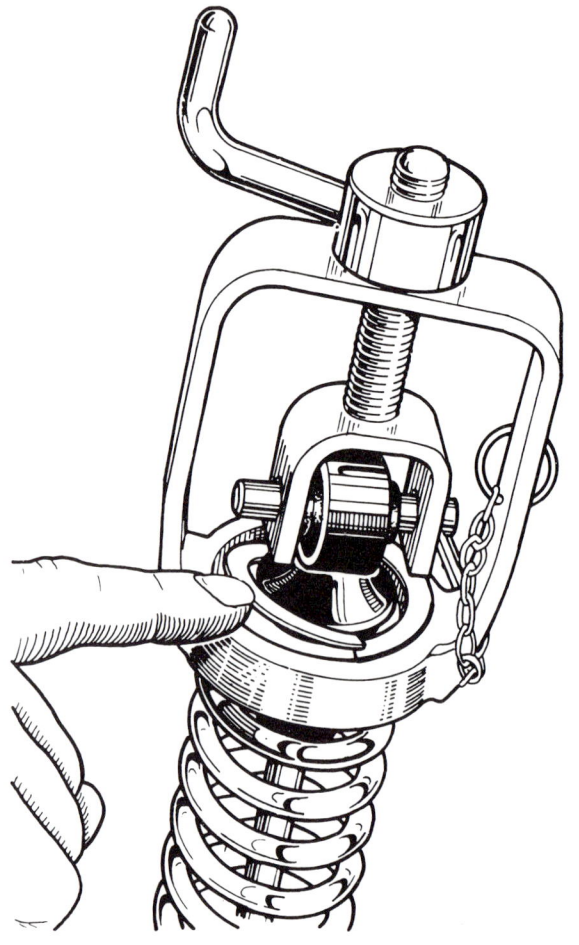

RIGHT *Special tool for compressing rear unit spring to release its split collets*

BELOW *Service article picture of 1954 A10 to illustrate rear unit spring load adjustment and an emergency-only method of rear spindle removal*

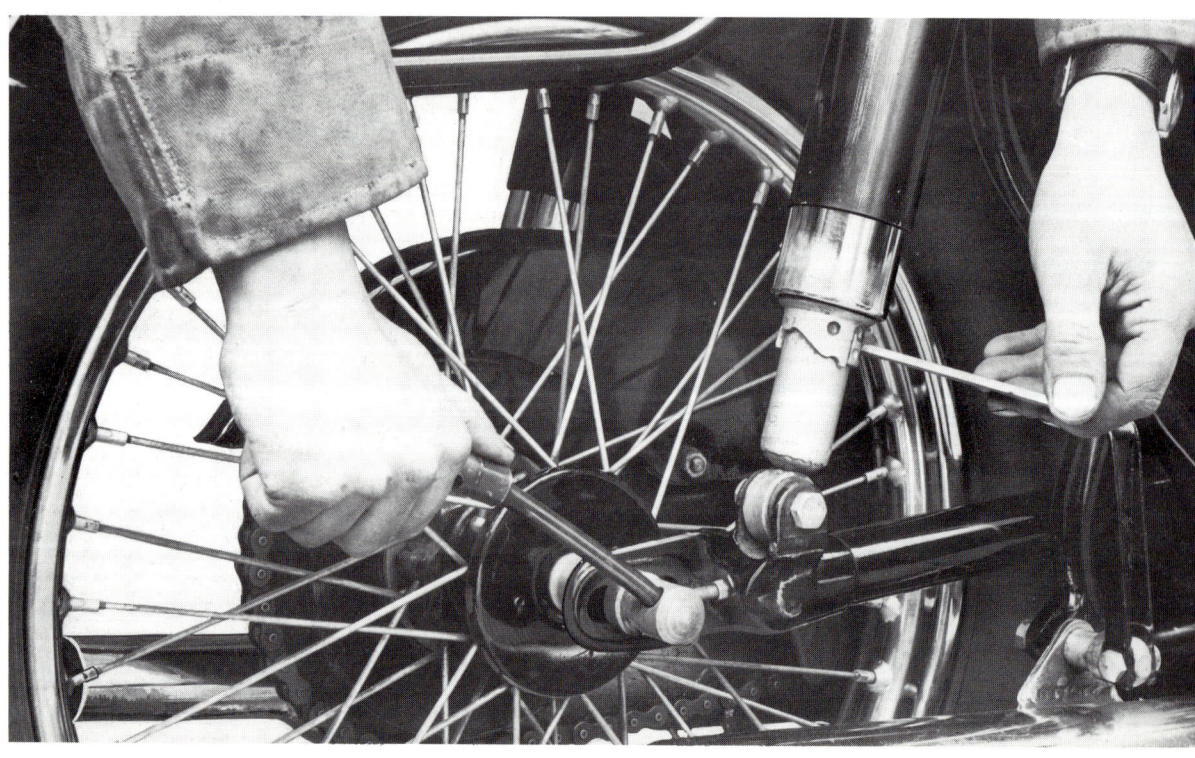

11 Painted parts and plated details

This title covers the mass of major parts and minor fittings that are mostly steel pressings and nearly all painted. A few are forged or diecast and some plated with either chrome or cadmium.

The steel pressings need to be checked over for repair. This may entail a simple bending job to straighten a bracket or a complex panel-beating job for such items as mudguards. Often the parts will need to be welded, either to mend cracks or to rejoin things that have come apart. Excess holes will need to be filled and the external signs of all this work removed before the finish is applied.

The problems in this area arise not so much with the repairs, which are usually straightforward, but in collecting all the parts and ensuring that what you have gathered up is correct for your model. In all too many cases changes did not affect fit, or if they did could be modified to suit. Thus, machines built up from parts can often have cycle details from many models included and worst of all can be the basket jobs.

These last need very careful checking over from the first. It is easy to see that you have a pair of mudguards, although less so to be sure they are the correct pair, but much more difficult to be sure you have a full set of engine plates or torque stays. The following sections are thus not concerned with the repair of the parts, which follows stock lines, but with their correct identification.

Knowledge, part numbers and changes will all help to ensure that the cycle spares bought from dealer or autojumble will be correct for your project

Engine and gearbox plates

The first A7 had one pair of front engine plates only as the rear fixing was direct to the frame. The two plates were both flanged in on their top and front edges to give a boxed-in effect between the duplex downtubes of the frame, and the right one was pierced to accommodate the dynamo. On the left the part was pressed into a dome to clear the dynamo end and between the two plates went an insert piece formed to enhance the smooth lines of the parts.

One owner's ideal. A composite in the style of the RGS but with later front brake, alloy tank and other nice parts. A lovely machine but a hybrid so buy for riding not originality

ABOVE *Following a 12,000-mile US tour on a B33 Joan Henley then changed to this 1951 A10*

RIGHT *Pipe brace and engine steady on a 1968 Royal Star with its US styling*

For 1949 the left plate was changed to have a piercing as the right to accommodate the longer dynamo fitted that year, but this pair of plates were only used up to 1950. That year they were joined by a similar pair that went onto the A10 and which still used the same insert piece. These parts were then used on the revised A7 in 1951 and on all plunger models to 1957.

They were joined by new parts in 1954 for the pivoted-fork frame and these machines had two front and four rear plates. The front ones looked similar to the early type, but the flange now ran continuously along the top and front without the gap for the insert, which was no longer used. To replace it the left plate had two distance tubes welded to it which ran across to meet the right plate.

At the rear there were two top plates with slots for gearbox adjustment and two L-shaped lower ones. Above the assembly went a cover pressing to enclose the area and neaten the appearance. All these parts went on all the pivoted-fork models with pre-unit engines and for the Spitfire there were a pair of round plates to blank off the dynamo holes in the front engine plates. The discs were to keep dirt from accumulating and were held by a cross-spoke and nipple.

The unit engine models had a simpler design with two triangular plates at the rear of the gearbox for all models from 1962 to 1970. For the 1971 oil-in-frame models there were two new rear plates, which were joggled and thus handed left and right.

Engine stays and steadies

These link the top of the engine to the frame and need

PAINTED PARTS AND PLATED DETAILS

to fit properly if they are to do their job. In addition, on the early A7 there are two rocker box steadies that are simple flat strips with two holes in each. They bridge the inlet and exhaust rocker boxes.

The original stays were two in number and each bolted to the underside of the rocker box lug on the cylinder head to run forward to the frame downtubes. They were tubular with flattened ends, which must be at the correct angles to fit snuggly and do their job without being strained on installation. These stays and the rocker box steady strip were only used on the A7 up to 1950.

That year a pair of new stays went onto the A10 and remained in use for all rigid and plunger models to 1957, except the Super Flash, which had its own pair.

The part was much as the first and requires the same treatment. For the pivoted-fork models there was a new arrangement with two angle brackets bolted to the top of the rocker box with a sleeve between them. This assembly was located to the frame by a pair of shaped stripes that ran back from a cross-bolt to the frame lug and went on all models to 1963.

For the unit engines there was a different arrangement with a single stay between the top front of the engine and the frame area just below the headstock. This stay continued in use to 1970 and was joined by one with a welded-on cross-plate in 1969. This part, with the addition, went on the Lightning and carried the relay for the twin horns.

The new 1971 frame used a different method with a

ABOVE *The factory trials A7 ridden by Bill Nicholson in 1948 and fitted with a crankcase shield. Never a production model*

BELOW *New unit twin in 1962 showing the fork top pressing, cable adjusters and twin switches on the left of the nacelle*

U-shaped pressing running forward from a lug on the underside of the frame top tube to the top of the engine.

Exhaust pipe and silencer brackets

These did not appear until the arrival of the unit models in 1962, when a pair of triangular plates supported the silencers. In 1966 these changed to similar but heavier plates handed for left and right. At the same time a tie between the exhaust pipes was introduced. The one for road models had the ends bent up, but the version fitted to the waist-level pipes was simply a flat strip.

For the Firebird in 1968 it was joined by a pair of small brackets, this model also having its own left and right silencer brackets. In 1969 only the Royal Star had a tie strap as the other road models adopted balance pipes, but the Firebird had a new pipe bracket and silencer support plus heat guard and clips to suit the twin waist-level installation on the left.

The 1969 silencer bracket was a rectangular plate with a vertical strip welded to it and bent in or out to reach its mountings. For 1970 this changed to a plate extended up for its top attachment and with a tube welded at the bottom. This tube ran along before curving down to its fixing.

For 1971 and the new frame there was a pair of new silencer plates for the road model and a new bracket for the Firebird much like the 1970 one.

Undershields

One of these was not listed until 1960, when it appeared on the Spitfire. It was simply a plate shaped to fit between the frame tubes and curve under the engine. Three pairs of lugs attached it to various frame bolts.

The next plate was for the unit models and was of simpler form and fastenings with a pair of U-bolts at the front. This was listed up to 1970, but for the following year a new one was used which used J-bolts for its forward fixing.

Drip shield

This was used on all pre-unit models to stop any petrol that leaked or flooded from the carburettor from dripping onto the magneto. It fitted into the inlet port between the cylinder head and the carburettor.

Two were listed, with the original one being joined by another in 1951 and both continuing to 1963. Both went on the Rocket engine at one time or another, so a parts list check should be made to ensure the correct fitment is made.

HT clip

This and a protection tube for the leads was only listed for 1949–50 and located the parts to the left of the induction manifold.

Headlamp cowl and nacelle

The cowl was first fitted in 1953, became a nacelle in 1958 and went after 1965. The original item was a single complex pressing that attached to the existing forks and remained the same for its five years of use. A rubber section sealed the top of the headlamp to it.

The nacelle adopted in 1958 comprised a tubular shell section that bolted to a pressing wrapped around the fork legs between the crowns. Between the two went a chrome-plated decorative ring and at the top a dished cover to clean that area up. There was also a small chrome flash on each side of the shell.

This design continued onto the unit models with new parts and in the process lost the side flashes and gained a rather more complex top pressing that enclosed the handlebar clamps and head race adjustment. The shell and top cover altered in detail, but otherwise this design continued to 1965.

Fork shrouds

These are also known as fork covers and in nearly all cases support the headlamp shell on welded-on-ears. They extend down the fork to reach the lower leg and cover the spring or may be cut off short at the bottom yoke and have gaiters below them to protect the stanchions. If they are not true they will scrape on the leg and damage the finish before continuing to wear themselves away. It is thus important to make sure they move freely over the leg when bolted into place with the headlamp.

The original shrouds were altered for 1949 and in 1953 lost their headlamp lugs as the cowl took over that job, except on the Super Flash. They continued on the Road Rocket in 1954 and on machines without cowl or nacelle to hold up their headlamps to 1963. In 1960 they were joined by a second pair used for models going to the USA and in 1962 by a shortened pair with rolled lower ends to suit the gaiters fitted and these went on the Rocket Gold Star. They were also available as an option and can be found on Super Rockets fitted with rev-counters and RGS styling parts.

The shrouds became part of the nacelle wrap-around pressing in 1958, so for models so equipped were not listed separately. This also continued to 1963. From 1960 shrouds without headlamp lugs were listed for the Spitfire and these were supplied with gaiters.

The unit models began with the nacelle with the shrouds as part of the assembly, but in 1964 the A65R came with RGS-style short shrouds and gaiters. For the A50C the shrouds with lugs from the 1960 USA models were listed and for models without lights the 1960 Spitfire type were used, both with gaiters. The Rocket models had a revised shroud for 1965 with the headlamp holes slotted to allow horizontal headlamp beam adjustment.

1966 brought new forks and all had short shrouds

ABOVE *1970 Royal Star showing headlamp shell and other features of that year*

BELOW *A BSA twin prepared for the 1952 Clubman's TT and showing the effect on looks of too much mudguard clearance*

and gaiters, with the Wasp and Hornet using the 1960 Spitfire part as they ran without lights. All were modified for 1967 and again in 1968 to suit new gaiters. One pair was listed for the Firebird and another for the other models, the first with a hole for the shell bolt and the second with a slot. The gaiters changed again for 1969 and 1970 saw the last fitment of the shrouds, which were not used on the 1971-type forks.

Headlamp shell

Most of these are very similar as they carry the same light unit, but there are variations. The shell is none too easy to repair, but ones from other models can often be used if necessary. Threads, general shape and condition need to be checked and the finish may be paint or chrome plate.

The 1947 shell carried a small panel with light switch and ammeter and changed in detail for the next two years. In 1952 the pre-focus light unit and underslung pilot light appeared and the next year went under the cowl, so the shell lost its small control panel except for the Super Flash. This continued onto the Road Rocket the next year and both types were revised for 1955, when the pilot light moved into the main housing behind the headlamp reflector.

From 1958 most models had a nacelle (so no shell), but the old style with its switch panel continued on export Super Rockets and on the RGS.

A separate shell did not appear on a unit model until 1964 – for the A65R – and it carried the ammeter and two switches. This design continued with a chrome-plated shell in 1965 and was joined by a second shell for the off-road models. When the nacelle went at the end of 1965 all models then used the chrome-plated shell, which was modified in 1968 to add one warning light and in 1969 to add a second. The shell changed once more for 1971, when a new shallow shape was adopted.

Mudguards, stays, front stand and lifting handle

All these parts are associated together and as there were a good few changes over the years some care is needed to ensure that all the correct parts are to hand. If they are not then the mudguards may be fabricated from others or from stock parts. The stays and supports can also be made from strip or tube as called for. When flattening the ends of a tube for the mounting hole add a piece of flat stock inside it. This will give more body and stop the walls cracking.

Above all else do make sure the mudguards are properly secured and cannot revolve round the wheel. Check that they sit correctly with a good line to the tyres and that all the stays and supports line up and bolt down without strain. Only when you are fully satisfied with the mechanical aspects should you move on and complete the finishing.

Front mudguard

The first A7 had a non-valanced guard supported by a bridge between the fork legs, a one-piece front stay and a similar rear one that doubled as a stand. Both stays were bolted to the mudguard and to single lugs to the rear of each fork leg close to the spindle. The bridge alone was modified for 1948, but in 1949 there were more alterations and a change to the fork legs.

There were two new mudguards that year, with the first much as the original and going onto the A7 models whether plunger or rigid. Its changes were to suit a new bridge, which became a simple loop of strip steel in place of the older part with joggled ends. The second mudguard went on the Star Twin and had deeply valanced sides that were able to accommodate a standard number plate; they were pressed with a flat section to do this.

As well as the new bridge there were new stays to suit the fork legs having lugs fore and aft of the spindle. Two front stays were listed, one for the A7 guard and a second with longer flat sections at the outer end to suit the Star Twin one with valances. This type would look odd on the A7 of course. A single rear stay was used by both models and was much as before with a slotted lug on each side to attach to the mudguard.

1950 brought the A10, which was fitted with the valanced mudguard from the Star Twin. It was supported by the same bridge and front stay but had its own rear stay-cum-front stand in the same style as the others. The A7 continued with its own guard and stays until 1953, when it adopted the valanced A10 parts and stays. Meanwhile in 1951 the Star Twin changed to the A7-style guard with single top-fitting number plate and the A7 stays.

1960 Super Rocket A10SR showing the new front mudguard with single rear stay

Stays and fork leg end of 1954 A10 with well worn front brake

During the period 1950 to 1953 the bridge remained common and the front mudguards were as above according to the parts list. However, there is some evidence to indicate that the Star Twin was also built with a valanced mudguard in 1952, and of course it was easy enough to change over as all bolted to the same fork legs.

For 1954 the plunger models remained as they were, with valances for the A7 and A10, which continued on the 1957, and a plainer blade for the Star Twin. The bridge was new, but both stays were the same with two types of each to suit the two types of guards. The new A7 and A10 with pivoted rear fork used the same stays and bridge but their own similar mudguard, still with its side panels to carry the front number plates. For the Shooting Star and Road Rocket there were blade guards with their own bridge and stays. The front stand was only held to the mudguard by a single nut on these models and the same style was also used on the earlier Super Flash, but chrome plated in that instance.

The mudguards all continued as they were for 1958, but the front stays, tourer stand and sports front stays all changed. For 1960 it was all change with a new mudguard common for all road models. It did without a front stay and was supported by a bracket on each side that tied it to the fork legs. At the rear went a stand with single nut fixing. For the Spitfire there was a chrome-plated blade supported by three strip stays on each side, the front and rear common parts, and all plated. A similar but different blade was to go on the RGS.

For the US market there were other arrangements, as was usual practice, with, for instance, the 1959 A10 using the sports Rocket guard and the export Rocket the same part chrome plated with the stays in the same finish. This continued for 1960, with a special blade for the 500 Flash, as the A7 was known, the Shooting Star and the Super Rocket with the last named chrome plated.

The unit models began with much the same style as the last pre-unit and used the same bridge brackets with a new blade and two strip stays, which replaced the old-style front stand. These were soon modified and joined by a US version of the blade. 1964 brought the A65R, with standard and US guards with chrome-plated finish, its own stays but the existing brackets. These details also went onto the first A65T/R along with the early US blade, while another one with three strip stays per side was listed for the A50C, A65S/H and A65L/R. The first two shared stays but a second type went onto the last.

1966 brought three new mudguards, one general, one for the MkII Spitfire and one for the Wasp and Hornet. Stays were again to suit and this arrangement continued with minor variations with another blade in 1967 plus left- and right-hand centre stays flanged for stiffness. The variations are such to warrant very careful checking of parts lists for all items. 1968 saw the Wasp and Hornet blade go as the Firebird used the US Spitfire one. Of the others one went on the home models and the other on the other three US variants.

They altered around again for 1969 with the US Lightning fitting the Spitfire blade, which had a loop front stay, while the Firebird had a new narrower blade supported by side brackets and a rear loop stay with single bolt fixing. This became a two-bolt arrangement for 1970, which meant new parts, but the other items stayed as they were.

Completely new mudguards were fitted to the 1971 models and these were made with a wire stay on each side. At the centre of each went two rubber bushes and these were clamped by a pair of brackets that bolted to the fork legs. Two blades were listed to cover the need for a front number plate, or not, and both were changed for 1972.

Rear mudguard

The first A7 had a rear mudguard with the tail able to hinge up. It was held by a loop stay that also acted as a lifting handle and two rear stays designed for easy release to allow the back wheel to roll out. In 1949 this design was joined by another, still with hinge, for the plunger-frame models. A pair of angle brackets went at the forward end of the blade and on each side a tube, bent at right angles, formed a vertical and rear stay with a fixing to the top plunger-frame lug.

The rigid mudguard and stays went at the end of 1951 and the plunger was changed for 1953 when a boxed-in number plate was fitted. They continued in this form on the plunger models to 1957 and were joined by a new type for the pivoted-fork models in 1954. For these a one-piece blade was used with a pair of supports and a front angle bracket. In 1956 this last was dispensed with and the blade and supports revised, with the result used to 1959 with the parts for

PAINTED PARTS AND PLATED DETAILS

ABOVE *The 1971 Lightning in its new frame with mudguards and side covers to suit*

RIGHT *Typical rear mudguard, stay and seat support of the period on a 1966 Thunderbolt*

the US Rocket chrome plated as had been the special Super Flash blade.

In 1960 the blade was changed again and its stays became simple struts that ran back to support the tail. With the standard item came a chrome-plated blade for the Spitfire using the older stays but with brackets welded to them and a chrome finish. The RGS had its own blade and brackets as at the front.

The unit models began with just one mudguard, but this was quickly joined by a second for the USA. In 1964 came a chrome-plated blade for the A65R and by 1965 a further eight blades were listed for various models. 1966 brought some rationalization with just three blades for six models at home and abroad.

The one used for the Spitfire and off-road models continued in 1967 for the Wasp and Hornet, while two other new ones were introduced. One took a number plate and went on the Lightning, Spitfire, Thunderbolt and Royal Star. The other was for export, so without plate holes, and went on the same list of machines plus the Firebird from 1968. For 1971 there was a single new mudguard also used in 1972.

Side panels

On the pre-unit models this enclosing job was done by the oil tank on the right and the toolbox on the left. It was not until 1962 and the unit machines that panels appeared to fill in the centre area including the carburettor.

The first unit models had different left and right panels for the A50 and A65, but before long the original A65 type went onto the A50 as well. All carried the circular BSA badge, which was made in left and right hands and continued the style used by the A10 for many years.

For 1964 new and slightly more bulbous panels were adopted for the two existing models and the A65R, the new shape chosen to allow twin batteries to

149

ABOVE *A 1973 exercise with a 750 cc engine in the Bandit or Fury frame designed for the 350 cc ohc engine*

LEFT *Side cover of a 1965 Lightning Clubman shaped to clear the carburettors even when air filters were fitted*

be encompassed. These panels continued for 1965 and were joined by three pairs moulded to clear twin carburettors without enclosing them. Both styles were to remain in use to 1970, each chosen to suit the carburettor layout.

For 1966 there were three pairs of panels with the more enclosing going on the Royal Star and Thunderbolt, a twin carburettor pair for the Lightning, Hornet and MkII Spitfire, and another of similar form to suit the smaller-engined Wasp.

1967 was a year of confusion with some nine pairs of panels being listed. This arose in part because the home ones were fitted with winged BSA badges as usual but the US models had transfers. Thus there were home panel pairs for the Royal Star, Thunderbolt, Lightning and Spitfire with further sets for the US Royal Star, east coast Thunderbolt, west coast Thunderbolt, Lightning and both the Spitfire and Hornet, which shared. In addition to all the panels there were three types of transfers in place of the single pair of badges.

It was simpler in 1968 as all models had transfers, but there were five in all of these. As regards the panels, the Royal Star had new ones but the Lightning and Thunderbolt used the 1967 US types and the Spitfire and Firebird shared the 1967 US Spitfire and Hornet one. The transfers were all new and all changed again for 1969 along with the side panels, which were down to four pairs, one for each model. There were three home transfers and four US ones, with the Firebird having different ones for left and right.

For 1970 the Thunderbolt took the Royal Star panels, the Lightning was unchanged and the Firebird kept one and used one from the Lightning. Three new transfers were listed plus a pair for the Firebird.

The new 1971 frame brought the size of the panels down with a single pair for all models. The Thunderbolt used its 1970 transfer but the others were new. They and the panels were all changed for 1972.

Front number plate

Although these are no longer a legal requirement in the UK, many owners like to keep them and either display the registration number or the model type and year. On many pre-unit models the sides of the front mudguard formed the plate backing and the actual number plate was fixed to these.

For other models a conventional plate was fixed to the top of the mudguard using two clips. The original plate served from 1947 and extended well forward of its front fixing. Its successor came in 1960 and had the fixing moved forward, so there was less of an overhang.

It went on the early unit models but was soon replaced by the one able to accommodate the suffix letters first added to UK registration marks in 1963. It was revised again for 1967 and replaced in 1971 by a cast-alloy part.

PAINTED PARTS AND PLATED DETAILS

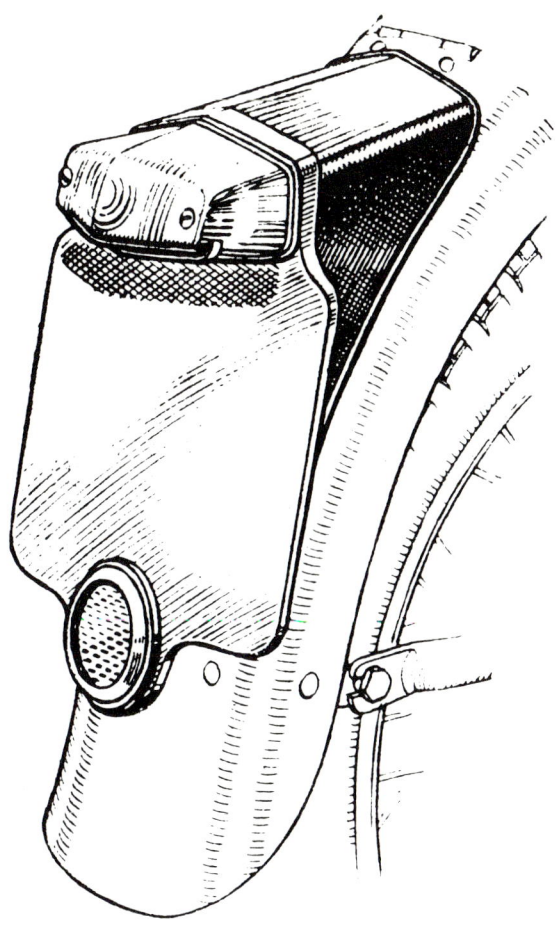

ABOVE *Rear number plate adopted for 1953 with boxed in sides*

RIGHT *By 1968 and this A50 there was just a bracket fitted for the plate as part of the rear light assembly*

Rear number plate

Still required and governed by local regulations so that in the end the company listed the brackets but kept the plate a home-market item. In many areas it was then up to the dealer to find and fit the necessary plate. Not so in earlier days, when white numbers would be painted directly to the plate. Later came transfers, plastic self-adhesive numbers, pressed-aluminium plates and finally the modern reflective one in yellow.

The first rear plate carried its light in the top centre and this was used to 1950, when it was joined by a second type. This was first used for some export markets but became the standard fit for 1951–52. It was changed for 1953 to a boxed-in form that fitted neatly to the rear mudguard. It also carried a rectangular rear lamp and a reflector at its base. This last went for 1956, but the plate remained in use on plunger models to 1957. The Super Flash used a plate from the Bantam Lucas D1 model.

For the pivoted-fork models of 1954 there was a new plate which was revised for 1960. The RGS had its own plate to match its own special mudguard.

The last pre-unit style of plate was carried onto the unit machines and continued on the tourers after an early modification. The Rocket version of 1964 revived the open type of plate, which was listed in two forms. This all changed in 1966, when a new style was brought in with a lamp support and a cross strip to carry the plate. The lamp plate and cross strip changed for 1967, when the number plate was listed again. All these details continued on to 1970. The support itself changed for 1968, when it was fitted with a reflector on each side on the line of the rear lamp.

The design had its last change for 1971 when a one-piece lamp bracket bolted to the mudguard with the number plate below it and mounted on twin brackets. The same parts were used for 1972.

Battery carrier and air cleaner body

This assembly was only used on rigid- and plunger-frame models so existed up to 1957. The original went on the rigid models only and was altered from frame ZA7-110 early in 1949 to accept an air cleaner element held by three bolts in place of the original four. The second type also went onto the plunger models and was joined by another version for the A10 in 1950. For that year alone a separate battery carrier was listed for the plunger-frame A7 models, but from 1951 only the A10 type was used and this ran on to 1957.

The battery carrier is often one of the most corroded parts of the machine, but fortunately the details are not too difficult to make, although to do this the hinge pins will have to come out.

Battery carrier

Where this item is alone it is still very likely to be corroded but again is one of the easier items to refurbish. Other than the brief listing in 1950 the carrier did not appear by itself until 1954 and the pivoted-fork frame. In its original form it comprised a platform bolted to the frame just above the rear fork pivot plus front, rear and top straps joined by bolts in swivel pins.

During 1960 this was superseded by a design that had the base and front formed into one with a wire clip with over-centre clamp lock to hold the battery in the same location. Two tray types were listed with one for the A7 from frame GA7-8855 and the A10 from frame GA7-8437, while the other was for the Shooting Star from frame GA7-8929 and the Super Rocket from frame GA7-8618. This latter also went onto the RGS in 1962.

The arrangement for the unit twins put the battery on the left under a side panel but continued to use the wire clip and over-centre lock. In 1964 this was joined by a second frame with hinged and bolted strap which was used when a 12-volt system was specified. In 1966 a new style of carrier was introduced in two forms to take either one 12-volt or two 6-volt batteries. Both comprised a U-shaped carrier bracket with flat top clamp and both were replaced for 1967. The replacement was of similar outline but held the battery in a moulded tray with a rubber strap. It did not change until 1971 and the new frame, when the mountings became round bushes on three sides with a separate angle piece and strap to secure the battery.

Battery carrier and side panel of a 1968 Thunderbolt

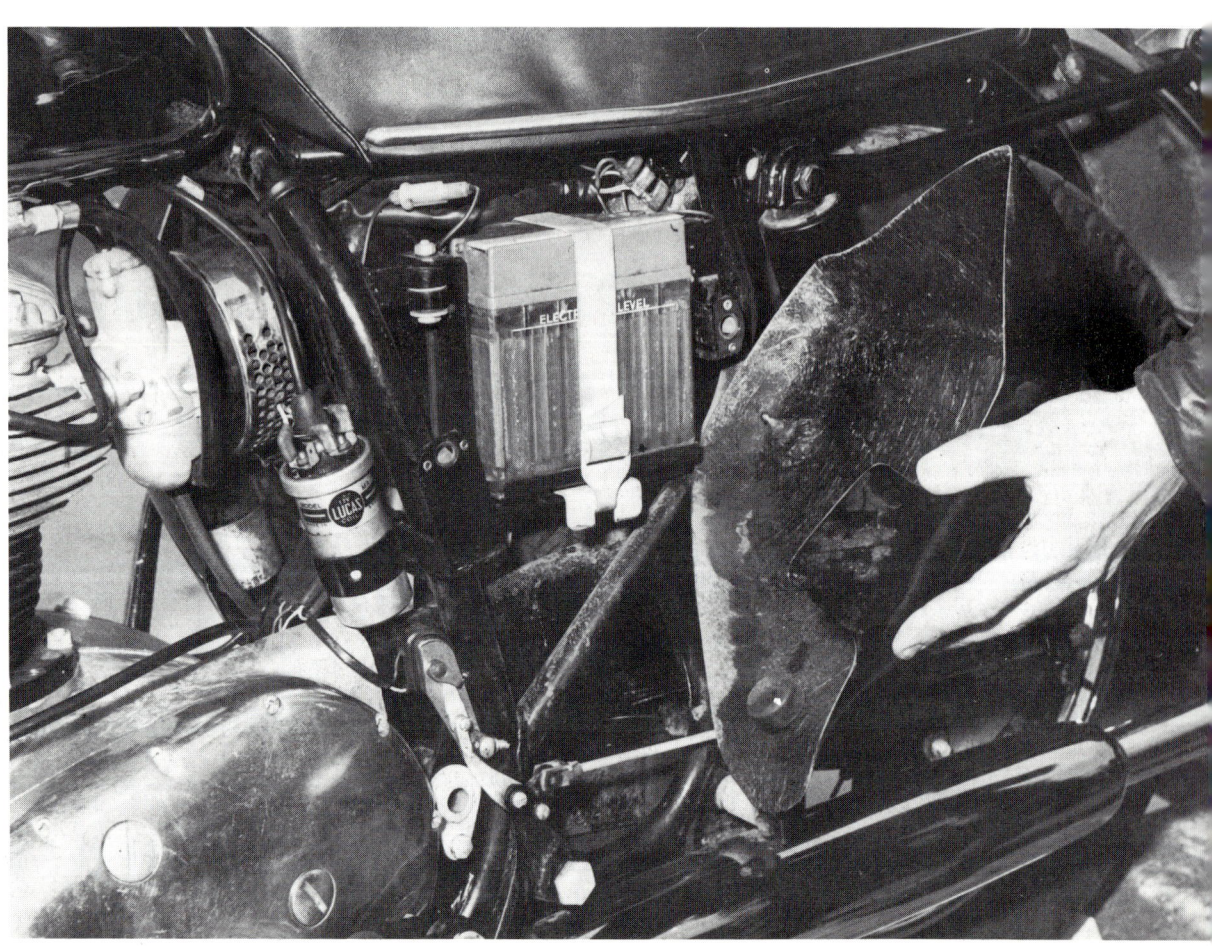

PAINTED PARTS AND PLATED DETAILS

Toolbox

The early models had a typical triangular toolbox fitted between the chainstays on the right side of the machine. The one box went onto all rigid-frame models and was joined by another similar one for the plunger frame in 1949. This was only used by the A7 models for that year and the next as a new toolbox appeared for the A10 in 1950. The following year it was in use on all plunger frame machines and continued to be fitted to 1957 except for the Super Flash, which had its own part.

A new toolbox was introduced for the pivoted-fork models in 1954 and this matched the oil tank. Its lid was more domed for 1958 and in 1960 it was joined by a second version to suit models fitted with a TT carburettor, but the first ran on to 1963.

The unit models had their tools tucked into the space behind and beneath the oil tank behind the right-side cover. The toolbox was squeezed into an open-topped container that also carried one of the cover fastener clips. The first toolbox had its outer side half closed in, but early on this went and the box became fully open sided. A second box appeared for the off-road models and it was this one that remained in use until 1971, when a tray went beneath the seat to carry the tools.

ABOVE *Toolbox of a 1957 Road Rocket which also housed the regulator. Battery under the seat which located onto a cross pin at the front.*

BELOW *1969 Lightning showing the cramped space provided for the tool bag which the oil tank kept nice and warm*

Once extracted, the 1969 toolroll did not offer much more than basic get-you-home items

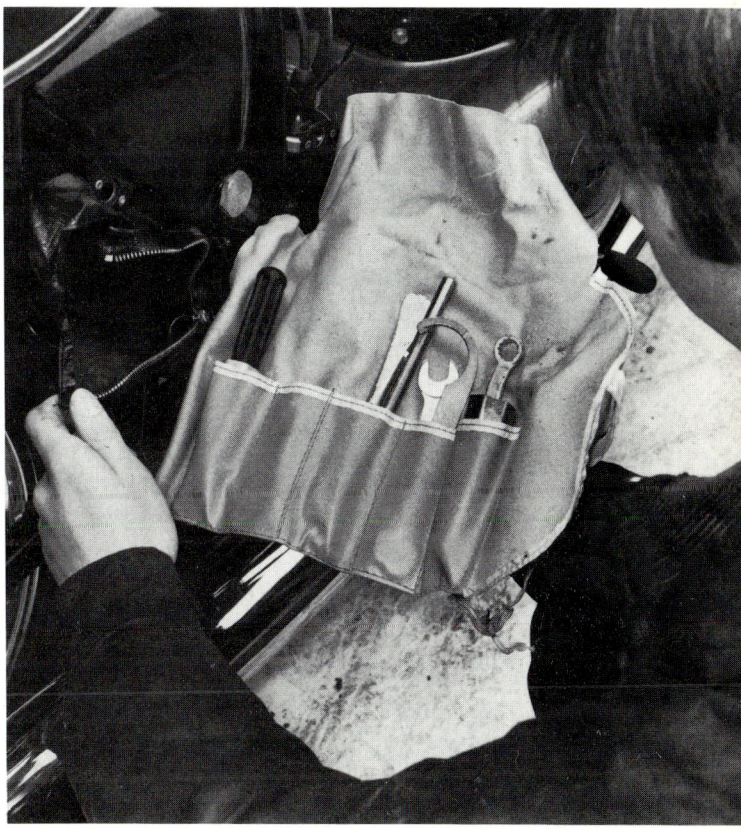

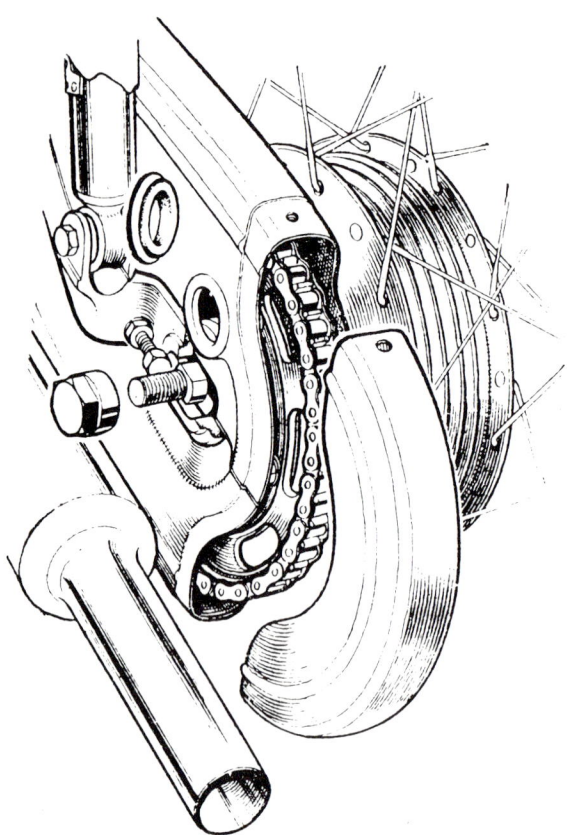

Chainguards

These are parts that are usually covered in grease, damaged by chains and bent or distorted by owners struggling to fit the rear wheel. So the first job is to clean what you have, which may take several sessions before you get all the grime off. Then repair and finish as any other steel item, making sure it fits as it should.

If there is any doubt, you will need to fit gearbox and rear wheel back into the frame assembly to check that the chain will run clear of the guard regardless of suspension movement. If it touches anywhere it will wear the finish away in no time and rattle always.

Chainguard and chaincase types

The first A7 had an upper and lower chainguard which were of a simple form. In 1949 they were joined by a single guard for the plunger frame. This gave more shield to the rear of the sprocket and was extended down inboard of the chain to shield the tyre from it.

LEFT *The 1956 optional full rear chaincase had a detachable rear section to let the chain out*

BELOW *Not standard but really not much changed is this A7 pictured in 1949 when Tornado Smith rode it on the Wall of Death*

For 1950 these guards remained in use until, from rigid-frame ZA7-7034 and plunger-frame ZA7S-4488, both upper ones were modified to add tyrepump clips and a pump guard plate. The lower chainguard as used by the rigid models continued as it was and with its new upper ran on to the end of 1951. For the plunger machines the new guard was fitted to 1957.

There was a new, and similar, chainguard brought in for the pivoted-fork models in 1954 and it was changed in 1956 for one with a longer deep inner side. This was to enable it to use the same fixings as the full chaincase introduced the same year as an option. This had one part fixed to the gearbox with the main enclosure divided into top and bottom sections that mated and were finished with a detachable tail around the rear sprocket. Both chainguard and chaincase remained in use to 1963 to be joined in 1960 by one for the Spitfire and in 1962 by another for the RGS.

The unit models continued in the same manner with an open chainguard fitted as standard and a two-piece chaincase available as an option. At the front went a shroud plate bolted to the engine and fitted to all models right through to 1972. The chaincase only lasted to 1965, after which it was guards only and why worry about chain life. A new guard of more abbreviated form appeared on the sports models in 1965 and was then fitted as standard until 1969. For that year the guard had an additional stay welded to it at the rear but was revised to a slimmer style for 1971.

Footrests

These are nice sturdy items that can usually be repaired. For once you have something to get hold of and the correct shape can be restored by heating the bent area and knocking it back to its right position. Clamp it in the vice to do this. If worn away, it may be necessary to build the material up again and then reshape it with a file.

BSA at first mounted their footrests on a plain taper formed as a lug on the frame. A stud was screwed into the taper and the rest held by a nut that had a left-hand thread for the left side and right for the right. Thus any creep of the rest round the taper tended to tighten the nut. A sharp tap will release the rest once the nut has been removed.

The original footrests went on all rigid and plunger frames, but for the pivoted-fork models a new arrangement was used. For these the rests were splined to tubes that were on a cross-stud and located by a pin to the engine plates. Once the end nuts were tightened the whole assembly was locked in place.

For 1958 the left tube and rest were altered with the rest curled in more to the tube instead of just running straight back. The tube was altered again for 1960 and joined by a pair of special rests for the Spitfire. These comprised a massive forging to form the rest and a clamping plate to match it. The two clamped to the frame tube and were shaped to locate to a cross-tube as well to prevent them from turning. Finally, in 1962 came a bracket and tube for the RGS when it wore its footrests in the forward position.

All models used the same footrest rubbers from 1947 to 1963 and they continued on the unit machines to 1966. These machines reverted to the 1947 style of footrest attachment and on the left side only had a special stud and lockplate fitted to the stud in the taper.

The fixed footrests used on the standard models were later joined by folding ones for the USA and competition. These were covered with their own style of rubber and continued to be listed to 1971. In 1967 the standard rest rubber was changed. The resultant plain item was again altered in 1969, when it was marked with BSA. The folding rest rubber also changed that year and was also marked.

For 1971 and the new frame there were new fixed and folding rests with new rubber for the first but a return to the pre-1969 type for the second.

On all models it is best to replace the rubbers if possible as new ones will help to put the final touch to a restored machine.

Pillion rests

These need to be cleaned up and straightened if necessary with particular attention to the pivot holes and threads. The pivot needs to be just tight enough to hold the rest in position without making it too hard to move.

The early models had a plain rest with turned-up end, but this was changed for 1955 to one of square section fitted with a rubber. Up to then the passenger had been expected to manage without that little luxury. There were other pillion rest assemblies for the RGS in 1962, but otherwise rest and rubber continued on for the early unit machines. Changes were made to the rest in 1966 and 1967 and to the rubber in 1969 and 1971, but the last of these was simply a reversion to the 1955 pattern.

Brake pedal

Another part that is often damaged but is not too hard to repair. The pivot may need to be machined true and bushed if worn. Heat to straighten and build up worn surfaces so they can be filed to shape.

The brake pedal used on the rigid frame was a one-piece part of pad, arm, bush and lever for the rod. It pivoted on a bolt screwed into the frame. For the plunger frame in 1949 a two-part assembly was used which pivoted in a hole in the frame. The parts comprised the pad on its arm, which was splined to a shaft to which was welded the rod lever. These items were used to 1951 for the rigid and 1957 for the plunger models.

For the pivoted-fork frame models in 1954 there was a return to the one-piece pedal turning on a pin screwed into the frame. Nuts and washers retained both pin and pedal, which now had a height adjuster bolt screwed into its vertical lever arm. This design was completely revised for 1956 to suit the full-width hub with the brake on the right. For that a cross-shaft was fitted inside the pivoted-fork spindle with the brake pedal splined to one end and a lever to the other. This connected to the brake via a cable. The design remained in use to the end of the pre-unit models, with changes to the pedal and cable in 1958 and 1960, with the lever also altering for the later year. For the RGS in 1962 with forward footrests, the 1954 pedal was listed.

During the first two years of the unit models two rear brake systems were used, the earliest with cable operation and the second with rods. Both retained the cross-shaft within the rear pivot and used the same pedal and lever. The cross-shaft dated from 1956. By 1964 the rod system had taken over and in 1965 was joined by a second pedal with single rod for models with the rear brake on the left. The first pedal had been formed with a small lever above the splined pivot to take the stop lamp switch lever. The second pivoted on a frame lug and had a rod lever with extra holes for a new stop lamp switch operation. This pedal continued as the standard fitment until 1971, when a new one was introduced.

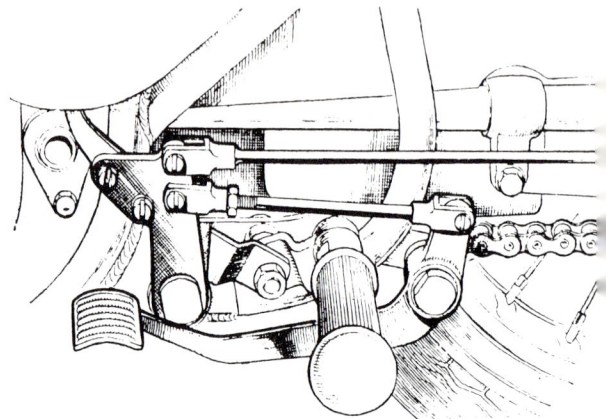

ABOVE *Remarkable factory linkage used on the 1965 Clubman models when fitted with rearsets. It does actually make sense if you use mainly stock parts*

BELOW *The 1967 Spitfire Mk III showing off its tank, side covers and other cycle parts*

Rear brake rod

For most years when a cable was not used BSA fitted a rod with a proper fork end at the front to connect to the pedal. Right at the end in 1971 standards dropped and the rod was simply bent at the end and secured with a split pin.

Rods need to be straight, the thread at the end in good condition and the fork hole not worn or the rod not worn where it bears in the pedal. Damage needs to be rectified.

One rod went on all rigid models and a second on all plungers. A third was used on the early pivoted-fork machines but from 1956 a cable took over. The next appearance of rods was on the unit models and the first design used two rods with a toggle to link them. From 1965 a left-side brake was in use and this had its own rod, which was replaced in 1971 by a bent-wire item.

Lift handle

On the rigid models this was a tubular part that went on the left of the machine. The tube had flattend ends for fixing and a loop at one end to stiffen it. It was joined in 1949 by a simple length of tubing that ran from the top of the plunger housing to the saddle spring lug on the left. The first continued to 1951 and the second was modified for 1954. This part ran on to 1957.

In 1954 a lift handle also appeared for the pivoted-fork frame and this continued to 1959. For the unit models there was no handle at first but one soon appeared, but only up to 1965.

Rear carrier

This was offered right from the start as an option and one part went on all rigid or plunger models up to 1957. A second part went on the pivoted-fork machines and was supplemented by a third, which was also designed to support pannier bag frames. In 1960 these last two were modified to suit changes in the machine and continued to the end of the pre-unit range.

The unit models had a similar pair of carriers soon after the launch and these were listed to 1965. After a lapse both appeared once more in 1967 in a revised form and were joined by a longer carrier for use when a single seat was fitted, as by the police and armed forces. These items remained available to 1970.

A 1954 A10 fitted with a rear carrier and very smart panniers

Legshields, crash bars and panniers

These were all listed on and off from 1951 to 1970 with changes to suit the frames and cycle parts of the machines. None are essential for a restoration, but the fitment of an optional extra from the correct period can set off a machine very well.

Most of the items were for pivoted-fork frames, but legshields and front bars were listed for the plunger models. Legshields were dropped after 1965 as the era was for café racer machines and not keeping the winter weather off.

Oddments

These need to be seen to just as much as any other item. The parts list will show what is needed and all must be collected, checked, mended and finished just as any larger part. Their fit can be important as they may align other pieces, so care with these details can pay dividends.

1962 A65 with Watsonian sidecar showing off screen and legshields

12 Wheels and brakes

This is an area where a good few operations have to follow one another in a definite sequence. Due to this an early start is advised to avoid a hold-up later on when it may not be convenient. Once the machine is without wheels it becomes very hard to move about unless reduced to parts. It may be worth considering slave wheels if this could be a problem to you.

Restoration begins by removing the wheels, taking the tyres off and separating the brake backplate from the wheel assembly. Each can then be dealt with in turn.

Trueing up a brake drum in a lathe. After this it may be necessary to fit oversize brake linings and machine to suit

Spoking pattern and rim offset

The wheel assembly consists of the hub assembly, the spokes, their nipples and the rim. Before doing anything else get your notepad out and measure the rim offset and draw the spoke pattern. This first is a vital piece of data and the second will give you real problems if you have to work it out from scratch. This can be done but it is not easy.

The rim offset is taken by placing a straight edge across the mouth of the brake drum and measuring from it to the edge of the rim. Just to make sure, also

measure from a firm point at the other end of the hub and take the rim width. Take several measurements to see if there is any variation.

If the rim is buckled or has been taken apart, it is back to basics. You will have to work out where the rim should be in relation to the frame and you have two points of reference to help. First is that the wheels are normally central to the frame and forks. Second is the sprocket offset, which you can measure on the gearbox and wheel.

Or find another machine and measure that.

You may have to do this if you start with the bare hub and don't know the spoking pattern, but with a complete machine you can make notes. You consider each side and start by checking the rim to see which way round it is. No problem with a full-width hub, but when it is offset the spoke lengths and angles differ from side to side.

Now note where the valve hole is and check that the spokes either side run away from it to give the best access. If they don't, the wheel has been built incorrectly at some time and you can expect to find most of the spokes bent near the thread. Note how the spoke to one side of the valve hole runs, whether its head points out from the wheel or into its centre and any feature of the hub that will enable you to locate that spoke into the same hole.

Relating the rim, spoke lay and hub for that first spoke will give the key to the wheel build. From it the others will fall into a pattern. Working round the rim the spokes will alternate from one side of the hub to the other. Every third spoke will be laid the opposite way to the first and its head will face the reverse way unless straight spokes are fitted. Every fifth spoke will echo the first in angle and lay.

To finish the notes for side one you need to work out the spoke cross-pattern. On one side a spoke may cross one running the other way two, three or four times. Note the position of the first spoke and the one that crosses it nearest to the hub. Trace it to the rim and note its position there from the outer end of the first spoke.

Now note how side two relates to side one. Don't forget you reverse things if you turn the wheel over. One spoke on side two will give you the start to the pattern, but check it out anyway as a double-check on your side-one notes.

A 1957 Road Rocket giving a clear picture of its spoking pattern

WHEELS AND BRAKES

Wheel dismantling
If you want to repaint the hub you will have to take the wheel apart and later rebuild it. Hence the notes above. The rim is removed by undoing all the spoke nipples, which may be easy or could call for penetrating oil and a little heat. Note that there can be four types of spoke in each wheel with differences in length and head angle, so these points need checking. Keep the spokes in batches and note which goes where on your spoke diagram or you will have to sort that out as well. Note that for some wheels certain spokes cannot come away until others have been removed. This sequence must be known, as the rebuild has to be done in the reverse order.

You now have a rim, 40 nipples and batches of 10, 20 or 40 spokes, plus the hub assembly with attendant brake drum and rear sprocket in the one case.

Hub, drum and rear sprocket
Various forms of assembly were used by BSA for these items and the bearings and spindle they turned on. The bearing retaining rings need to be removed, some having left-hand threads, and all the parts dismantled, cleaned and inspected. Before removing the spindle check the hub and brake drum for any run-out, which will need correcting. This should not be attempted until the hub is on its new bearings to ensure accuracy.

Many BSAs used a built-up assembly as hub and drum and if all is well there is no need to disturb. If there is any doubt the parts should come down and all be indivdually inspected. This construction does allow replacement of brake drums if scored and rear sprockets if hooked, but for many models the two were combined, so changing one meant doing this for both. Make sure the new parts run true when on their new bearings.

If renewal is not feasible it is possible to skim the brake drum. This measure will also deal with oval or belled drums. The sprocket teeth can be built up and recut by a specialist.

The hub itself should be closely inspected for any signs of damage. Repair can be awkward, depending on the construction, and not attempted unless you are confident that the result will withstand the loads placed upon it. Check the rivets of the crinkle hub as these are known to work loose.

The various parts will need careful masking before finishing and threads must be left clean or the locating rings may bind. Check this before assembly.

Front hub types
The first A7 was offered with quickly detachable and interchangeable wheels, so front and rear were of the same design. This used the famous BSA crinkle hub with the bearing tube in an outer whose flanges were formed in a crinkle pattern to permit the fitment of straight spokes. The two tubes were connected by rivets and the inner was finely splined on one end to mate with similar internal splines formed in the back of the brake drum. The drum was further supported by a thrust ball race fitted just behind the brake backplate. An end cover kept dirt out of the end of the hub.

This design was only used for two years and was replaced for 1949 by a one-piece hub built up from

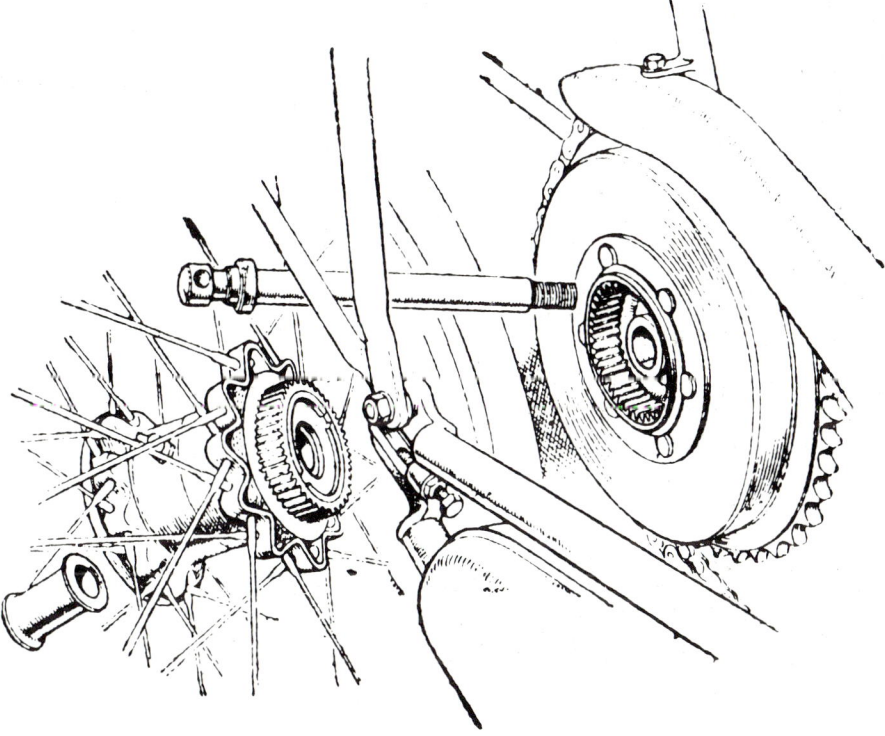

The quickly detachable hub and brake drum used for both wheels of the first twins. Famous crinkle hub which allowed the use of straight spokes

Front hub of a 1966 Thunderbolt. Note knock-outs which can be removed to improve brake ventilation

ABOVE *For 1969 the nave plate lost its slots and was peened into place*

RIGHT *1968 Spitfire Mk IV with the slotted front hub nave plate*

tubes and pressings welded and riveted together. The spoke flanges changed with the brake side one round the outside of the drum and angled spokes were fitted. The smaller flange had the typical BSA slotting between each adjacent pair of holes and this can be another reason for the spoking to go wrong on a rebuild.

Both these brakes were of 7 in. diameter with shoes $1\frac{1}{8}$ in. wide, and they were joined by a new hub for the A10 in 1950. This was of 8 in. diameter with shoes $1\frac{3}{8}$ in. wide and was cast in a high-grade iron alloy known as Millenite. For 1951 the Star Twin was fitted with this hub, having managed with the 7 in. up to then, and for 1953 so were the A7 and Super Flash.

The same hub remained in use on the new pivoted-fork frame models in 1954 and 1955, while a new but similar hub went onto the plunger-frame models from then up to 1957. For the pivoted-fork machines in 1956 there was a change to full-width, light-alloy hubs, ribbed for cooling and webbed for rigidity.

Steel bearing housings and iron brake liners were cast into place and the drums were 7 in. diameter with $1\frac{1}{2}$ in. wide brake shoes.

This design only lasted two years, as for 1958 a new full-width brake appeared in 7 and 8 in. sizes, with the smaller going on the A7 and the larger on the other models. Both hubs were of composite construction with a central tube brazed to two conical pressings, which were riveted to a cast-iron hub shell and brake drum. A plated end cover sealed off the hub at the end away from the drum and these hubs continued to the end of the pre-unit models.

For the Rocket Gold Star the 8 in.-diameter single-sided brake with $1\frac{3}{8}$ in.-wide shoes was fitted as standard, but also available as an option was the 190 mm full-width unit with 2 in.-wide shoes.

The unit models commenced with the same hubs with the 7 in. for the A50 and the 8 in. for the A65 until 1965, when the 8 in. unit went on the A50 as well. For the off-road and competition models in 1964

and 1965 the old-style single-sided brake was revived and went on the A50C, A65T/R, A65L/R, A65LC and A65SH models of that period.

This situation continued into 1966 with all models except the Spitfire, which was fitted with the full-width hub with 190 mm brake. There was no change for 1967 and none for the Royal Star or Thunderbolt for 1968, but the Lightning, Spitfire MkIV and Firebird of that year were all fitted with a twin leading shoe brake in a full-width hub. This had a nave plate with slots in it and retained to the hub by three screws. For 1969 all models had the full-width hub and twin leading shoes, but the nave plate lost its slots and was peened into place. There was no change for 1970, but 1971 brought the conical hub, which continued for 1972.

Rear hub types

The first A7 rear hub was the same part as the front one and they interchanged. Because the splines had to transmit the driving as well as the braking power the drum had a splined drive flange bolted to it to spread the load out. The drum was formed in one with the sprocket and the bolts holding the drive flange against one side carried a ball race housing on the other. This went on the short part of the spindle, which held the drum in place in the frame when the main spindle and wheel were removed.

This concept remained in use on BSA models for many years, but was altered in detail in 1949 to suit both rigid and plunger frames. Two new hubs of the same crinkled form appeared along with four different one-piece brake drums, which incorporated the sprocket and ball race housing. There were four parts to give the solo and sidecar number of teeth and to cope with the two frame types. The plunger type differed from the others in that the main spindle went right through the other and had a nut on its left end.

The rigid hubs went after 1951, but the plunger ones continued to 1957. In 1954 the pivoted-fork frame appeared and this used the 1949 rigid frame hub with a one-piece drum and sprocket first introduced for the rigid A10 in 1950. When searching for a replacement drum and sprocket remember to count the teeth, as 42, 45, 46 and 49 were all used on rigid and plunger models.

In 1956 the pivoted-fork models were fitted with a full-width rear hub to match the front and this had a separate, bolted-on, sprocket. The design changed for 1958 to a cast-iron, one-piece hub and drum to match the front, but the bolted sprocket remained, although of a different type. In both these designs it was necessary to undo four fixings as well as to pull out the main spindle to remove the wheel. The rear sprocket was modified in 1960, while the Rocket Gold Star fitted the older-style single-sided brake.

The unit models continued with the full-width hub cast in iron and separate sprocket, and this was used on the standard models to 1965 and also the A65T/R. All the more sporting or off-road models reverted to the crinkle hub and at first used the one from the 1949 rigid A7.

For 1966 the old-style single-sided brake was used, but with detail changes and universal use of a separate sprocket, which had only applied to some models the year before. The hub was further revised for 1967 along with the brake drum, but then continued until replaced by the conical hub in 1971.

Wheel bearings

All models used ball races with a pair in each hub and a third in the drum of quick detachable wheels. Both wheels began in 1947 with the same bearings and the rear gained a third one of another size in 1949. This odd one remained in use to 1965, but the front pair and ones in the rear hub all changed in 1958. This new size also continued to 1965, when it was joined by the 1947 bearing to suit the single-sided brakes at the front.

The same bearing went into all three locations for the 1966 rear hubs, but only two continued to 1967 as the drum one changed. 1967 also saw a new race in the front, which was used to 1968 and was joined by another that same year. In 1971 came new races to suit the conical hubs with the same type used front and rear.

Rear hub and brake drum of a 1966 Thunderbolt which was not much different from a 1947 A7

Ball races need to be a good fit in the hub and on the spindle. The second is easy to replace if damaged, but for the first it may be necessary to use Loctite to ensure the race does not move. Races must be fitted square and the drift or press used must bear directly on the race being inserted and not load the balls and their tracks.

Sometimes it will be found that once assembled the wheel spindle is tight. What can happen is that as you push the outer home the inner is held back by the spindle so finishes out of line from its nominal position. To correct you use a hammer as a precision tool and just lightly tap in the required direction.

Brakes

Most are single leading shoe, but regardless of type they require the same attentions. Strip, clean and examine for wear, damage, distortion or cracks. Repair as required. Check the fit of the backplate to the wheel spindle, the condition of the cams, the cam levers and the return springs. If the last are tired, replace them.

You are likely to fit new brake shoes or to reline the ones you have. With the former first check that the brake drum is the standard diameter and has not been skimmed at some time. If it has not, still beware of pattern shoes as some have minimal lining material and will seem to be worn out even when new.

If you reline yourself you will need clamps to hold the liners in place, drill and counter-bore to form the holes and riveting tools. Work out from the centre and chamfer when finished.

Should you go to an expert he will, or should, want the wheel and backplate. He will check and skim the drum first if this is needed and then reline the brakes with oversize liners, which can be turned down to fit.

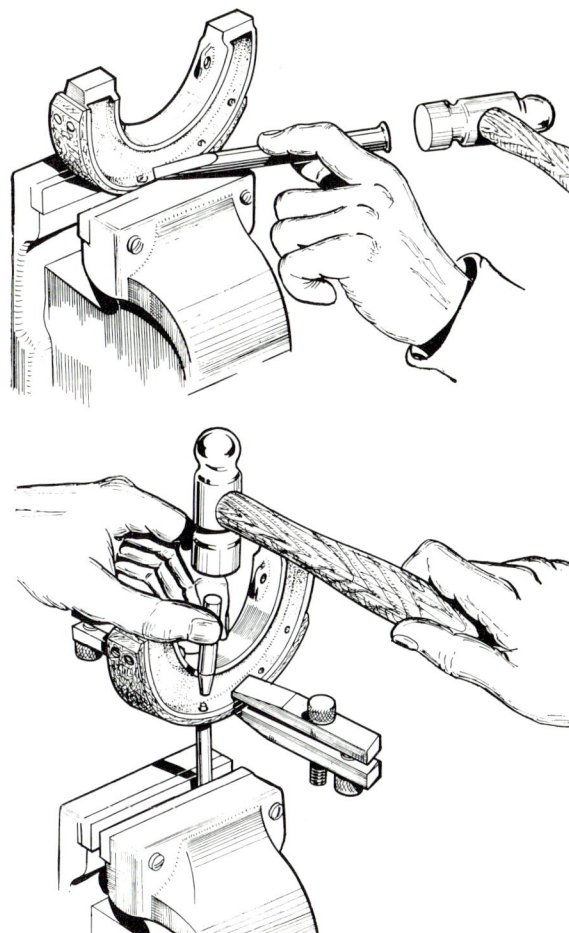

Two stages in renewing brake linings. Removing the old (above) and fitting the new (below)

Front brake types

The A7 began with a simple single leading shoe brake in 1947 and some details remained in use to 1957. The backplate changed in 1949, when a new hub type was fitted. This was joined by parts for the 8 in. brake for the A10 in 1950. This was held in place by a torque stay but the others just locked to the fork leg with a lug in a hole or slot.

This situation continued until the appearance of the full-width, light-alloy hub in 1956. It had a wedge adjuster and specially shaped shoe ends to suit. Operation was still by cam in the usual way and a torque stay held the backplate.

In 1958 the brake design reverted to normal and the backplate was formed to locate on a lug on the fork leg. For 1962 floating brake shoes were fitted which centralized themselves to the drum automatically. Previously the rider was required to do this and not all of them did, with predictable results.

This design continued on the unit models to 1965, but where a single-sided hub was fitted the older design prevailed along with a torque stay. This continued for 1966–67, but in 1968 the first twin leading shoe brake appeared for the Lightning, Spitfire and Firebird. For that year only the cable swept in from the rear to a cast stop on the backplate and to the front cam lever, which was extended. It was linked to the rear lever by an adjustable rod and each cam was formed to do its job on one shoe and act as a pivot for the other.

The design was changed for 1969, with the front lever moved round so the cable could run down the fork leg to its stop and the lever connection. As the link between the levers had to remain as it was, the front lever became a bell crank. In 1971 this was replaced by the conical hub with a new backplate and shoes operated by very short cam levers connected directly to the inner and outer of the cable.

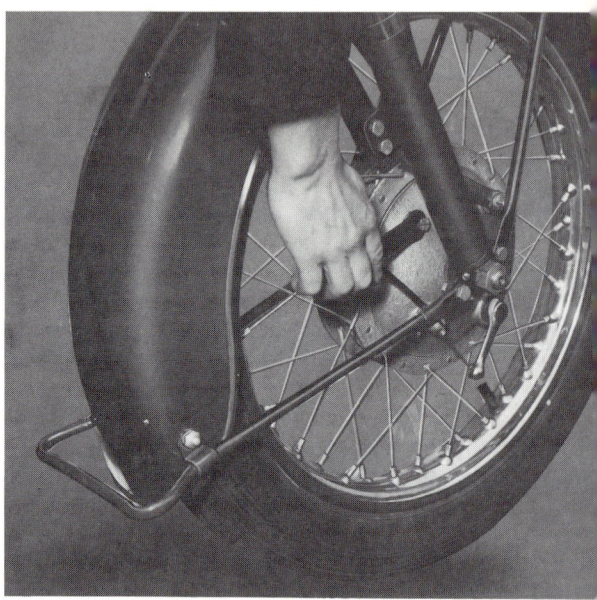

ABOVE *A 1956 A7 showing the wedge adjuster of the full width, light alloy hub brake*

LEFT *Early type brake on a 1954 A10*

BELOW LEFT *The floating brake shoe assembly adopted for the 1962 models*

BELOW *The 1969 bell crank front brake with twin leading shoes. A variation from the 1968 layout*

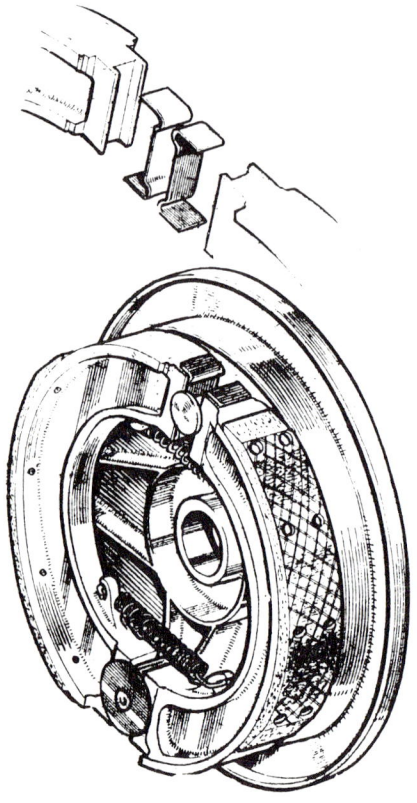

The 1971 conical front hub on a Lightning. Very short cam levers with direct operation

ABOVE *Conical rear hub as adopted from 1971*

LEFT *The bolted-on rear sprocket of a 1969 Thunderbolt whose rear hub was much as that of the A7 in 1947*

Rear brake types
All brakes were of 7 in. diameter and all except those used in 1956–57 of $1\frac{1}{8}$ in. width. The two odd years had $1\frac{1}{2}$ in. shoes. There was little change from the first type after the plunger version had appeared in 1949 until 1954. Several new parts went into the pivoted-fork brake, but this did have a torque stay, unlike its predecessors, which used a slot and a frame lug.

1956 brought the full-width, light-alloy hubs with wedge adjuster as at the front and still with a torque stay. The 1958 one that replaced it was similar but had the cable stop cast into the backplate. This practice was not continued with on the 1960 version. That year the cam lever was moved to point down instead of up and in 1962 the floating shoes were adopted.

The unit models had a similar brake assembly, which was then joined by the older single-sided design for the more sporting or off-road machines. In 1966 only this type was used, so all models had their brake on the left, where it had first been in 1947. The backplate had changed for 1966 and did again for 1967, while the cam was altered for 1969. For 1971 and the conical hub it was all new parts except for the shoe springs, which dated from 1947.

Spokes and nipples
These need to be straight and with good threads. It is false economy to just replace some if more than one or two are past redemption; better to re-spoke completely. Check carefully the length, gauge and head angle you require before shopping and inspect what you buy to make sure you do get what you want.

WHEELS AND BRAKES

If the spokes are being replaced a new set of nipples are worth getting as well. Remember that their diameter is to suit the spoke gauge and that the rim holes must suit.

It is possible to buy stainless steel spokes, although opinions vary as to how this material can cope with the bending of the head angle and the stress pattern spokes are subject to. If made to really close tolerances they should be no trouble, but avoid anything cheap or poorly finished.

Wheel rims

Most BSA twins have steel rims of the WM section form. Diameters used were 18 and 19 in. and width numbers 1, 2 and 3. All had 40 spoke holes and security bolts were listed from 1967 for most models. Light-alloy rims were listed as options for the RGS and as standard for the unit Spitfire.

If the rim is damaged or rusty it will have to be replaced as you are unlikely to find anyone who can repair the first or willing to strip and replate to correct the second. Thus you will need a new rim. The first point to consider is the tyre size you will finally fit. In many cases it will be worth going to a WM3 section rather than keeping to the listed WM2 if you wish to fit a fatter tyre.

Next is the dimpling and the holes. For a really strong wheel the spokes must lay at the correct angle in both directions and to achieve this the rim must be pierced to suit. You also need holes for the tyre valve and any security bolts. Inspect the join in the rim as, unless smooth, you will never get the wheel to run really true.

The rims used for the various models are set out in an appendix along wih their listed tyre size.

The rim finish is either chrome plating or the same with a painted, lined centre. Unless you are very sure that you can produce this really well, send it to an expert. It is an area where any flaw will be only too obvious so the cost will be worth it.

1960 Shooting Star showing off its full width, composite construction front hub

Wheel rebuilding

This is an area that many people fight shy of, but with care and patience good results can be obtained. Your notes will make the job much easier and should be consulted as to the order of assembly and the precise location of each item. The rim must be the right way round.

Simply fit the first spoke and start its nipple so it cannot shift and scratch the rim. Then continue this process until you have all 40 in place. It should be obvious if you have made a mistake as either spokes won't connect at all or will be at the wrong angle. As long as spoke one is correct, the rest will fall into place.

You now have to true the wheel and could consider sending the assembly to an expert for this final important stage. Or you can do it yourself. Set the wheel vertical with the spindle held so you can spin the rim. Place a marker clear of the rim and try it for truth. Adjust spokes to suit, but work to get the radial position correct first and then go on to deal with the sideways error. If you start with a good rim and work carefully you should not have much trouble. Make sure every spoke is nicely tensioned without being overstrained.

Tyres, tubes and rim tapes

Your first problem could be finding something to fit. Much easier with some models than others. You now have the choice of 'old-fashioned' sizes, or some of them, more up-to-date low-profile tyres or the latest metric offerings, which are low profiles with their inches translated into millimetres.

Regardless of which you decide on, do fit a rim tape in good condition after you have checked the spoke nipples for protruding spoke ends. A new inner tube really is mandatory, don't even think of patches. The tyre itself must suit the rim section and the front and rear must be compatible. The faster the machine, the more important are the tyres and their type; they must never be ignored.

If you fit modern tyres you must make certain that there is ample clearance for the fatter section in all positions of the rear suspension. Fit them with care and use your slim, smooth, polished tyre levers. Don't forget the security bolt. Do forget the tyre pressure table in the old manuals, which has no relevance to modern tyres. Establish the wheel loading and check the tyre data for the correct pressure. Check the rolling diameter or revolutions per mile for the old tyre and the modern replacement in case it affects the speedometer reading to any real extent.

The 1964 A65 which continued with the composite front hub for some years

13 Cables, controls, instruments

There are a few things that look worse on a restored motorcycle than cables drooping in loops and obviously far too long or ones with the adjuster screwed right out and hanging on the last thread. There are few more dangerous than cables that are tight and which could be pulled by the forks as they move.

The control cables should be the proper length, run on the right route, be neatly clipped out of harm's way and in correct adjustment. They should also be of the correct gauge for the job or the throttle will feel heavy and the front brake full of sponge.

Every cable is an assembly of inner, outer, outer ends and wire nipples at a minimum and normally all have at least one adjuster in their length. To these parts can be added end stops and fittings to attach the cable to its lever and the machine. In just about all cases the outer length determines the sweep of the final job, while the inner must be chosen to suit the wear on the parts and the length of adjustment available.

Each end fitting needs to be checked over and repaired or replaced where needed. This operation should include any plating required. Nipples may be re-used but must be fully cleaned first. It is best to remove all the old solder using heat so you can properly assess the condition of the part. If past recall, they should be replaced, and if exactly the right size is not available, it may be machined from another, larger, nipple. Do make sure it is a good fit on the cable, free to slide into place but no more.

Control layout of the 1947 A7 with speedometer in petrol tank. Very clean apart from the horn and dipswitch wires

Soldering stages showing wire tinning, cutting to length, splaying to fit the nipple, filing to fit the lever and one lubrication method

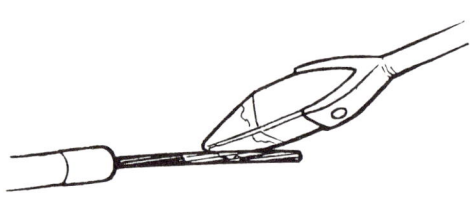
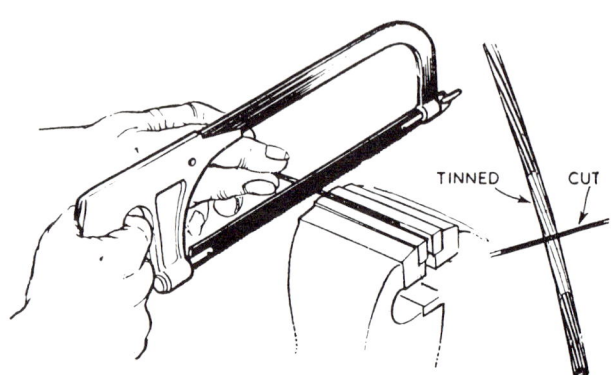

Soldering

This is the technique used to attach nipple to wire and the secret of success is clean parts. Solder will not adhere to surfaces that are dirty, tarnished or greasy but is no problem on a clean surface.

The tools you need are soldering iron, solder and flux. The first may be electric, heated over a gas flame or heated by butane. The slim type used for electrical work will not have enough heat for cables and something of 60 to 70 watts is necessary. If you use a gas flame first clean up the iron tip with a file and let the flame play on the iron an inch back from the tip to keep it clean. When hot it can be dipped in flux to remove any oxidation and given a thin coat of solder.

The solder you use comes in a stick. Do not use flux-cored electrician's solder as it is not up to the job, being designed for electric wires, not steel cables. The flux can be a paste in a tin or a liquid. My own preference is for the first as it is convenient to be able to open it and dip the iron or cable in. A match is handy for putting flux onto areas where it is needed.

To cut an inner to length you use sharp, heavy-duty cutters or a cold chisel and block or a hacksaw. Before cutting you must tin the cable to stop it unwinding. The process is the same as any soldering. First clean the wire really well, next tin the iron and third use the iron to tin the wire, adding solder if needed. Keep it to a minimum and try to avoid blobs.

You can now cut the wire and solder a nipple on the end. To do this successfully you have to splay the wire ends out to sit in the countersink in the nipple and this operation can be done as follows. Clamp the wire vertically in the vice with the nipple sitting on top of the vice jaw. Before holding the wire firmly, slide it down to about level with the top surface of the nipple. Clamp but don't crush and then tap the wire top with the ball end of a light hammer to splay the strands. This can be started using a tack if needed.

Now hold the wire lightly in the vice with a clothes peg between the nipple and the vice jaws. Leave the vice slack enough for you to pull down on the wire. Tin the iron and apply solder to the nipple to build up as required. While it cools keep a light pull on the wire

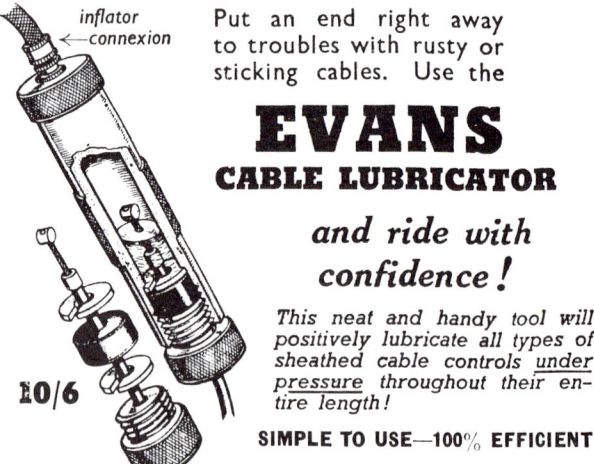

I find this oiler good but messy. Price reflects the 1960 date of advert and there are others as good

and watch. The surface appearance will change as soon as it hardens. Leave for a short while and give it a good tug. Better it flies off in the workshop than on the road. File to shape and make sure it fits its lever and can turn if necessary.

CABLES, CONTROLS, INSTRUMENTS

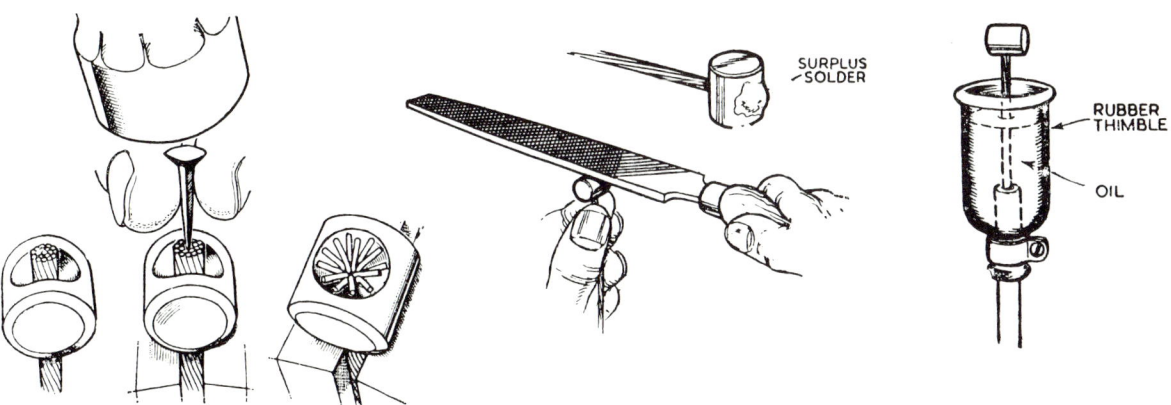

Cable making

There are two ends to a cable so there are two soldering jobs to do. As there are at least three and sometimes four or five cables to do it takes some time to make a full set from scratch.

Start with the outer and determine its run and thus its length. Fit its ferrules having checked that they in turn will fit their housings at both ends. Solder on one nipple to the inner and assemble to the outer complete with all fittings. Some owners like to lubricate the cable at this point, but this practice means that the end has to be cleaned again. My own preference is to assemble, clean, solder and then oil.

In either case the important aspect is to get the inner wire length correct. To do this connect the already soldered end and offer up the other. No need to clip anything to the frame or even have the parts on the machine at this stage as long as the operation at the ends is correct. Set the adjusters to suit the controls. Thus screw the front brake one right in if the brakes have been relined as movement will all be in one direction. The clutch is better in mid-travel as this will allow for wear and swelling plates if you have the latter problem. The throttle, air and magneto cables should be set up to allow the controls to work to their inbuilt stops without the adjusters hanging out of their housings.

Now solder the second nipple in place and clean it up. The cable can now be lubricated and the only way to be sure the oil has gone all the way through is to pour it in one end until it comes out of the other. Funnels formed round the end are a common suggestion, but my own method is to use a pressure device that goes round the end and is pumped up with a bicycle pump. Rather messy but very effective, and there are others available.

Controls

The handlebars fitted to the 1947 models had end plugs, but they were changed for the next year and this new type continued in use to 1963. In 1960 it was joined by three others, one a Western style for general use, one an American bar for the Spitfire and the third a Western bar for the USA.

There was a little more variety on the unit models with a high-rise bar appearing very early on. In 1965 more varieties were available, including one from the 1960 list, but for 1966 there was simply one, another from the 1960 list. In 1967 it was joined by a second and both were replaced by a single part in 1971.

The controls also varied over the years and careful reference needs to be made to the parts list to ensure the correct item. Early machines have the air lever under the seat and others have the horn button and dipswitch held to the back of the clutch and front brake bodies by small screws.

Each control needs to be stripped, cleaned, inspected, renovated as required and assembled. Care will be rewarded by smooth operation and pleasant feel. Twistgrip and left bar grips should be replaced if required and the right part will enhance the final result.

The handlebars themselves may well have been changed or bent. If the former, the criterion is whether they are comfortable for you the new owner or whether you want to change them to be original. On the latter, much the same applies, but beware of straightened bars as they have been known to snap due to the metal being stretched.

Instruments

The ammeter has been mentioned, which just leaves the speedometer and rev-counter.

Two types of mechanism were used in the speedometers and rev-counters fitted by BSA, with the chronometric type being superseded by the magnetic in 1964. The first was generally held to be the more reliable in the long term, but is a complex mechanical device that just became too expensive for a mass-produced product. It has a camshaft, balance wheel, gears, levers and springs. To get at these you first have to unscrew the bezel ring without marking it, which will then allow the works to be removed.

If you are an instrument fitter you should be able to strip, repair and rebuild a chronometric speedometer. If you are an instrument mechanic it could be as well

ABOVE *Impossible to read ammeter of the nacelle models, this being a 1955 Shooting Star*

BELOW *Easy to read instruments of a 1957 Road Rocket which also has all controls to finger. Centre button is cut-out, not the horn one which is with the dipswitch*

ABOVE *The A65R in 1964 with ring assembly of minor electric controls*

BELOW *Spitfire Mk III layout in 1967 with twin cable twistgrip*

to stop at the mileage recorder, which is easier to work with although it still needs delicate care.

The later magnetic type is easier to work on but only once you get inside it, for the bezel is rolled on. This means care and maybe a special tool to unroll it plus another to replace it. Once inside, it is much less complex but just as delicate as any other.

From the point of repair the rev-counter is simply a speedometer mechanism minus the distance recorder. The case is basically the same and just the dial differs with its own calibration.

Along with the instrument head must be considered its mounting and its drive. The first must be in good order and the second consists of the cable and the drive box. The cable needs to be inspected and replaced if either inner or outer are damaged, while the drive box must operate smoothly. For many years the speedometer was driven from the gearbox, but late models used the rear wheel and the rev-counter various drive schemes.

Speedometer types

The first point on any speedometer is the direction of rotation of the needle, which must match the cable. Next is the maximum scale reading, then whether in miles or kilometres and, most important, the revolutions per mile figure.

This is normally written on the scale just under the part number and for many models a figure around 1600–1700 can be expected if it is calibrated in miles, this reducing to about 1000 for the metric measurement. This is also the cable speed in rpm at 60 mph by definition as at that speed one mile takes one minute to travel, so if the cable turns, say, 1620 times in the distance, it has done the same in the time.

The final points in speedometer selection are the presence of total and maybe trip distance recorders, the method of returning the trip one to zero and the mounting of the instrument.

For 1947 only the speedometer was mounted in the petrol tank on the right side, but from 1948 moved to the fork crown. In 1953 it moved into the cowl and in 1958 to the nacelle, except for the Super Flash and Road Rocket models. The nacelle went after 1965 and before then the fork top mounting was used for the sports models for some markets and where matching speedometer and rev-counter were fitted.

When hunting for a replacement speedometer, most of the requirements are easy to determine and to check, except for the important revs-per-mile needed to match the machine. For rear wheel-driven machines the factors are the tyres' revs-per-mile and the ratio between wheel and cable. The latter is controlled by the speedometer gearbox and the ratio is usually around 2:1. Where the drive is from the machine's gearbox the tyre, final drive gearing, sleeve gear ratio and layshaft skew gear pair all play their part and have to be allowed for. If any change so does the speed of the instrument cable, so adjustment is needed to allow for a change of tyre size or the fitting of a wide-ratio sleeve gear pair.

Dials of the 1967 Spitfire Mk III but 150 mph seems as unlikely as 10,000 rpm

The optimum cable speed can be found by calculation using the data available for the model in question and applies provided it is to standard specification in respect of the features that affect it. If all is well, this is the figure to seek on the replacement speedometer, or something close to it.

On occasion the sum has to be used in reverse, in effect. If a good speedometer is to hand but with the wrong cable speed, it may be possible to achieve the correct readings by using an alternative wheel gearbox. Calculators make it easy to do the sums once the data has been collected.

CABLES, CONTROLS, INSTRUMENTS

ABOVE *Side view of the instruments and controls of a 1968 Thunderbolt*

BELOW *The rev-counter drive from the oil pump adopted by the Super Rocket for 1960 and later used by the unit twins*

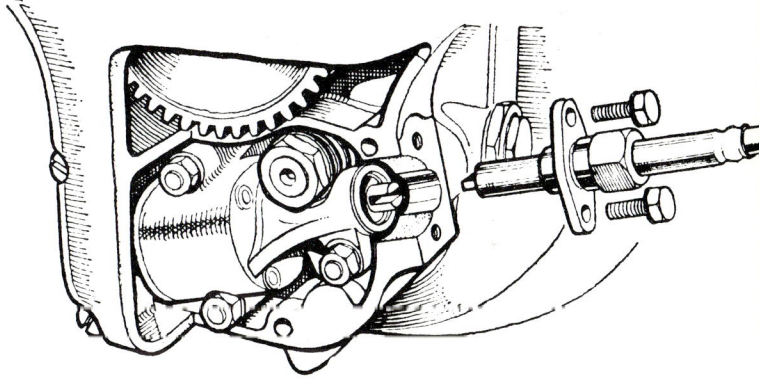

Rev-counter types

Both chronometric and magnetic types were used driven from the magneto gear via a drive box bolted to the timing cover or from the oil pump shaft. The first used a 1:1 box, so the cable shaft ran at half engine speed, but the second ran at one-third so a different head was fitted.

A 4:1 head could be used with a 2:1 box in the first instance but any other variation will give an error. This will at least be consistent so re-marking the dial becomes possible.

Instrument bracket types

After the initial tank location the speedometer was mounted on a small bracket common to several models. It continued to be used, after the fork cowl appeared, on both Super Flash and Road Rocket models. For these it was either fitted alone to carry the speedometer or as two-off to carry the rev-counter alongside the speedometer, both being mounted on a plate held by the fork top nuts to the crown.

For the Super Flash and Rocket there was a second bracket used when a rev-counter was fitted alone; this was a little longer and formed to tilt the instrument to suit a racing application. This arrangement continued to 1963 and was joined in 1962 by a pair of brackets used solely by the RGS.

BSA TWIN RESTORATION

The standard unit models had the nacelle mounting to 1965 and this was joined by the old 1948 bracket in 1964 for the A65R. This bracket was mounted on another small one fixed under the fork leg nut and with two such assemblies could support the two instruments. 1964 also saw a change over to magnetic heads, and on the Rocket these had a new form of mounting. This was a substantial plate that bolted to the fork crown and carried both instruments, each in its own moulded cup and held in place by a top rubber. Much the same arrangements continued for 1965 plus a new sheet plate to carry two instrument brackets and held by the fork nuts as before.

The 1964 instrument plate changed for 1966 and was joined by a single-head version for use when a speedometer was fitted alone. A further sheet plate appeared for the Hornet and Wasp which also had only one instrument and required it to be well tucked in. It changed to a shaped pressing with a flange all around for 1967, and that year new instrument cups also appeared and with them a new instrument plate.

For 1968 yet another single mounting plate was devised, while 1969 brought new cups once more. The major redesign for 1971 was unable to leave the instruments alone and each went into another new cup which fitted into a ring casting held by the fork top nut, one on each side.

Layout of the 1971 Lightning with switches built into the lever blocks and new style headlamp with turn switch and three warning lights

14 Petrol tank

This has already been mentioned under Finishing and the tank truly is the crowning glory of any motorcycle, so its finish is important if you want the machine to look nice, but not to the extent that it does not match the rest of the machine. If the general paintwork is reasonable but a touch shabby, a super tank job will stand out and show up against it. Maybe better to leave the tank to blend in with the rest or you may find yourself renovating all the paint you meant to leave alone for a season or two.

Any tank must be checked out for damage which could be dangerous. This means looking for splits and cracks, checking brackets, examining tap bosses and badge screw threads, and looking closely at the tank bolt holes in the base. If bolts of too great a length have been used or washers left out at any time, the base of the threaded hole may have been lifted so that a small crack exists. All these faults need to be corrected.

The fit of the tank cap should also be checked early on in case attention is needed in this area. Where there is no real damage but the tank interior is rusty this needs to be removed as far as possible. If left, either the rust will block the carburettor or the rust area will develop a leak or both. To remove the worst of the rust, drop a handful of small nuts and bolts or sharp stones into the tank and give it a good shake. Then wash out well. After this a swill with a rust inhibitor fluid is well worth the trouble and, when the finish is complete, the inside should be treated with Petseal. This two-part liquid forms a coat on the inside of the tank and seals any small pinholes or doubtful areas, so is well worth using in any tank that has a query over it. However, do look on it as an extra insurance and don't expect it to hold a cobweb of steel together with petrol in it.

The tank appearance is dependent on its external

1951 A10 with tank just painted and lined without chrome plating due to the nickel shortage

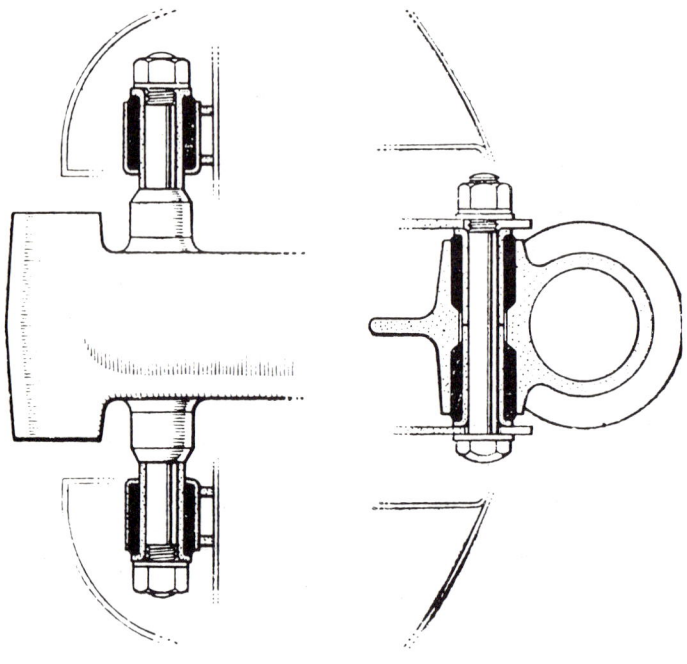

ABOVE *Rubber tank mountings adopted for 1953 by the twins*

BELOW *A 1956 A7 showing the new centre bolt tank fixing used by BSA for a long time*

shape and if dented this will require attention. This is specialist work, as has already been mentioned, and usually entails cutting the tank open for access and re-welding it afterwards. Before deciding what work is needed, first remove all the loose items from the tank such as taps, cap, badges and panels. Then examine it to establish if it has any filled patches. If it has and you want a good job, they must be cleared away.

Work on the tank, even if minor, usually means a welding torch and many are the horror stories on the subject. The problem is removing all the petrol and the fumes before the torch is lit up. Methods used are to wash it out with water or to allow a car exhaust to flow into it or both of these. After this many experienced workers will stand well back, light the torch and point it into the tank. The theory, and it works, is that if there is any vapour left you burn it then and there while expecting a bang. You may not be disappointed, in which case you will remember to wash the tank out better next time. What you avoid with this method is a bang when welding close up to the tank.

Tank finish

This can be simply paint with the style coming from the badges and trim, or paint plus lining, or two colours of paint plus separating line, or, worst of all to cope with, chrome plate plus painted panels plus lining or painting with chrome side panels.

The tank style, fixing and trim of a 1968 Thunderbolt

This last was used for many years and is very specialized. The sequence of jobs is plate, paint and line and a good job will be expensive. It will also be worth the money.

As with any finish, preparation is all and for other than plated tanks follows the same lines as any other sheet steel item. The exception is the avoidance of polyurethene lacquer, which would react with spilt petrol to lift the paint. Otherwise the final result will simply reflect the care with which the metal surface has been prepared and the skill with which the paint is applied, rubbed down and polished up. As with mudguards a brush finish can be fine as long as you can keep the dust off it. Care will be repaid by a smooth, glossy surface. An internal coat of Petseal may be a good idea depending on what you discovered during your early examination. Protect the tank finish while applying as a dent at this stage could annoy.

Tank types

For the first year only the A7 had the speedometer set in the tank top, but from 1948 this went. A new and slightly larger tank appeared in 1949 for the Star Twin and the two continued into 1950 up to frame ZA7-4487 and ZA7S-7034. After these numbers new tanks were fitted with both having the same capacity as the earlier Star Twin. The fitting changed with the rear attachment lugs having slots in place of holes so their bolt only needs to be slackened to allow the tank to be removed.

1950 also brought the A10, and this was fitted with a larger tank than the A7 models in its standard export guise, although for home use at first it used the smaller A7 tank. For 1951 the big A10 tank continued, but the two A7 machines were fitted with a common new tank with just the finish to distinguish one from the other.

All three tanks changed for 1953, when they became rubber mounted with the front bushes in the frame and the rear ones in the tank lugs provided for them. One tank with a choice of finish continued to look after the A7s and a larger one went on the A10. In addition there was a two-gallon tank for the Super Flash to suit the US styling needs.

For the A7 plunger-frame model in 1954 the tank was modified to accept a round plastic badge, but the Star Twin and A10 continued with the 1953 type, the latter to the end of the plunger frame in 1957. The pivoted-fork frames had a new series of tanks that were rubber mounted on pads and held down by a single bolt in the tank top aft of the filler cap. A rubber bung marked BSA closed off the tube set in the tank for this arrangement.

Two- and four-gallon tanks were listed for the A7, A7SS and A10 and all were different. Only the four-gallon one was listed for the Road Rocket and this was the same part as the A7 tank. In 1956 a two-gallon tank appeared for this model.

The four-gallon tanks were altered in appearance for 1958 when a single tank served for the A7, A10 and A10SR with another for the A7SS. The 1954 two-gallon tanks mainly continued with the A7 and A7SS types running on to 1962, while the A10 took the A7 tank and used it to 1963. A two-gallon tank continued to be listed for the Super Rocket and this size was also used by the Spitfire.

A single new four-gallon tank appeared in 1960 for all road models and carried pear-shaped badges. Some Shooting Star models were built with round badges and the older tank, but otherwise the older style only continued on the two-gallon tanks. In addition to the existing pair of this size of tank another was also listed for the range.

These tanks continued to the end of the pre-unit models and were joined by a trio for the Rocket Gold Star in 1962. The standard fitment was in steel with a wing bolt filler cap and breather pipe, but there were options for two gallons in steel or light alloy and another for five gallons in the alloy.

The unit models began wih a single four-gallon tank with pear-shaped badges, but this was soon joined by a second tank with round badges and no kneegrips. These continued to 1965, when they were joined by a four-gallon tank for the Lightning with pear-shaped badges while the Thunderbolt used the one from the standard models. In addition there were two-gallon steel tanks listed, one for the Thunderbolt and another for the Lightning and the A50C, plus one in fibreglass for the Hornet.

For 1966 the original tank continued on the Royal Star and the Thunderbolt kept its 1965 one, which also went on the Lightning. Besides these there were two new tanks with hinged filler caps and a capacity just under two gallons that went on any of the road models. In addition there were three fibreglass tanks of the same size, one each for the Wasp, Hornet and Spitfire MkII. For the last of these this was soon joined

1957 A10 in its US style with chrome-plated tank panels carrying the familiar winged BSA badge

The wing bolt type of tank cap used as early as 1953 on the Super Flash and seen here on a 1966 Thunderbolt

by a five-gallon version that sat rather better above the twin GP Amals it had to feed.

The 1965 Thunderbolt tank became the standard four-gallon road model fit for 1967 along with a new two-gallon one. There were new fibreglass tanks for the Wasp and Hornet, while both large and small continued on the Spitfire that year and the next. For the Firebird in 1968 there was a new tank and for the road models two- and four-gallon tanks with snap-action filler caps.

These continued for 1969 and were joined by a fibreglass tank with sculptured sides on the Firebird. The four-gallon tank continued on all road models in 1970, but the two-gallon one was only listed for the 650s. The fibreglass one for the Firebird was replaced by one in steel but of the same form and was joined by another of conventional shape. The four-gallon tank on the Lightning was changed early in the year to one similar to that of the Firebird with shaped sides and made in steel.

New tanks of two and four gallons were introduced for the new frames in 1971 and the larger was modified for 1972 with a cross-brace under the front.

Filler cap

The first A7 had a quarter-turn bayonet cap and this item was still in use in 1966. Up to 1964 it went on all models except the Super Flash in 1953 and the Rocket Gold Star in 1962. For them there was a quick-action hinged cap with wing bolt fastener. This type went on the Lightning and A50C models in 1965 while the fibreglass Hornet tank had a snap-action cap.

All three types continued in use for 1966, but for 1967 the road models used the wing bolt cap and the fibreglass ones the snap action. All tanks had this type of cap for 1968 and this continued to 1970, along with a bayonet cap for the normal shape Firebird tank. Another bayonet cap was introduced for 1971 and was modified for 1972.

ABOVE *Star transfer used as the tank badge for a 1967 Spitfire Mk III*

One of the plastic moulded tank badges used by BSA over the years

BELOW *The die-cast light alloy tank badge which replaced the earlier plastic moulding in 1968*

Rider's eye view of tank and controls of a 1970 Firebird Scrambler with chrome-plated knee grip areas on the petrol tank

The 1970 Lightning had a tank much as the Firebird in steel and with snap action filler cap

Tank badges

Handle with care. Check that they are not damaged and fit as they should. Make sure the fixing screws do fit and don't bottom in their holes.

The first A7 models used their own version of the small rectangular, winged BSA badge held in place by a pair of screws. For the Star Twin in 1949 there were star-shaped transfers and for the A10 the next year a round, winged BSA badge made in left and right hands and each with the legend Golden Flash beneath the maker's name.

1953 brought the first round plastic badge for the Star Twin in green. With it came new, handed, badges for the A7 with a round area carrying the letters BSA and an extension running back to the kneegrip with horizontal styling lines on it.

There were changes for 1954 with the introduction of a round plastic badge carrying the piled arms insignia and this went on the A7 and Rocket models to 1959 and on the A10 for 1958–59. Note that the badge colouring of export models often differed from home-market ones and that it changed to suit the model colour.

In 1960 pear-shaped badges were generally adopted, but with the round star and piled arms ones still listed for the two-gallon tanks. Both were joined by a new design in 1961 which had a large star with the marque letters superimposed on it, but the 1958 star badge style continued in use on the Rocket Gold Star for 1962–63.

The unit models began with the 1960-type pear-shaped badges, which were joined by the 1961 star badge for the alternative tank. Two more types were listed in 1965, for the A50C and A65L/R, but a new pair were listed for all the steel tanks and transfers went on the fibreglass ones. In 1968 the badges became alloy die castings, which were modified for the following year. In 1971 it was back to the beginning with a winged BSA badge being used on some models. For home and general export a transfer was listed, but not for 1972.

Kneegrips

These were a feature of machines from the 1920s and gradually became more common as speeds rose and the need for something to clamp onto became more pressing. As tanks fattened in the 1930s they served also to protect the finish.

The original 1947 pair were changed for 1951 and the new pair continued in use to 1963. In 1960 the larger petrol tank changed to pear-shaped badges and with these came new kneegrips without the BSA name moulded into them. They were produced also as a pair for American models.

These unmarked grips continued on the unit models in a grey colour at first but quickly in black also. After 1965 only the black was listed, although not for all tanks, and from then on only on the four-gallon tank. In 1969 new kneegrips appeared for the Firebird tank which were shaped to fit the knee recesses moulded into it. The black kneegrips were listed for 1970, but not the others, as both the Firebird and Lightning tanks of this style had the recesses chrome plated that year. No kneegrips were fitted after then.

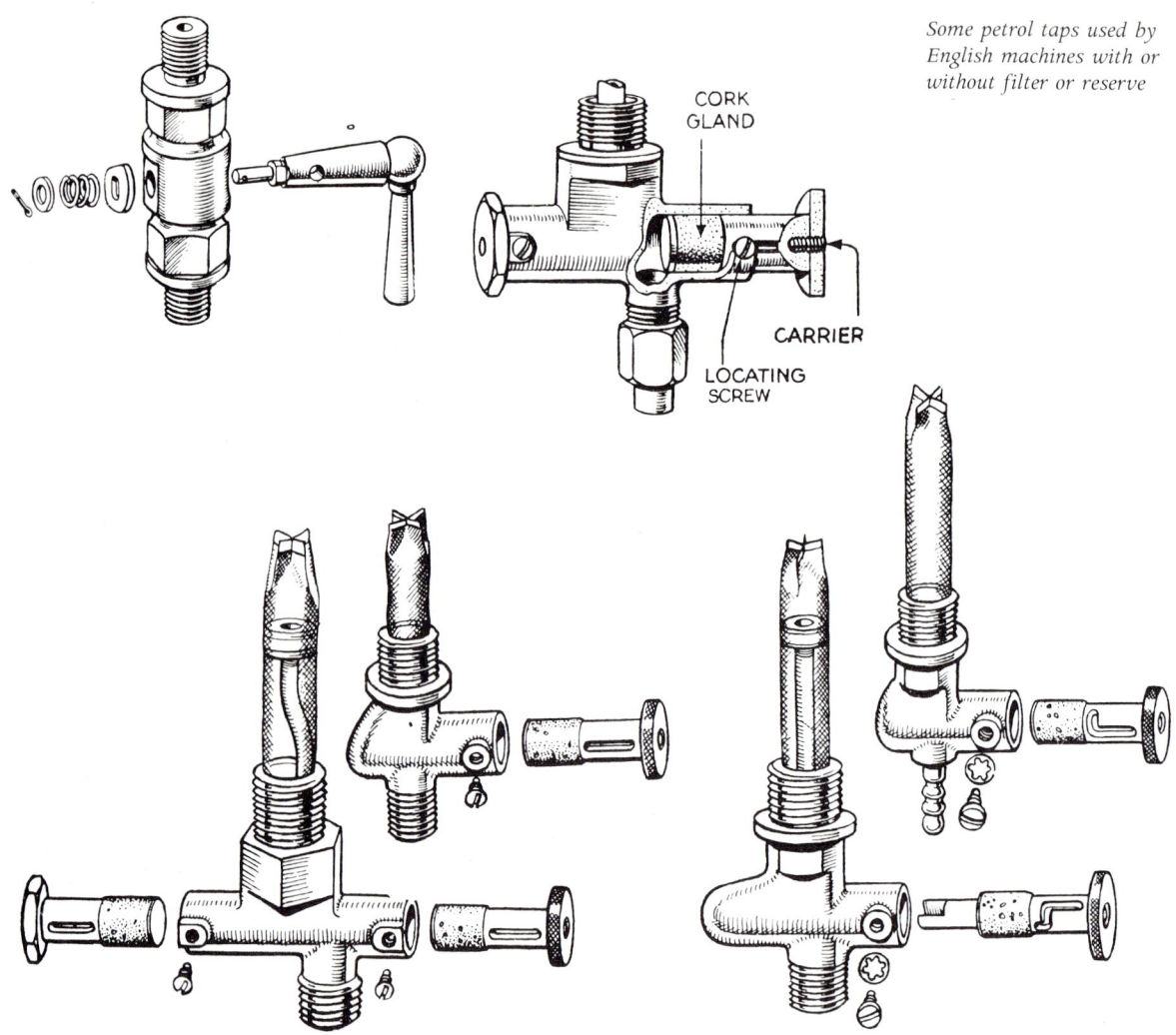

Some petrol taps used by English machines with or without filter or reserve

Taps

These either have a cork seal or a taper cock fitting. In either case they may need to come apart and the sealing arrangements checked over and repaired as required. Then check that the filter is undamaged and that the taps work freely. Make sure the taps don't leak and do pass a full flow of petrol before they are used on the machine. Leaks at that stage are a bind and a fire risk.

The original machine had two push/pull taps, but those on the Star Twin had a reserve lever as well. The type used on the A10 lacked this feature but differed from the A7 ones in that they could accommodate a banjo connection beneath the tap which was used to join the two tank halves together. During 1950, from frame number ZA7S-7035, this type also went onto the Star Twin.

A new tap type with cork plunger was fitted in 1951 and remained in use on the plunger-frame models. It was also used on the 1954 pivoted-fork machines, but for the Road Rocket and 1955 models a change was made to the 1947 design. The Super Flash used a proper racing taper cock tap for its supply but the other models continued with the push/pull or the cork plunger to 1963. The exception was the Rocket Gold Star, which repeated the use of the taper cock taps.

The unit models began with a pair of cork plunger taps with pipe connection in line with the plunger and these remained in use to 1970. In 1965 they were joined by an in-line version and in 1966 by a taper cock pair for the Spitfire Mk II. Another six tap variations were used during 1969 and 1970, but all went for 1971, when a pair of lever taps were fitted, one with a reserve.

ABOVE RIGHT *The centre-bolt tank fixing of a 1954 A10 which should be hidden by a rubber plug. Centre button on bars is magneto cut-out*

BELOW RIGHT *The A10 in 1953 when it had chromed tank panels and not quite its original appearance*

PETROL TANK

15 Seating

LEFT *Separate saddle and pillion on a 1953 A10 in use in Australia*

ABOVE *The BSA dualseat of 1955 shown on a Shooting Star*

The seating on BSA twins began as a saddle and pillion pad, which was fitted up to 1951 and the end of the rigid frame. In 1952 the dualseat was first listed as an option for all models and in 1954 was fitted as standard to the pivoted-fork models while remaining an option for the plunger-frame ones.

From then on only a dualseat was fitted, although a saddle remained available up to 1963, for the police, and in 1967. In addition, some machines had a handrail from 1954 on.

Saddle

A saddle is an assembly and should be treated as such. On top is the cover, which is sewn to shape and then fitted with clips riveted around the edge. Under that went a felt underlay and this tends to wear and fray on the springs beneath. With felt and cover removed what is left is the main frame and a series of suspension springs that run fore and aft.

At the rear of the assembly the two main springs were attached and a pivot bolt went at the front. This was supposed to pivot in a greased hole in the frame but is an area often neglected and the holes may well need repair. A good fit will allow the saddle to rise and fall on its springs as it should without side sway, which can be disconcerting.

The parts need to be refurbished as with any others and then re-assembled. Once complete a new cover with underfelt can be fitted and retained with its clips. Fit the back first and work the material forward to the nose.

Saddle types

The original fitting was a Terry saddle, which went on both the A7 and Star Twin models with rigid or plunger frames to 1949. The next year there was a change to Lycette saddles with two listed, one for the A10 and the other for the two A7 models. The first remained in the list to 1957 for use with the plunger frame and was joined by a saddle to suit the pivoted-fork frame in 1954. This continued in the lists to 1963 and along with it was a Terry Dominion saddle listed for the police.

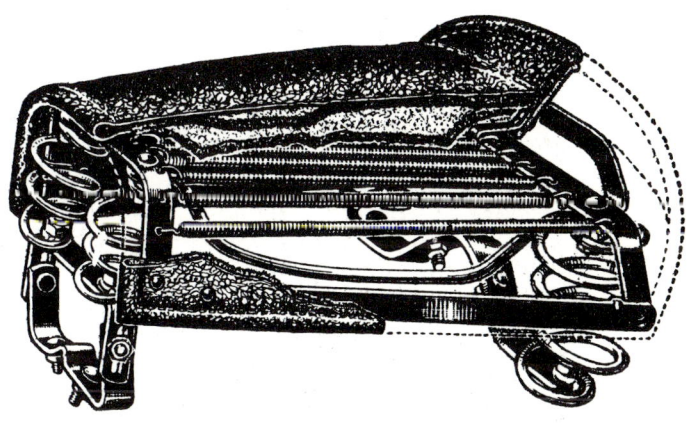

The construction features of a Camden pillion seat which was built on the same lines as a saddle

ABOVE *Latter dualseat and handrail seen on a 1964 Thunderbolt Rocket in US style*

RIGHT *A 1956 A7 showing the seat fixing to a pin at the front with two bolts to hold it down at the rear*

Pillion pad

When separate from a saddle passenger seats could be either sprung and built up like the saddle or simply a rubber pad with a cover. BSA opted for the latter, which was listed from 1947 to 1949 as one type and for 1950 only as another. In both cases the pad was simply bolted in place.

If water has got into the interior it is unlikely that it can be used any more so replacement will be necessary. Again, if the cover is damaged, a new one will be needed. Make sure you have sorted out the fixing to the mudguard before that item is finished.

When saddles and pillion seats were standard wear, it was common practice to fit a proprietary seat for the passenger. If this has been done it may require repair. If of the spring type, this is done in the same manner as for a saddle, and again the fixing to the machine needs to be finalized before finishing and not after.

Dualseat

These can be more of a problem as there were a good few variations used by BSA over the years and they can be awkward to mend. They consist of a steel pan, which can rust, a moulded interior, which can rot, and a cover, which may tear or split.

The interior moulding is the greatest problem as replacement may be the only answer and unless you can locate a suitable one you will not get the desired final seat shape. The pan can be refurbished as for any other steel part and the cover replaced by another, which may be stitched from basic material.

Restoration is thus a specialist job and one you can expect to farm out in most cases as not being practical for most owners. There are always exceptions of course, depending on the size of the problem and the skills and resources of the person dealing with it.

Dualseat types

The first dualseat was for the plunger frame and bolted to brackets attached to the saddle nose lug on the frame and the rear mudguard supports. It was modified for 1954 and continued in this form to 1957. A seat with brackets to suit the pivoted-fork frame appeared in 1954 and was modified for 1960, with a deeper skirt for the passenger's area. At the same time the two-level aspect became more accentuated and this seat was also used on some Super Rocket models during 1959. It went onto the Rocket Gold Star in 1962 while for the Spitfire there was a special short version.

The unit models began with an all-black seat on the A65 and a two-tone one on the A50, with light grey sides and dark grey top, which later went onto the larger machine. There was also a short seat for use by the police or with a special rear carrier. The A65R used the all-black seat and in 1965 a humped tail seat appeared for the Clubman racing models.

For 1966 there was a new touring-style seat for the Royal Star, Thunderbolt and Wasp, while the Hornet, Lightning and Spitfire had a racing style. For the benefit of passengers its hump was soft and collapsed under their weight to enable two to ride in comfort. The rear of the seat carried the BSA name and its lower edge was trimmed with a chrome-plated strip.

A new seat went onto all models in 1967 and this had a rear hump and a small one between rider and passenger. It continued to be fitted as standard to all models up to 1970 and with it was also listed a short seat. This was first seen in 1967 as a fitting for the Hornet when in West Coast USA guise and next in 1969, when the early unit one was listed to special order only. It also appeared in the 1970 lists, but for that year without any nose bracket. For 1971–72 there was just the one hinged seat for all models in the new frame.

Handrail

This is a tubular, chrome-plated part that bolts to or around the rear of the dualseat. It first appeared in 1954 as an option for the pivoted-fork frame models and continued on the pre-unit models in this way with changes for 1958 and 1960.

Two were listed for the early unit models, one for general use and the other for America. Two more appeared in 1965 to suit the revised and sporting dualseats, but for 1966 just one new one was listed. It was modified for 1967 and replaced by a new design for 1969. This had the rail welded to the rear seat loop, which ran back to support the mudguard. Two versions were listed, one for the Firebird and the other for the three road models. The Firebird one continued for 1970, but the road models went back to a bent tube that bolted to the seat, and this was also listed for the Firebird.

For 1971 a new design was used with a rear seat loop with the handrail welded to it and side reflectors fitted at the junction. The complete part was fixed to the frame and rear mudguard as standard and continued for 1972.

Dualseat with rear hump on a 1969 Lightning also fitted with a handrail

16 Assembly

This is often the most satisfying part of a restoration or rebuild, culminating in that heady moment when you swing on the kickstarter and the engine bursts into life.

It is also a time for making haste slowly as rushing matters can easily damage something you have spent time, money and effort on. Slow and sure is best, with plenty of reference to your notes, so that you work in the right sequence. In the build-up to final assembly you should have checked the fit of bolts to holes as you went along. All this work will now pay off in a straightforward fitment of the parts without snags.

The greatest problem is protecting the finish you have lavished so much care on, so cover, pad and mask

A 1951 A10 on show at Bethnal Green Town Hall for a road safety week

where necessary and work slowly to avoid damage. Have a think about the order in which you intend to assemble the parts and arrange the items of each stage so they are together. It is good practice to do this as it is a further check that you have everything and that each item has been reworked as required. It will also ensure that you are not caught off balance with something partly together and you short of a vital bolt and with no free hand to locate it. If this does happen, go back and dismantle rather than chance damage occurring while your back is turned.

Start the assembly with the frame and fit the rear fork, the head race cups and the main stand whether this is centre or rear. You can now put the skeleton on your machine bench and prop the front end up. If you have any doubt at all on stability, clamp the stand down. Now fit the fork crowns and the forks themselves. Add the front wheel. If you fit the mudguard at this stage, it will need protection for sure, so is best omitted for the time being.

The rear guard may well have to be fitted early on and it may be necessary to add the wiring harness at this stage or at least fit the rear section if this is threaded through frame and mudguard tubes and guides. If the machine is balanced on its centre stand, either fit the rear wheel or anchor the rear fork end to your bench.

Once you have a stable frame that is not going to rock about, fit the engine and gearbox while you have the most room to move in. Don't forget to check that you have not left anything out that must be fitted first.

Sort out all engine fixings, plates and spacers in advance and place to hand. Spare rods to locate on may well be needed.

You are more likely to damage something while fitting the engine than at any other time, so first protect everything you can. Don't try to lift the weight into place unless you have at least two helpers to take the load while you slide the fixings in. With only two people, something is sure to be scratched.

Blocks underneath are one way to take the strain, but better is a means of lifting it from above. In view of the cost of a rebuild, it is well worth the price of a car engine hoist, which will be able to carry the load easily. Arrange the lifting sling so it is secure and holds the engine in the correct plane for its fixings to line up. If you have to tilt the engine to achieve this, you are more likely to have an accident and crushed fingers. Better to adjust the sling so the engine just drops into place.

Then fit all fixings and tighten. As with any assembly work it is best to complete a sequence fully and not leave the final tightening for later in case you forget. This is not always possible, in which case leave the nut undone and give it a marker to remind you.

Continue the assembly as you wish and as the design dictates but leave the tank and seat as late as possible. Check wheel alignment once both are in place for good and adjust the chain tension correctly.

Don't try to start the engine until all is ready and keep the battery on the shelf until near the end. Before connecting it use your meter to check that the wiring

Posed show picture with Geoff Duke and Doug Hele beside a 1955 Shooting Star

is not shorting to earth somewhere and make sure you connect it the right way round. It should be fine, but better to be sure than chance a spark at this stage. Then disconnect the battery again while you fill the oil tank and check the gearbox and primary chain levels.

If the machine is still up on the bench, you will need help to get it down safely. Take care that you don't drop it at this stage and give yourself plenty of room to work in. Once down, you can prepare to start up by opening the workshop doors to let the exhaust fumes out.

The petrol tank will best have been left off while you get the machine down to ground level so now fit it, connect it up and pour a small amount of fuel in. Half a gallon or two litres is fine to start with. Turn on and check for leaks. Connect battery and start the engine. Keep the engine speed low and check that oil is returning to the oil tank. Hold your finger on the return to force some into the rocker box as soon as possible. Check that the generator is charging.

Next put the machine on its stand and run it up through the gears to make sure all is well in that area. Have a good look round the pipe connections to make sure there are no leaks and do your ignition timing strobe check if this is called for.

Try the machine gently to check the operation of the clutch and brakes. If you have done your paperwork and are taxed and insured, you can now get your helmet and go for a ride. If not, you will have to put it away for the moment.

For most owners in the UK that first ride of the restored machine is the prosaic one to the local dealer for its official test. Rather irksome after all your work but look on it as a top mechanic may regard scrutineering at a race meeting – a check that nothing has been overlooked. It may help to go to a dealer who knows something of older machines and who will believe that, for instance, taper roller bearing wheels should have some side play and that a 7 in. sls drum brake may lack the bite of a double disc with hydraulic operation.

A chat when booking the appointment is well worth the effort and can smooth the way to your pass.

With the machine legal, enjoy a ride. After a few miles check the oil level and give the machine a lookover to see if anything has worked loose. Get some more petrol before you run short and roll off some more miles.

Then take the machine back to the workshop. Check items such as chains, brakes and cables which may have settled down a touch. Go and do your carburation check.

Enjoy your BSA twin.

Final assembly of an A7 for the Swedish War Office in 1949 with Fred Rist waiting to check the machine out on the road

17 Paperwork

PAPERWORK

In this modern age, ownership and use of any road vehicle involves pieces of paper and some of these are documents issued by the authorities. This chapter concerns these in general and those specific to the United Kingdom in particular. Details for other countries will vary and must be checked as necessary.

The first piece of paper was mentioned in the opening chapter and is the receipt for the machine, or the bundle of receipts for parts if that was the way you obtained your model. It is very desirable that they contain the engine and frame numbers so you have proof of ownership of what you actually do have. Make sure they agree with what is stamped on the machine and beware of anything that looks altered.

The other documents you will need in the UK are registration form, test certificate and insurance certificate. The first is currently known as a V5, the second as VT20 and the last is obtained privately. With them you can then tax the machine for road use.

You should consider insurance long before you get to the road as the parts and the machine as a whole need to be covered against fire or theft as soon as you get them. Try to obtain an agreed value for the machine and make sure you adjust this in line with the market. The insurance will need to be extended to cover road risks before you ride in public and it is worth shopping around for a company that specializes in older machines and caters for them. Otherwise your relatively sedate Golden Flash will be lumped in with modern 900 cc models of far higher performance and spares prices.

The V5 and VT20 are to an extent linked and also involve the number plate of your machine. Where a machine has been in use on a fairly continuous basis its original buff or green log book will have been replaced by a V5, which will record the correct engine and frame numbers along with the original registration number as displayed on the number plate.

As nothing is perfect there are even discrepancies when the documentation is all in order. For example a BSA twin is bought from a dealer. It suffers an engine problem and the complete unit is changed. This is not recorded at the time, the machine is eventually withdrawn from use and finally sold off. The new owner rebuilds it and on coming to register it compares paper numbers with actual markings to find they don't tally. As they have not done for many years.

More difficult is a machine that has not been used for a period and has no V5. For the authorities to issue a form either with the existing registration number, if known, or one appropriate to the machine's year, they need further proof and the onus is on the owner to provide it.

It is necessary to link the number to the machine and for this old MoT certificates or old license discs are acceptable. Where not available or to back them up a letter from a recognized authority to confirm the date of the quoted engine and frame numbers and stating whether or not they were likely to have begun life together should be obtained. Acceptable sources are the owners club, Vintage MCC, service-page writers of the specialist magazines (I am one of these) or the holders of the original records of the firm.

It is not normally possible to trace the original registration number from scratch and much of the

LEFT *The right papers would keep this Singapore policeman happy, otherwise his sidearm could come into use. His machine is a 1948 A7*

RIGHT *Swede Lennart Strand, who held the world 1500 metre record in 1947, on his 1951 A10*

official record no longer exists. The procedure needed would be to look at the firm's records to match engine and frame numbers. If this is in order the records will then give the name of the dealer to whom the machine was sent. He in turn would then need to be sought out and his records would give the registration number.

In practice few dealers from those days are still in business and fewer have kept such records for the 20 or 30 years likely to be involved.

So you have to call on your Local Vehicle Licensing Office and take all your documents with you. There you fill up a form, as you would expect to do at any government office. This will trigger off a series of events that will culminate with the issue of a V5, if all goes well.

The first thing likely to happen is a visit from the authorities or their agents to inspect your machine. This is done to check that the numbers all agree with those quoted on the form and that the machine is what you say it is and does exist.

This visit is not always carried out, but for it the machine is best assembled to some degree. It is often desirable to register the machine long before the restoration is complete or there is any need to tax it for the road. At the very least it allows you to get the number plate finished.

After the visit and if all is in order, the vehicle documents can be issued. If the evidence is good the original registration number, or mark as they call it, will be retained and entered on the main computer at Swansea. If this cannot be done but there is evidence as to the age of the machine, the authorities will try to issue it an appropriate number for its period. Should there be no way of linking the machine to any period, which may happen with a hybrid, a number with a letter Q suffix will be issued.

Following this the machine will have to go for its official test as mentioned in the previous chapter. Book the test, make sure you have insured the machine for road use, pass the test as after all this I would be most disappointed if you did otherwise, and you can then tax the machine for the road.

Keep all the paperwork, first in case there are any queries at any time and second to go with the machine should you ever come to sell it.

Now you have to decide what to restore next year.

Once you have restored your 1950 A10 you can take it for a run but one this far is not mandatory

APPENDICES

1 Engine and frame numbers

Year	Model	Engine	Frame
1947	A7	XA7-101	XA7-101
1948	A7	YA7-101	YA7-101
1949	A7	ZA7-101	ZA7-101
	A7 (pl)	ZA7-101	ZA7S-101
	A7ST	ZA7S-101	ZA7S-101
1950	A7	ZA7-7001	ZA7-4001
	A7 (pl)	ZA7-7001	ZA7S-6001
	A7ST	ZA7S-4001	ZA7S-6001
	A10	ZA10-101	ZA7-4001
	A10 (pl)	ZA10-101	ZA7S-6001
1951	A7	AA7-101	ZA7-6001
	A7 (pl)	AA7-101	ZA7S-14001
	A7ST	AA7S-101	ZA7S-14001
	A10	ZA10-4001	ZA7-6001
	A10 (pl)	ZA10-4001	ZA7S-14001
1952	A7	AA7-5001	ZA7-8001
	A7 (pl)	AA7-5001	ZA7S-26001
	A7ST	AA7S-1001	ZA7S-26001
	A10	ZA10-12001	ZA7-8001
	A10 (pl)	ZA10-12001	ZA7S-26001
1953	A7	BA7-101	BA7-101
	A7 (pl)	BA7-101	BA7S-101
	A7ST	BA7S-101	BA7S-101
	A10	BA10-101	BA7-101
	A10 (pl)	BA10-101	BA7S-101
	A10SF	BA10S-101	BA10-101
1954	A7 (pl)	BA7-2001	BA7S-8950
	A7 (s/a)	CA7-101	CA7-101
	A7ST	BA7S-2001	BA7S-8950
	A7SS	CA7SS-101	CA7-101
	A10 (pl)	BA10-7001	BA7S-8950
	A10 (s/a)	CA10-101	CA7-101
	A10SF	BA10S-701	BA10S-701
	A10RR	CA10R-101	CA7-101
1955	A7	CA7-1501	} CA7-7001
	A7SS	CA7SS-501	
	A10 (s/a)	CA10-4501	
	A10RR	CA10R-601	
	A10 (pl)	BA10-11001	BA7S-15001

Year	Model	Frame	
1956	A7	CA7-2701	} EA7-101
	A7SS	CA7SS-2301	
	A10 (s/a)	CA10-8001	
	A10RR	CA10R-2001	
	A10 (pl)	BA10-14001	BA7S-18001
1957	A7	CA7-	} EA7-
	A7SS	CA7SS-	
	A10 (s/a)	CA10-	
	A10RR	CA10R-	
last	A10 (pl)	BA10-16036	BA7S-20289
1958	A7	CA7-5001	} FA7-101
	A7SS	CA7SS-4501	
	A10	DA10-651	
	A10SR	CA10R-6001	
1959	A7	CA7-5867	} FA7-8522
	A7SS	CA7SS-5425	
	A10	DA10-4616	
	A10SR	CA10R-8193	
	A10 Spitfire	CA10SR-776	FA7A-101
1960	A7	CA7-7101	} GA7-101
	A7SS	CA7SS-6701	
	A10	DA10-7801	
	A10SR	DA10R-101	
	A10 Spitfire	DA10SR-101	GA7A-101
1961	A7	CA7-8501	} GA7-11101
	A7 (alt)	CA7A-8501	
	A7SS	CA7SS-8001	
	A10	DA10-13201	
	A10 (alt)	DA10A-13201	
	A10SR	DA10R-3001	
	A10 Spitfire	DA10SR-401	GA7A-401
1962	A7	CA7-9714	} GA7-21120
	A7 (alt)	CA7A-9714	
	A7SS	CA7SS-9277	
	A10	DA10-17181	
	A10 (alt)	DA10A-341	
	A10SR	DA10R-5958	
	A10 Spitfire	DA10R-5958	GA7A-536
	A10RGS	DA10R-5958	GA10-101
	A50	A50-101	} A50-101
	A65	A65-101	

200

APPENDIX 1 ENGINE AND FRAME NUMBERS

	A50 (rod brake)	A50-101	A50A-101
	A65 (rod brake)	A65-101	
1963	A10	DA10-17727	GA7-23643
	A10 (alt)	DA10A-17727	
	A10SR	DA10R-8197	
	A10 Spitfire	DA10R-8197	GA7A-748
	A10RGS	DA10R-8197	GA10-390
	last A10RGS	DA10R-10388	GA10-1914
	A50	A50-823	A50-2288
	A65	A65-1947	
	A50 (rod brake)	A50-823	A50-2701
	A65 (rod brake)	A65-1947	
1964	A50	A50A-101	A50-5501
	A50 (police)	A50AP-101	
	A65	A65A-101	
	A65 (police)	A65AP-101	
	A65R	A65B-101	
	A65R (with rev counter)	A65C-101	
	A65T/R	A65B-101	
	A50C (USA)	A50B-101	A50B-101
	A65L/R	A65D-101	
	A65SH	A65E-101	

Letter C after model indicates close-ratio gearbox and was used 1964–67.

1965	A50	A50A-686	A50-8437
	A50 (police)	A50AP-121	
	A65	A65A-1134	
	A65 (police)	A65AP-267	
	A65R	A65B-334	
	A65R (rev-counter)	A65C-1082	
	A50C (US road)	A50D-101	A50B-4001
	A50CC (US off-road)	A50B-507	
	A50C (UK)	A50DC-101	
	A50CC (UK)	A50DC-101	
	A65L/R	A65D-1742	
	A65SH	A65E-701	
	A65L	A65DC-2158	
	A65LC	A65DC-2158	

1966	A50 Royal Star	A50R-101	A50C-101
	A50 Wasp	A50W-101	
	A65 Thunderbolt	A65T-101	
	A65 Lightning	A65L-101	
	A65 Hornet	A65H-101	
	A65 Spitfire MkII	A65S-101	

1967 on – engine and frame used same number.

1967	A50 Royal Star	A50RA-101
	A50 Wasp	A50WA-101
	A65 Thunderbolt	A65TA-101
	A65 Lightning	A65LA-101
	A65 Hornet	A65HA-101
	A65 Spitfire MkIII	A65SA-101
1968	A50 Royal Star	A50RB-101
	A50 Wasp	A50WB-101
	A65 Thunderbolt	A65TB-101
	A65 Lightning	A65LB-101
	A65 Firebird	A65FB-101
	A65 Spitfire MkIV	A65SB-101
1969	A50 Royal Star	A50RC-101
	A65 Thunderbolt	A65TC-101
	A65 Lightning	A65LC-101
	A65 Firebird	A65FC-101

1969 and onwards

During 1969 a new coding system was introduced using a two-letter prefix for the month and model season year, plus model type code and a number that began at 00101 for each model year and ran on irrespective of the model it was stamped on. Model season was taken to start in July 1969 for 1970 and August for 1971 and 1972.

First letter was month and code is:

A January	D April	H July	N October
B February	E May	J August	P November
C March	G June	K September	X December

Second letter was year and code is:

D July 1969 to July 1970
E August 1970 to July 1971
G August 1971 to July 1972

The model codes for 1970 were A50R, A65T, A65L and A65F, and engine and frame numbers were the same. For 1971 the engine codes were A65T, A65L and A65FS with the frames stamped XE.00101 A65 up. For 1972 the engine codes were A65T, A65L and A70L, while the frame marking became XG.00101 A65 up.

2 Model chart

A7/A10	1947	1948	1949	1950	1951	1952	1953	1954	1955	1956	1957	1958	1959	1960	1961	1962	1963
A7	——	——	——	——	——												
A7 (pl)				——	——	——	——	——									
A7 (s/a)									——	——	——	——	——	——	——	——	——
A7ST				——	——	——	——	——									
A7SS										——	——	——	——	——	——	——	——
A10				——	——												
A10 (pl)				——	——	——	——	——									
A10 (s/a)									——	——	——	——	——	——	——	——	——
A10SF							——	——	——								
A10RR								——	——	——	——						
A10SR												——	——	——	——	——	——
A10 Spitfire												——	——	——	——	——	——
A10RGS																——	——

A50/A65		1962	1963	1964	1965	1966	1967	1968	1969	1970	1971	1972
A50		——	——	——	——	——	——	——				
A50CC (US)			——	——								
A50C (US)				——	——							
A50C (UK)				——	——							
A50CC (UK)				——	——							
A50W					——	——	——					
A65		——	——	——	——	——	——	——	——	——	——	——
A65T						——	——	——	——	——	——	——
A65R			——	——								
A65T/R		——	——									
A65L/R			——	——								
A65L				——	——							
A65L						——	——	——	——	——	——	——
A65LC				——	——							
A65 Spitfire		——	——	——	——	II	III	IV				
A65SH			——	——								
A65H					——	——	——					
A65FS								——	——	——	——	——
A70L												——

3 Model alterations

These notes have been compiled from the main text and are to provide a quick guide for checking a machine for its year. The starting point should always be the engine and frame numbers and the following is mainly concerned with external details that can be inspected when purchasing.

The notes run on and are generally applicable to later models of the same series. If in doubt, refer to the main text.

The first section deals with general changes that apply to all, or most, models then in production and the feature normally continues until the end of the model or when changed as noted. The start and finish of each model run is included in this section. See also the data in the other appendices.

General

1947 A7 start, speedo in tank, qd hubs front and rear, special crankshaft, special centre stand. During year revised crankshaft fitted, normal type of centre stand and oil feed to exhaust rockers added.
1948 Speedo on fork top.
1949 A7ST start, plunger frame, two-part frame construction for rigid and plunger, left front engine plate pierced for dynamo, E3L dynamo, MCR2 cvc, inlet rocker oil feed, revised front mudguard stay lugs on fork legs, one-piece front hub.
1950 A10 start, revised gearset, tyre pump on chainguard. Longstroke A7 and A7ST end.
1951 Revised A7 and A7ST start, positive earth electrics, first use of manual advance magneto. Rigid frame end.
1952 Pre-focus headlamp and underslung pilot light, dualseat option available, ball-ended extension for centre stand.
1953 A10SF start, headlamp cowl (not A10SF), boxed-in rear number plate, rubber mounted petrol tank, rectangular rear lamp, separate rear reflector.
1954 A7SS, A10RR start, pivoted-fork frame introduced with pre-unit construction, one-bolt petrol tank fixing and dualseat as standard on new frame. Plunger A7, A7ST, A10SF end.
1955 Pilot light set in headlamp reflector, steering lock added to top fork crown, general adoption of Monobloc carburettor (not plunger A10 or A10RR).
1956 Full-width, light-alloy hubs front and rear, combined rear lamp and reflector, brake cross-shaft in rear fork pivot.
1957 End of semi-unit construction and plunger frame. Plunger A10, A10RR end.
1958 A10SR, A10 Rocket Scrambler start, nacelle replaces cowl (not A10RS or export A10SR), new full-width hubs with composite front and one-piece rear, RB107 cvc, oval feet for centre stand, split front fork ends.
1960 A10 Rocket Scrambler becomes A10 Spitfire, pear-shaped tank badges, plain kneegrips, deeper dualseat skirt, chaincase standpipe, RB108 cvc, centre stand spring on left, no front stay for front mudguard, simplified rear mudguard stays.
1962 A10RGS, A50, A65 start, floating brake shoes. A7, A7SS end.
1963 A10, A10SR, A10 Spitfire, A10RGS end.
1964 A50CC offroad, A65R, A65T/R, A65L/R, A65SH start, needle race layshaft bearings. A65T/R end.
1965 A50C (USA), A50C, A50CC, A65L, A65LC start, close-ratio gears listed. A50CC off road, A50C (USA), A50C, A50CC, A65, A65R, A65L/R, A65LC, A65SH end.
1966 A50 becomes A50R, A50W, A65T, A65S, A65H start, exhaust pipe tie, rear wheel speedo drive, three-spring clutch, top-access cap in chaincase, 12-volt electrics standard, two-way front fork damping.
1967 Finned rocker box lid, rotor access cover in chaincase. A50W, A65H end.
1968 A65FS start, general use of Concentric carburettors, Lucas 6CA contact points. A65S end.
1969 RM21 alternator, forks with split ends and shuttle damping, points and rotor covers with BSA cast into them, oil pressure switch, exhaust balance pipe (not A50R), twin leading shoe front brake with plain nave plate.
1970 Three-ball clutch lift, plunger piston oil release valve. A50R end.
1971 New frame with built-in oil tank, slim-line forks, conical hubs, cast-iron oil pump body. A65FS end.
1972 A70L start. A65T, A65L, A70L end.

Notes on specific models

A7SS
1954 Light-alloy cylinder head, separate inlet manifold.
1956 Integral cylinder head and manifold.

A10
1950 8 in. front brake.

A10RR
1954 Light-alloy cylinder head.

A10SR
1960 Rev-counter driven from oil pump.

A65
1964 12-volt option for electric system.

A65S
1967 Concentric carburettors fitted.

A65L, A65S, A65FS
1968 Twin leading shoe front brake, slotted nave plate.

A65L
1969 Twin horns.

4 Finish codes

There is a series of suffix numbers that was added to a component part number to indicate the finish required. These numbers were mainly used for petrol tanks, wheels, rims, mudguards and fork seal holders, which could all vary in appearance depending on the year of manufacture and whether an option finish had been taken up or not. The suffix was separated from the part number by a stroke and thus the A7 petrol tank was 67-8015/17 for the standard black panels in 1949 but 67-8015/12 if in the optional red. Codes used by models other than twins have been included for interest and assistance.

1 Cadmium
2 Dull chrome
3 Bright chrome
4 Dull green Dutch
5 Sand (Egyptian)
6 Rustproof black
7 Black enamel
8 Service green (matt)
9 Green enamel
10 Khaki green
11 Khaki green (No. 3 gasproof)
12 Chrome plate and Devon red, lined gold
13 Chrome plate and matt silver, lined black
14 Chrome plate and blue, lined gold
15 Chrome plate and green, lined gold
16 Matt silver, lined black
17 Chrome plate and black, lined gold
18 Mist green
19 Chrome plate and matt silver, lined red
21 Polished aluminium
23 Polychromatic grey
24 Polychromatic silver beige
25 Swedish army grey
26 Chrome plate, silver beige, lined red
34 Devon red
36 Maroon and chrome lined gold
37 Maroon only
38 Metallic green and chrome plate lined dark green
39 Metallic green
40 Dark green
41 Chrome rim and maroon hub
42 Chrome rim and dark green hub
43 Chrome rim and beige hub
44 Chrome rim and black hub
78 Brilliant red and chrome
88 Nutley blue or sapphire blue (in 1966)
100 Almond green

101 Gunmetal grey
102 Princess grey
109 Royal red and chrome (tank)
120 Black and chrome (tank)
127 Metallic grey and chrome (tank)
142 Devon red and chrome (tank)
146 Blue and chrome (tank)
165 Silver
167 Flamboyant blue
170 Flamboyant red
174 Flamboyant blue and chrome, single white line
175 Flamboyant blue, single white line
176 Flamboyant red and chrome, single white line
177 Flamboyant red, single white line
201 Mandarine red
202 Mandarine red and chrome
208 Red and black
223 Peony red, ivory panels, single gold line
226 Peony
227 Flamboyant aircraft blue
228 Flamboyant aircraft blue, chrome panels, single white line
229 Flamboyant aircraft blue, single white line
233 Black, chrome panels, single white line
234 Black, single white line
261 Firebird red
268 Blue tank centre, white lining, chrome side panels (1970 A65L)
269 Blue tank centre, white lining, chrome side panels (1970 A65F)
270 Grey tank centre, white lining, chrome side panels
271 Blue (1970 A65L)
272 Blue (1970 A65F)
274 Grey
276 Flamboyant red, white lining
277 Flamboyant red tank centre, white lining, chrome side panels
288 Dove grey
295 Polychromatic golden metallic bronze upper and white lower
296 Polychromatic golden metallic bronze
297 Sterling Moss polychromatic green upper and white lower
298 Sterling Moss polychromatic green
306 Instrument matt black
307 Silver sheen
322 Etruscan bronze
330 Chromed, Firebird red with white lining

5 Colours

Numbers in parentheses refer to BSA finish codes.

A7

1947–50 All painted parts either black (7) or Devon red (34), this including frame, forks, oil tank, battery carrier, chainguard and mudguards. Petrol tank chrome plated with black panels (17) lined in gold or Devon red panels (12) gold lined. Wheel rims chrome plated with either black or Devon red centres gold-lined. Chrome-plated headlamp rim, handlebars, tank cap, brake backplates, battery strap, fork oil seal holders and exhaust system.

1951 As 1947 all in black or with petrol tank panels alone in Devon red (12).

1951–52 Due to nickel shortage chrome plating restricted so tank finished in matt silver with red or black panels gold lined. Painted brake backplates, otherwise as 1947 in black.

1953 All painted parts in maroon (37). Petrol tank maroon with chrome-plated side panels lined gold (36) and carrying new tank badges. Wheel rims chrome plated and laced to maroon hub (41). Chrome plating as 1947.

1954–55 As 1953 except round tank badges for both plunger and pivoted-fork models. Chrome-plated front brake backplate, painted rear.

1956–57 As 1955 except for alloy hubs and backplates. Black option available.

1958–59 Black frame, forks, chainguard, hubs, hub cover plate centre and brake backplate centre. Rims of last two polished (21). Princess grey (102) mudguards, mudguard stays, oil tank, toolbox, air cleaner box and petrol tank, which has chrome-plated side panels lined red. Chrome-plated wheel rims, headlamp rim, fork oil seal holders, handlebars and exhaust system. Black option available.

1959 USA model as UK except colour sapphire blue for petrol tank and mudguards. Other painted parts black and all of brake backplate and hub cover plate polished. Gold lines on tank and mudguards.

1960–62 Finish as 1958 in black (7) and Devon red (34) for mudguards, stays, oil tank, toolbox and air cleaner box with the petrol tank Devon red with chrome-plated side panels (142). Option in black with black and chrome tank (120). Devon red also referred to as fuchsia red in 1960–61 and royal red in 1962. Pear-shaped tank badges.

A7ST

1949–51 Generally as 1947 A7 in black. Petrol tank chrome plated with matt silver panels lined red (19) and wheel rims chrome plated with matt silver centres lined red (19).

1951–52 As 1949 except tank all matt silver with panel outline in red. Painted brake backplates.

1953–54 Frame dark green (40). Mudguards, forks, chainguard, oil tank and toolbox metallic green (39). Petrol tank metallic green with chrome-plated side panels lined dark green (38). Wheel rims chrome plated and laced to dark green hubs (42). Chrome-plated headlamp rim, exhaust system, handlebars, tank cap, fork oil seal holders and brake backplates. Round plastic tank badges.

A7SS

1954–55 As 1953 A7ST except rear brake backplate painted dark green (38).

1956–57 As 1954 except for alloy hubs and backplates.

1958–62 In style of 1958 A7 with metallic green (30) in place of princess grey. No air cleaner and tank as before (38). No options. From 1960 pear-shaped tank badges.

1959 USA model as UK except all painted parts black with gold lines on tank and mudguard.

A10

1950–51 All painted parts black (7) or polychromatic silver beige (24) as for 1947 A7. Petrol tank chrome plated with black panels lined gold (17) or beige panels lined red (26). Wheel rims chrome plated with black centres lined gold (17) or beige centres lined red (26). Chrome plated as A7. Round winged BSA tank badge with 'Golden Flash' motif.

1951–52 As 1950 except tank all beige with panel outlined. Painted brake backplates.

1953 As 1950 except petrol tank black or beige with chrome-plated side panels lined gold or red. Wheel rims chrome plated and laced to black (44) or beige (43) hubs. Chrome plating as 1947 A7.

1954–55 As 1953 except painted rear brake backplate.
1956–57 As 1954 except for alloy hubs and backplates for pivoted-fork model.
1957 USA model all black except petrol tank bright red with chrome-plated side panels lined gold (78).
1958–59 In style of 1958 A7 with black (7) or beige (24) in place of princess grey. Round plastic tank badge.
1959 USA model as US A7.
1960–63 As for 1958 in black or beige plus option in nutley blue (88) for mudguards, oil tank, toolbox and air cleaner box. Petrol tank in black and chrome (120), beige and chrome with red lining (26) or blue and chrome (146). Pear-shaped tank badges. Blue also referred to as sapphire blue.

A10SF
1953–54 As A7ST in black with chrome-plated mudguards and stays. Petrol tank with chrome-plated side panels and top-painted matt silver and lined red (19) or metallic green and lined dark green (38) with 1950 A10-style badges on sides and transfer on top. Wheels with chrome-plated rim and black hub (44).

A10RR
1954–55 Black frame, forks, hubs, oil tank, toolbox, headlight shell and chainguard. Petrol tank matt silver with chrome-plated side panels lined red (19) or bright red with chrome-plated side panels lined gold (78) or green and chrome. Chrome-plated wheel rims, mudguards, mudguard stays, headlamp rim and exhaust systems.
1956–57 As 1954 except alloy hubs.

A10SR
1958 Generally as 1958 A7. First colour option had mudguards red with black oil tank and toolbox and petrol tank red with gold-lined, chrome-plated side panels. Second option was silver sheen for mudguards, oil tank and toolbox with petrol tank to match in silver with red-lined, chrome-plated panels. Chrome-plated mudguards for export models.
1959 UK as 1958. USA model with petrol tank in sapphire blue with gold-lined panels and chrome-plated mudguards, stays and fork top shrouds. All of brake backplate polished for US model.
1960 As 1958 in revised colours. First with royal red petrol tank with gold-lined, chrome-plated side panels (109), royal red mudguards (27) and black (7) oil tank and toolbox. Second with black and chrome (120) petrol tank and black for all other painted parts. Third with metallic grey petrol tank with chrome-plated side panels (127) and metallic princess grey (102) for oil tank, toolbox and mudguards. Pear-shaped tank badges.
1961–63 As 1960 except no all-black option.

A10 Spitfire
1959 USA model in black with chrome-plated mudguards, polished brake backplates and red tank with gold-lined, chrome-plated side panels.

A10RGS
1962–63 Black frame, fork legs, oil tank, toolbox and headlamp shell. Chrome-plated wheel rims when in steel, headlamp rim, exhaust system, mudguards, chainguard and fork top shrouds. Petrol tank matt silver with chrome-plated side panels lined red and round star badges.

A50
1962–65 Black (7) frame, forks, headlamp nacelle, chaincase and oil tank. Mudguards and side covers metallic green (39) and petrol tank metallic green with chrome-plated side panels lined gold (38). Pear-shaped tank badges and round winged BSA badges on side covers. Star badge on points cover for early models only. Chrome-plated wheel rims, headlamp rim and exhaust system. Silver sheen hubs and brake backplates with polished rims. All-black option also available.
1966 As 1962 except no nacelle, side covers flamboyant red (170), mudguards flamboyant red with white lining (177) and petrol tank flamboyant red with chrome panels and white lining (176). Badges as 1962. Chrome-plated parts as 1962 plus headlamp shell and brake backplates. Black hubs.
1967 As 1966 except colour flamboyant blue and codes are side covers (167), mudguards (175) and petrol tank (174).
1968 As 1966 except die-cast alloy tank badges and transfers for side covers.
1969–70 As 1968 except colour aircraft flamboyant blue and side covers lined as mudguards so code of both is 229 and petrol tank is 228. Code for the blue by itself is 227. New side cover transfers each year.

A50C and A50CC
1965 Side covers metallic gold with red lining, petrol tank the same plus chrome-plated side panels. Badges as 1962 A50. Chrome-plated headlamp shell, fork shrouds, mudguards, wheel rims, exhaust system and brake backplates. Black frame, fork legs and hubs.

A50W
1966 Side covers and petrol tank sapphire blue (88) with round winged BSA badges on first and transfers on second. Chrome-plated mudguards, fork shrouds, exhaust system, wheel rims, chainguard and brake backplates. Black frame, fork legs and hubs.

APPENDIX 5 COLOURS

A65
1962–65 As 1962 A50 except colours are nutley blue (88) for mudguards and side covers and blue and chrome (146) for the petrol tank. Options in black (as A50) and in flamboyant red, codes 170 and 176.

A65R
1964–65 As A65 in flamboyant red except mudguards and fork shrouds, which were chrome plated.

A65T
1966 As 1966 A50 except colour flamboyant blue and codes as 1967 A50.
1967 As 1966 except colour black.
1968 As 1968 A50 with colour flamboyant red.
1969–70 As 1968 in black with white lining. Code for side panels and mudguards 234 and for petrol tank 233. Option of chrome-plated mudguards. New side cover transfers each year.
1971 Frame dove grey (288), side covers and air filter boxes in Sterling Moss green (298), petrol tank in Sterling Moss green upper and white lower (297), headlamp shell, wheel rims and mudguards chrome plated.
1972 Frame black; side covers, air filter boxes and petrol tank in Etruscan bronze (322). Chrome plating as 1971.

A65L and A65LC
1965 As 1965 A50C.

A65L
1966–67 As 1966 A50 except mudguards chrome plated.
1968 As 1968 A50.
1969 As 1968 with new side cover transfers.
1970 As 1968 with revised side cover transfers. Also with tank in flamboyant red with chrome-plated kneegrip areas lined white. Also in blue with codes 268, 229 and 271.
1971 As 1971 A65T except colour bronze (296) or bronze and white (295).
1972 As 1972 A65T except colour firebird red (261).

A65 Spitfire
1966 MkII. Side covers and petrol tank flamboyant red with round winged BSA badges on first and transfers on second. Tank lined in ivory and gold. Chrome-plated mudguards, fork shrouds, headlamp shell, exhaust system, chainguard and rear brake backplate. Alloy rims and front hub. Black frame, fork legs and rear hub.
1967 MkIII. As 1966 except colour royal red.
1968 MkIV. As 1967 except transfers for side covers.

A65H
1966 As 1966 A50W except colour Mandarin red (201).

A65F
1970 As 1970 A65L or in blue with codes 269, 229 and 272.
1971 As 1971 A65L.

A70L
1972 As 1972 A65L.

6 Pistons

500 cc, pre-unit, 62 mm
67-195	6.6	1949–50
67-81	7.0	1947–50
67-103	7.5	1948–50
67-93	8.6	1948–49

500 cc, pre-unit, 66 mm
67-460	6.7	1951–59
67-466	7.25	1951–53
67-533	7.25	1951–57
67-1422	7.25	1960–62
67-566	8.0	1953–57
67-1442	8.1	1958–62
67-1558	8.5	1960–62

650 cc, pre-unit 70 mm
67-304	6.5	1950
67-423	6.7	1951–52
67-423	6.5	1953–57
67-365	7.25	1950
67-429	7.25	1951–57
67-1416	7.25	1958–63
67-572	8.0	1953–57
67-1370	8.26	1958–63
67-594	8.5	1954–57
67-1552	8.75	1960–63
67-545	9.0	1951–57
67-551	14.0	1951–57

500 cc, unit, 65.5 mm
68-266	7.25	1962
68-453	8.5	1963–66
68-434	9.0	1963–70
68-505	10.0	1963–67

650 cc, unit, 75 mm
68-250	7.25	1962
68-819	7.5	1969–72
68-427	8.0	1963–66
68-484	9.0	1963–65
68-749	9.0	1966
68-784	9.0	1967
68-906	9.0	1968–72
68-891	10.0	1967–68
68-742	10.5	1966
68-568	11.0	1963–66

750 cc, unit, 75 mm
71-2710	9.5	1972

7 Camshafts

Part number	Timing				Used
	i.o	i.c	e.o	e.c	
67-690	24	65	60	21.5	A7 1947
67-695	24	65	60	21.5	A7 1947–50, A7ST 1949–50
67-334	30	70	65	25	A7 1951–58, A10 1950–58
67-356	42	62	67	37	A7ST 1951–54, A7SS 1954–62, A7 1959–62, A10 1959–63, A10SF 1953–54, A10RR 1954–57, A10SR 1958–61
67-357	51	68	78	37	A10SR 1961–63, A10RGS 1962–63, A10 Spitfire 1960–63
68-103	40	60	65	35	A50 1962–70, A65 1962–65
68-473	51	68	78	37	All other A50 and A65 models 1964–72

8 Valve spring lengths

Model	Year	Inner	Outer
A7, A7ST, A10	1947–50	1.531	1.875
A7, A7ST, A7SS, A10	1951–63	1.531	1.875
A10RR, A10SR, A10RGS	1954–63	2.000	2.125
A50, A65, A65R	1962–66	1.625	2.031
A50, A65	1967–72	1.437	1.750
A50W	1967	1.500	1.625

All lengths are in inches.

9 Magnetos

All Lucas with automatic advance for A7, A10 and A7ST for 1947–51. All years of A7SS, A10SF, A10RR, A10SR, A10RGS, A10 Spitfire and A7ST from 1952–54 have manual advance.

10 Spark plugs

Model	Year	Listed recommendation Champion	Modern equivalent	
			NGK	Champion
A7	1947–59	L10S	B6HS	L85
	1960–62	L7	B7HCS B7HS	L85
A7ST	1949–51	L10S	B6HS	L85
	1952–54	L11	B7HS	L5
A7SS	1954–59	NA10	B8ES	N3
	1960–62	N3	B8ES	N3
A10	1950–59	L10S	B6HS	L85
	1960–63	L7	B7HCS B7HS	L85
A10SF	1953–54	L11S	B7HS	L5
A10RR	1954–57	NA10	B8ES	N3
A10SR	1958–59	NA10	B8ES	N3
	1960–61	N3	B8ES	N3
	1962–63	N4	B7ES	N4
A10RGS	1962–63	N4	B7ES	N4
A50	1962–70	N4	B7ES	N4
A50W	1966	N3	B8ES	N3
A65	1962–65	N4	B7ES	N4
A65R	196465	N4	B7ES	N4
A65T	1966–70	N4	B7ES	N4
	1971	N3	B8ES	N3
	1972	N4	–7ES	N4
A65L	1966–72	N3	B8ES	N3
A65S	1966–68	N3	B8ES	N3
A65H	1966–07	N3	B8ES	N3
A65F	1968–71	N3	B8ES	N3
A70L	1972	N3	B8ES	N3

209

11 Carburettor settings

Model	Year	Type	Size	Main	Pilot	Slide	Needle pos.	Needle jet
A7	1947–48	276 CG	$\frac{15}{16}$	140		6/3	2	.107
	1947–48	276 CY	$\frac{15}{16}$	140		6/3	3	.107
	1949–50	276 DP	$\frac{15}{16}$	140		6/3	3	.107
	1951–54	276 EU	$\frac{15}{16}$	140		6/4	4	.107
	1955–57	376/4	$\frac{15}{16}$	210	25	$3\frac{1}{2}$	2	.107
	1958–59	376/83	$\frac{15}{16}$	210	25	$3\frac{1}{2}$	2	.1065
	1960–62	376/238	$\frac{15}{16}$	210	25	$3\frac{1}{2}$	2	.106
500 Flash (USA)	1960–62	376/212	$\frac{15}{16}$	210	25	$3\frac{1}{2}$	2	.106
A7ST	1949–50	275AR 275AS	$\frac{7}{8}$	110		5/4	3	.107
	1951–54	276 FD	1	160		6/4	3	.107
A7SS	1954	276 GK	1	160		6/4	3	.107
	1955	376/15	1	270	30	$3\frac{1}{2}$	3	.107
(export)	1955	376/16	1	270	30	$3\frac{1}{2}$	3	.106
	1956–57	376/15	1	270	30	$3\frac{1}{2}$	3	.1065
	1958–59	376/86	1	270	30	$3\frac{1}{2}$	3	.1065
	1960–62	376/239	1	270	30	$3\frac{1}{2}$	3	.106
(USA)	1960–62	376/213	1	270	30	$3\frac{1}{2}$	3	.106
A10	1950	276 EL	$1\frac{1}{16}$	170		6/4	2	.108
	1951–53	276 ER	$1\frac{1}{16}$	170		6/4	2	.108
(plunger)	1954–57	276 GG	$1\frac{1}{16}$	170		6/4	2	.107
	1955–57	376/1	$1\frac{1}{16}$	240	25	4	3	.1065
	1958–59	376/80	$1\frac{1}{16}$	240	25	$3\frac{1}{2}$	3	.1065
	1959	376/014	$1\frac{1}{16}$	240	25	$3\frac{1}{2}$	3	.106
	1960–63	389/45	$1\frac{1}{8}$	250	30	$3\frac{1}{2}$	3	.106
Royal Tourist (USA)	1960–63	389/48	$1\frac{1}{8}$	250	30	$3\frac{7}{8}$	3	.106
A10SF	1953–54	TT9	$1\frac{1}{16}$	360		6	4	.109
A10RR	1954–55	TT9	$1\frac{1}{16}$	340		7	3	.109
	1956–57	TT9	$1\frac{1}{16}$	340		6	4	.109
	1959–60	389/31	$1\frac{1}{8}$	290	30	$3\frac{1}{2}$	3	.106
A10SR	1958	376/80	$1\frac{1}{16}$	240	25	4	3	.1065
	1958–59	389/36	$1\frac{1}{8}$	290	30	$3\frac{1}{2}$	3	.106
(no air filter)	1958–59	389/37	$1\frac{1}{8}$	400	30	$3\frac{1}{2}$	3	.106
	1959	376/97	$1\frac{1}{16}$	240	25	$3\frac{1}{2}$	3	.106
	1960–63	389/46	$1\frac{5}{32}$	420	25	3	2	.106
(USA)	1960–63	389/47	$1\frac{5}{32}$	290	25	3	2	.106
(home and USA)	1960	TT9	$1\frac{5}{32}$	410		7	4	.109
	1963	389/94	$1\frac{5}{32}$	310	25	3	2	.106
A10 Spitfire	1957–58	376/89	$1\frac{1}{16}$	400	25	$3\frac{1}{2}$	4	.106
	1960	TT9	$1\frac{5}{32}$	410		7	4	.109
	1960–61	389/47	$1\frac{5}{32}$	290	25	3	2	.106
A10RGS	1962–63	388/80	$1\frac{5}{32}$	420	25	3	2	.106
	1963	389/94	$1\frac{5}{32}$	310	25	3	2	.104
	1962	389/81	$1\frac{3}{16}$	440	30	4	2	.107

APPENDIX 11 CARBURETTOR SETTINGS

Model	Year	Type	Size	Main	Pilot	Slide	Needle pos.	Needle jet
A50	1962–65	376/282	0	250	25	$3\frac{1}{2}$	3	.106
	1966–67	376/321	1	260	25	$3\frac{1}{2}$	3	.104
	1968–69	626/7	26	200	25	$3\frac{1}{2}$	2	.106
	1970	626/19	26	200	25	$3\frac{1}{2}$	2	.106
(USA)	1963–64	376/284	1	260	25	$3\frac{1}{2}$	3	.106
(USA)	1966–67	376/319	1	260	25	$3\frac{1}{2}$	3	.106
A50C (West US)	1965	376/310	$1\frac{1}{16}$	180	25	$3\frac{1}{2}$	3	.106
(East US)	1965	376/316	$1\frac{1}{16}$	170	25	$3\frac{1}{2}$	2	.106
A50W (home)	1966	389/200 689/227	$1\frac{1}{8}$	200	25	$3\frac{1}{2}$	2	.106
(USA)	1966–67	389/230 689/230	$1\frac{1}{8}$	190	25	$3\frac{1}{2}$	2	.106
A65	1962	389/67	$1\frac{1}{8}$	300	25	$3\frac{1}{2}$	2	.106
	1963	389/67	$1\frac{1}{8}$	300	25	3	2	.106
	1964–65	389/67	$1\frac{1}{8}$	300	25	$3\frac{1}{2}$	3	.106
(USA)	1963–64	389/70	$1\frac{1}{8}$	310	25	3	2	.107
A65R	1964–65	389/201	$1\frac{11}{16}$	300	25	$3\frac{1}{2}$	3	.106
A65T/R	1964	389/202	$1\frac{1}{8}$	310	25	$3\frac{1}{2}$	3	.106
A65T	1966–67	389/233	$1\frac{1}{8}$	300	25	$3\frac{1}{2}$	3	.106
	1968–69	928/2	28	230	20	$3\frac{1}{2}$	1	.106
	1970	928/6	28	230		$3\frac{1}{2}$	1	.106
	1971	928/17	28	230		$3\frac{1}{2}$	1	.106
	1972	928/11	28	230		$3\frac{1}{2}$	1	.106
(USA)	1966–67	389/234	$1\frac{1}{8}$	310	25	$3\frac{1}{2}$	3	.106
A65L/R, A65S/H	1964–65	389/206	$1\frac{1}{8}$	220	25	$3\frac{1}{2}$	3	.106
A65L, A65H	1966–67	389/229 689/229	$1\frac{5}{32}$	270	25	3	3	.106
(USA)	1966–67	389/228 689/228	$1\frac{5}{32}$	270	25	3	3	.106
A65L	1968–69	930/21	30	190	20	$2\frac{1}{2}$	2	.106
A65F	1968	930/22						
A65F	1969	930/24 930/25	30	190	25	$2\frac{1}{2}$	3	.106
A65L, A65F	1970	930/34 930/35	30	180		3	1	.106
A65L	1971–72	930/70 930/71	30	220		3	1	.105
A65F	1971	930/72 930/73	30	230		3	1	.106
A65S (MkII)	1966	GP2	$1\frac{5}{32}$	250	25	5	3	.109
(MkIII)	1967	932/1	32	190	20	3	2	.107
(MkIV)	1968	932/2						
A70L	1972	930/78 930/79	30	250		3	1	.106

211

12 Capacities

Petrol tank (Imp. gall.)

Model	Year	Size
A7	1947–49	3.0
	1950–54	3.5
A7 s/a	1954–62	4.0
A7ST	1949–54	3.5
A7SS	1954–62	2 or 4
A10	1950–57	4.25
A10 s/a	1954–63	2 or 4
A10SF	1953–54	2.0
A10RR	1954–55	4.0
	1956–57	2 or 4
A10SR	1958–63	2 or 4
A10RGS	1962–63	2, 4 or 5
A10 Spitfire	1960–63	3.0
A50	1962–65	4.0
A50RS	1966	3.5
	1967–68	2.75
	1969–70	2.75 or 4
A50W	1966	1.87
A65	1962–65	4.0
A65T, A65L	1966	3.5
	1967	2.75
	1968–70	2.75 or 4
	1971–72	2.5 or 4
A65SS	1966	1.87 or 5
	1967–68	1.87 or 4
A65H	1966–67	1.87
A65F	1968	1.87
	1969–71	2.5

Part number	Badge	Capacity	Used	Fibreglass
68-8003	P	4	1962–65	
68-8042	R	2	1963–65	
68-8065	P	3.5	1964, 1966–7	
68-8066	R	2	1965	
68-8082		2	1965	yes
68-8093		2	1966	yes
68-8094		2	1966	yes
68-8095		2	1967	yes
68-8105	P	2	1966	
68-8107	P	2	1966	
68-8145	P	2	1967–68	
68-8147		2	1967	yes
68-8150		2	1967	yes
68-8165		5	1967–68	yes
68-8188	P	2.8	1968–70	
68-8189	P	4	1968–70	
82-8446		2	1968	yes
82-9609		2.5	1969	yes
82-9801		2.5	1970	
83-2262	BSA	2.5	1971–72	
83-2881	BSA	2.5	1971	
83-4316		4	1972	

Badges: P – pear shape, R – round, BSA – winged

Oil tank (Imp. pint)

1947–57	Rigid and plunger models – 4
1954–63	S/a models – 5.5
1962–65	Unit models – 5.5
1966–72	Unit models – 5

Primary chaincase

1947–51	284 cc or 0.5 pint
1952–53	90 cc or 0.17 pint
1954–57	Plunger models 115 cc or 0.2 pint
1954–63	S/a models 225 cc or 0.4 pint
1962–72	Unit models 142 cc or 0.25 pint

Gearbox

1947–55	568 cc or 1 pint
1956–61	400 cc or 0.7 pint
1962–63	S/a models 425 cc or 0.75 pint
1962–72	Unit models 500 cc or 0.875 pint

Front forks

1947–51	142 cc or 0.25 pint
1952–63	212 cc or 0.375 pint
1962–72	Unit models 190 cc or 0.33 pint

13 Transmission

Gearbox internal ratios

Gearbox	Date fitted	Mainshaft				Layshaft				3rd	2nd	1st
		4	3	2	1	4	3	2	1			
1 Pre-unit standard	1947–63	26	24	20	16	17	19	23	27	1.211	1.759	2.581
2 Pre-unit wide	1947–57	26	22	18	14	17	21	25	29	1.460	2.124	3.168
3 Spitfire	1960–63	25	22	19	16	18	21	24	27	1.326	1.754	2.344
4 RGS (RRT2)	1962–63	25	24	22	19	18	19	21	24	1.099	1.326	1.754
5 Unit	1962	28	26	22	17	20	22	26	31	1.185	1.655	2.553
6 Unit standard	1963–72	23	26	22	14	17	22	26	26	1.145	1.599	2.513
7 Unit close	1965	23	26	23	16	17	22	25	24	1.145	1.471	2.029
8 Unit close	1967–72	23	23	22	16	17	25	18	24	1.107	1.471	2.029

Sprockets, boxes and overall gear ratios

Semi- and pre-unit models

Model	Year	Sprockets				Overall ratio	Box number
		E	C	G	R		
A7	1947–54	27	54	18	46	5.111	1
A7 s/a	1954–62	18	43	19	42	5.281	1
A7 s/c	1947–54	27	54	18	49	5.444	1
A7 s/a s/c	1958–62	18	43	17	42	5.902	1
A7ST	1949–50	27	54	18	46	5.111	1
	1951–54	27	54	18	45	5.000	1
A7ST s/c	1949–54	27	54	18	49	5.444	1
A7SS	1954–62	18	43	19	42	5.281	1
A7SS s/c	1958–62	18	43	17	42	5.902	1
A10	1950–57	27	54	19	42	4.421	1
A10 s/a	1954–63	21	43	19	42	4.526	1
A10 s/c	1950–57	27	54	19	49	5.128	1
A10 s/a s/c	1958–63	18	43	19	42	5.281	1
A10SF	1953–54	27	54	19	42	4.421	1
A10SF s/c	1953–54	27	54	19	49	5.158	1
A10R	1954–63	21	43	19	42	4.526	1
A10R s/c	1958–63	18	43	19	42	5.281	1
A10 Spitfire	1960–63	17	43	16	42	6.640	3
A10RGS	1962	23	43	19	46	4.526	4
	1963	22	43	19	46	4.732	4

Optional gearbox sprockets, semi-unit engines, 18 and 19T for 1947–57. For pre-unit models 16, 17, 18 and 19T gearbox sprockets 1954–63 and 17, 18, 21, 22 and 23T engine sprockets also. Wide gearbox ratios listed 1947–50 and 1954–57. RGS gearbox options as Gold Star: standard, wide, close or very close.

Unit models

Model	Year	Sprockets				Overall ratio	Box number
		E	C	G	R		
A50	1962	28	58	17	42	5.118	5
	1963–65	28	58	17	42	5.118	6
	1966–70	28	58	18	47	5.409	6
A50 s/c	1962	28	58	16	42	5.437	5
	1963–65	28	58	16	43	5.567	6
	1966–70	28	58	17	47	5.727	6
A50C	1964–65	28	58	17	42	5.118	6 or 7
	1965	28	58	21	42	4.143	6 or 7
	1966	28	58	17	47	5.727	6
A50W	1966–67	28	58	18	47	5.409	6 or 8
A65	1962	28	58	20	42	4.350	5
	1963–65	28	58	20	42	4.350	6
A65 s/c	1962	28	58	17	42	5.118	5
	1963–65	28	58	17	42	5.118	6
A65R	1964–65	28	58	20	42	4.350	6
A65T/R	1964	28	58	19	42	4.579	6
A65T	1966–72	28	58	20	47	4.868	6
A65T s/c	1966–71	28	58	18	47	5.409	6
A65L/R	1964–65	28	58	19	42	4.579	6
A65LC	1965	28	58	19	42	4.579	6 or 7
A65L	1965	28	58	19	42	4.579	6 or 7
	1966–72	28	58	20	47	4.868	6 or 8
A65L s/c	1969–71	28	58	18	47	5.409	6
A65S	1966	28	58	21	47	4.636	6
	1967–68	28	58	20	47	4.868	6 or 8
A65S/H	1964–65	28	58	21	42	4.143	6
	1966	28	58	20	47	4.868	6
	1967	28	58	17	47	5.727	6
A65 S/H (West)	1966	28	58	17	47	5.727	6
A65F	1968–70	28	58	20	47	4.868	6
	1971	28	58	18	47	5.409	6
A70	1972	28	58	21	47	4.636	6

Optional gearbox sprockets:
1962	17 and 20T
1963–64	16, 17 and 20T
1965	16, 17, 19, 20 and 21T
1966–70	17 to 21T
1971–72	18 to 21T

Before using check that it will fit your engine year.

Chains

Primary

Semi-unit: 0.375 pitch × 0.250 roller diameter × 0.225 in. between inner plates duplex – 80 links, triplex to order
A10SF and unit: 0.375 × 0.250 × 0.225 in. triplex – 80 links
Pre-unit: 0.5 × 0.335 × 0.305 in.

A7, A7SS	1954–55	67 pitches
	1956–58	68
	1959–62	67
A10, A10R	1954–55	67
	1956	68
	1957–63	69
A10 s/c	1958	68
	1959–63	67
A10RGS	1962	69
	1963	70

Final 0.625 × 0.400 × 0.380 in.

		solo	sidecar
A7 rigid	1947–51	102	103
A7 plunger	1949–50	102	103
	1951–54	102	104
A7, A7SS s/a	1954–55	96	—
	1956–62	98	97
A7ST	1949–54	102	104
A10 rigid	1950–51	100	104
A10 plunger	1950–57	100	104
A10 s/a	1954–55	97	—
	1956–59	98	98
	1960–63	97	98
A10R	1954–55	97	—
	1956–59	98	—
	1960–63	97	—
A10RGS	1962–63	99	—
A50	1962–65	98	—
	1966–70	105	—
A50C	1965	103	—
A50W	1966	105	—
A65	1962–64	100	98
	1965	99	98
A65R	1964	100	98
	1965	99	—
A65T	1966–70	106	103
	1971–72	110	—
A65L	1965	103	—
	1966–70	106	—
	1971–72	110	—
A65S	1966–68	106	—
A65H	1966–67	106	—
A65F	1968–70	106	—
	1971	110	—
A70L	1972	110	—

14 Wheels

Brake sizes

Fronts varied a good deal more than rears with three diameters and five widths to be found. At the rear all were 7 in. diameter and width was 1.5 in. for 1956–57 and 1.12 in. for all other years from 1947 to 1972. Front brake usage was:

7 × 1.12 in.	A7 1947–52 and 1958–62, A7ST 1949–50, A50 1962–64
7 × 1.5 in.	A7, A7SS, A10 s/a, A10RR 1956–57
8 × 1.12 in.	A7SS, A10, A10SR 1958–63, A10 Spitfire 1960–63, A50 1965, A65 1962–65, A65R 1964–65
8 × 1.37 in.	A7 1953–55, A7ST 1951–54, A7SS 1954–55, A10 plunger 1950–57, A10 s/a 1954–55, A10SF 1953–54, A10RR 1954–55, A10RGS 1962–63, A50 1966–68, A50C 1964–65, A50W 1966–67, A65T/R, A65L/R, A65SH 1964–65, A65T 1966–68, A65L 1965–67, A65H 1966–67
8 × 1.62 in.	A50, A65T 1969–70, A65L 1968–70, A65S 1968, A65F 1968–70
8.0 in.	A65T, A65L 1971–72, A65F 1971, A70L 1972
190 mm × 2.0 in.	A10RGS 1962–63, A65S 1966–67

Rims – part numbers and use

Model	Year	Front	Rear
A7	1947–48	67-6005	67-6005
	1949–52	65-5871	67-6005
	1953–55	67-5543	67-6005
	1956–57	42-5637	42-5637
	1958–62	42-5810	42-5810
A7ST	1949–50	65-5871	67-6005
	1951–54	67-5543	67-6005
A7SS	1954–55	67-5543	67-6005
	1956–57	42-5637	42-5637
	1958–62	42-5810	42-5810
A10	1950–57	67-5543	67-6005
	1956–57	42-5637	42-5637
	1958–63	42-5810	42-5810
A10SF	1953–54	67-5543	67-6005
A10RR	1954–55	67-5543	67-6005
	1956–57	42-5649	42-5644
A10SR	1958–63	42-5866	42-5866
A10 Spitfire	1960–63	42-5810	42-5833
A10RGS	1962–63	42-5514 / 42-5901 / 42-5903 / 42-5905 / 42-5907	42-5866 / 42-6379 / 42-6377
A50	1962–65	41-6006	41-6006
	1966	67-5543	65-6306
	1967–68	68-5556	42-6371
	1969–70	37-1230	42-6371
A50C	1965	42-5514	42-6371
A50W	1966	68-5548	42-6371
	1967	68-5556	42-6371
A65	1962–65	41-6006	41-6006
A65R	1964–65	41-6007	41-6007
A65T/R	1964	41-6007	41-6007
A65T	1966	67-5543	65-6306
	1967–68	68-5556	42-6371
	1969–70	37-1230	42-6371
	1971–72	37-3818	37-3784
A65L/R	1964–65	42-5514	65-6306
A65L	1966	67-5543	65-6306
	1967	68-5556	42-6371
	1968	42-5810	42-6371
	1969–70	37-1230	42-6371
	1971–72	37-3818	37-3784
A65S	1966–67	42-5905	68-6086
	1968	37-2207	68-6086
A65 S/H	1965	42-5514	42-6371
A65H	1966	68-5548	42-6371
	1967	68-5556	42-6371
A65F	1968	42-5810	42-6371
	1969–70	37-1230	42-6371
	1971	37-3818	37-3784
A70L	1972	37-3818	37-3784

Note: RGS front rim type depends on hub.

APPENDIX 14 WHEELS

Rims – sizes

Part number	Size	Used
37-1230	WM2-19	1969–70
37-2207	WM2-19 (LA)	1968
37-3784	WM3-18	1971–72
37-3818	WM2-19	1971–72
41-6006	WM2-18	1962–65
41-6007	WM2-18	1964–65
42-5514	WM2-19	1962–65
42-5637	WM2-19	1956–57
42-5644	WM2-19	1956–57
42-5649	WM2-19	1956–57
42-5810	WM2-19	1958–63, 1968
42-5833	WM3-19	1960–63
42-5866	WM2-19	1958–63
42-5901	WM1-19 (LA)	1962–63
42-5903	WM1-19 (LA)	1962–63
42-5905	WM2-19 (LA)	1962–63, 1966–67
42-5907	WM2-19 (LA)	1962–63
42-6371	WM3-18	1965–70
42-6377	WM2-19 (LA)	1962–63
42-6379	WM2-18 (LA)	1962–63
65-5871	WM2-19	1949–52
65-6306	WM2-19	1964–66
67-5543	WM2-19	1951–57, 1966
67-6005	WM2-19	1947–57
68-5548	WM3-19	1966
68-5556	WM2-19	1967–68
68-6086	WM3-18 (LA)	1966–68

Tyre equivalents

Section

Original	Low profile	Metric
3.00	3.60	90/90
3.25	3.60	90/90
3.50	4.10	100/90
4.00	4.25/85	110/90

Revolutions per mile

3.50 × 18	825
4.00 × 18	812
3.50 × 19	795
4.00 × 19	783
3.50 × 19 s/c	803

Data from Avon Tyres Ltd or by calculation.
Sidecar tyre included for reference from modern list.

Security bolts

Fitted as part 68-9575 to A50, A65T and A65L in 1967–69, A50W and A65H in 1967, and A65F in 1968–69. Fitted as part 37-3468 to A65T and A65L in 1970–72, A65F in 1970–71 and A50 in 1970.

Tyre sizes

Model	Year	Front	Rear
A7	1947–62	3.25 × 19	3.50 × 19
A7ST	1949–54	3.25 × 19	3.50 × 19
A7SS	1954–62	3.25 × 19	3.50 × 19
A10	1950–63	3.25 × 19	3.50 × 19
A10SF	1953–54	3.35 × 19	3.50 × 19
A10RR	1954–57	3.25 × 19	3.50 × 19
A10SR	1958–63	3.25 × 19	3.50 × 19
A10 Spitfire	1960–63	3.25 × 19	4.00 × 19
A10RGS	1962–63	3.00 × 19	3.50 × 19
		3.25 × 19	
A50	1962–65	3.25 × 18	3.50 × 18
	1966	3.25 × 19	3.50 × 19
	1967–70	3.25 × 19	4.00 × 18
A50C	1965	3.25 × 19	4.00 × 18
A50W	1966–67	3.50 × 19	4.00 × 18
A65	1962–65	3.25 × 18	3.50 × 18
A65R	1964–65	3.25 × 18	3.50 × 18
A65T	1966	3.25 × 19	3.50 × 19
	1967–72	3.25 × 19	4.00 × 18
A65L	1965–66	3.25 × 19	3.50 × 19
	1967–72	3.25 × 19	4.00 × 18
A65S	1966–68	3.25 × 19	4.00 × 18
A65H	1966–67	3.50 × 19	4.00 × 18
A65F	1968–70	3.50 × 19	4.00 × 18
	1971	3.25 × 19	4.00 × 18
A70L	1972	3.25 × 19	4.00 × 18

15 Headlamp, ammeter, switches

These varied and moved about over the years, and while much of the data given below is also to be found in the main text a summary may help. The headlamp may have a separate shell by itself or with a cowl or be fitted to a nacelle.

A7
1947 Separate shell with small panel carrying ammeter and light switch. Horn button on front brake lever block and dipswitch on clutch block. Speedometer in tank.
1948–50 As 1947 except speedometer on fork crown.
1951 Cut-out added on left or centre of handlebar.
1952 Underslung pilot lamp.
1953–54 Cowl added around shell with ammeter on right, speedometer central and light switch on left. Horn and dipswitch as 1947, cut-out as 1951, underslung pilot lamp.
1955 As 1953 except pilot in main reflector and steering head lock added.
1956–57 Combined horn button and dipswitch on left.
1958–59 Nacelle with ammeter on left, central speedometer and light switch on right. Combined horn button and dipswitch on left. Cut-out on bar centre.
1960–62 Horn button, dipswitch and cut-out in one ring-shaped assembly on left bar, otherwise as 1958.

A7ST
1949–50 As 1948 A7.
1951–54 As A7, year by year.

A7SS
1954–62 As A7, year by year.

A10
1950–63 As A7, year by year.

A10SF
1953–54 As 1952 A7.

A10RR
1954 As 1952 A7.
1955 As 1954 except pilot in main reflector and steering head lock added.
1956–57 Combined horn button and dipswitch on left.

A10SR
1958–59 As 1958 A7 for home market. For export as 1948 A7 except horn and dip controls combined on left. Speedometer by itself and central or on left if with rev-counter, which went on right.
1960–63 Change as for A7.

A10RGS
1962–63 As export A10SR.

A50
1962–65 Nacelle with ammeter on right, central speedometer and two switches on left. Front one for ignition, rear for lights. Ring-mounted horn and dip unit on left.
1966–67 Separate shell with ammeter in centre and light switch behind it. Ignition switch in steering head gusset plate on left side. Ring horn and dip unit on left.
1968 As 1966 except light switch now toggle type but in same position, and red warning light for low oil pressure added to left of ammeter.
1969–70 As 1968 except red warning light now on right and green one for main beam on the left.

A50C, A50CC
1965 Separate shell with ammeter in centre, ignition switch on right and light switch on left. Ring horn and dip on left bar.

A50CC (off-road)
1964–65 Small separate shell with light and dip switches mounted in it.

A50W
1966–67 Cut-out button only.

A65
1962–65 As 1962 A50.

A65R
1964–65 As 1965 A50C.

A65T/R
1964 As 1965 A50C.

A65T
1966–70 As A50, year by year.
1971–72 Shallow shell, no ammeter, ignition switch in right side panel, turn-type light switch in shell top and three warning lights in top rear of shell. Light colours amber for turn signals, red for low oil pressure and green for main beam. Switches for turn signals, engine kill, dip and horn in bar lever blocks.

APPENDIX 15 HEADLAMP, AMMETER, SWITCHES

A65L/R
1964–65   As 1965 A50C.

A65LC
1965   As 1965 A50C.

A65L
1965   As 1965 A50C.
1966–70   As A50, year by year.
1971–72   As 1971 A65T.

A65S
1966–68   As A50, year by year.

A65H
1966–67   Cut-out button only.

A65F
1968   As 1968 A50 except horn button fitted by itself and dipswitch mounted in shell.
1969–70   As A50, year by year.
1971   As 1971 A65T.

A70L
1972   As 1971 A65T.

Notes

1 The model type indicated in the left column applies to all variants unless a further line is included for them. Thus the first listing is 'cylinder block A7', which covers A7, A7ST and A7SS. The next is A10 alone and the one after covers A10RR, A10SR and A10RGS.

2 A stroke between part numbers indicates that a change occurred during the year, as for the A7 crankshaft in 1947. This went from 67-621 to 67-615.

3 An ampersand (&) between numbers indicates that both were fitted.

4 A stroke plus single- or two-digit number indicates two parts, usually left and right, such as side covers 68-9212 and 68-9233 represented as 68-9212/33.

16 Part numbers

Pre-unit	1947	1948	1949	1950	1951
Cylinder block A7	67-50	←	←	←	67-378
A10				67-253	←
A10R					
Cylinder head A7	67-24	←	←	←	67-380
A7ST			67-182	←	67-524
A7SS					
A10				67-250	←
A10SF, A10R					
Inlet valve A7	67-29	←	←	←	67-394
A7ST/SS			67-189	←	67-531
A10				67-323	←
A10SF, A10R					
Exhaust valve A7	67-30	←	←	←	67-395
A7ST/SS			67-190	←	67-532
A10				67-324	←
A10SF, A10R					
Valve caps A7	65-209	←	←	←	
Valve guides A7, A10	67-31/32	←	←	←	67-31
A7SS					
A10SF, A10R					
Valve spring inner A7, A10	31-108	←	←	←	67-440
A10SF, A10R					
Valve spring outer A7, A10	31-106	←	←	←	67-439
A10SF, A10R					
Crank & flywheel A7	67-621/615	67-615	←	←	67-384
A7SS					
A10				67-664	←
A10R					
Crankcase time A7	67-1229/31	67-1231	←	←	
drive A7	67-1227	←	←	←	
time A7, A10 pl				67-293	67-455
drive A7, A10 pl				67-291	67-453
time A7 s/a					
drive A7 s/a					
time A10 s/a					
drive A10 s/a					
time A10R					
drive A10R					
Con rod left A7	67-219/228	67-228	←	←	67-386
right A7	67-228	67-228	←	←	67-389
left A10				67-268	67-317
right A10				67-268	←
left A10R					
right A10R					

Notes

1 The model type indicated in the left-hand column applies to all variants unless a further line is included for them. Thus the first listing is 'cylinder block A7', which covers A7, A7ST and A7SS. The next is A10 alone and the one after covers A10RR, A10SR and A10RGS.

2 A stroke between part numbers may indicate that a change occurred during the year, as for the A7 crankshaft in 1947. This went from 67-621 to 67-615. Or see note 4.

3 An ampersand (&) between numbers indicates that both were fitted.

4 A stroke plus a single- or two-digit number indicates two parts, usually left and right, for example side covers 68-9212 and 68-9233 are represented as 68-9212/33.

1952	1953	1954	1955	1956	1957	1958	1959	1960	1961	1962	1963
←	←	67-1070	←	←	←	←	←	←	←	←	
←	←	67-1074	←	←	←	67-1210	←	←	←	←	←
		67-1210	←	←	←	←	←	←	←	←	←
←	←	67-1061	←	←	←	←	←	←	←	←	
←	←	67-1063									
		67-1101	←	67-1121	←	←	←	←	←	←	
←	←	67-1065	←	←	←	←	←	42-0180	←	←	←
	67-965	←		67-1125	←	←	←	67-1548	←	←	←
←	←	←	←	←	←	67-740	←	←	←	←	
←	←	←	←	←	←	67-740	←	←	←	←	
←	←	←	←	←	←	67-742	←	←	←	←	←
	67-968	←	←	←	←	←	←	67-1551	←	←	←
←	←	←	←	←	←	67-741	←	←	←	←	
←	←	←	←	←	←	67-741	←	←	←	←	
←	←	←	←	←	←	67-743	←	←	←	←	←
	67-967	←	←	←	←	←	←	←	←	←	←
←	←	←	←	←	←	←	←				
		67-1110	←	67-1140	←	67-1110	←				
	67-931 & 932	←		67-1140	←	67-31	←				
←	←	←	←	←	←	←	←	←	←	←	←
	67-957	67-883	←	←	←	←	←	←	←	←	←
←	←	←	←	←	←	←	←	←	←	←	←
	67-956	67-884	←	←	←	←	←	←	←	←	←
		67-383	←	←	←	67-384	←	←	←	←	
		67-383	←	67-384	←	←	←	←	←	←	
←	←	67-663	←	←	←	67-1216	←	←	←	←	←
		67-1216	←	←	←	←	←	←	←	←	←
←	←	←	←	←	←						
←	←	←	←	←	←						
		67-1087	←	←	←	←	←	←	←	←	
		67-1085	←	←	←	←	←	←	←	←	
		67-1087	←	←	←	67-1080	←	←	←	←	←
		67-1085	←	←	←	67-1079	←	←	←	←	←
				67-1080	←	←	←	←	←	←	←
				67-1079	←	←	←	←	←	←	←
←	←	67-1201	←	←	←	←	←	←	←	←	
←	←	67-1202	←	←	←	←	←	←	←	←	
←	←	67-1203	←	←	←	67-1205	←	←	←	←	←
←	←	67-1204	←	←	←	67-1206	←	←	←	←	←
		67-1205	←	←	←	←	←	←	←	←	←
		67-1206	←	←	←	←	←	←	←	←	←

Pre-unit	1947	1948	1949	1950	1951
Timing main bush	67-646/48	67-648	←	←	←
Drive main race – ball	67-1240	←	←	←	
roller				67-670	←
Oil pump	67-1381	←	←	←	←
A10SR					
Timing cover inner	67-124	67-142	←	←	
				67-284	←
A10SR					
outer A7	67-128	67-146	←	←	
A7ST			67-157	←	
				67-287	←
(rpm)					
Exhaust pipe right A7	67-2675	←	←	←	←
left A7	67-2679	←	←	←	←
right A7 s/a					
left A7 s/a					
right A10 pl				67-2720	←
left A10 pl				47-2722	←
right A10 s/a					
left A10 s/a					
right A10 Spitfire					
left A10 Spitfire					
right A10SF, RGS					
left RGS					
siamese RGS					
Silencer right A7 rigid	67-2700	←	←	←	←
left A7	67-2701	←	←	←	←
A7, A10 pl			67-2711	←	←
right A7, A10 s/a					
left A7, A10 s/a					
right A10SR					
left A10SR					
A10SF, A10RGS					
track A10RGS					
Frame XA7-101 to 1100	67-4000				
XA7-1101 on	67-4050	←			
front			67-4056	←	←
rear rigid			67-4070	←	67-4102
plunger			67-4094	←	←
s/a					
A10RGS					
Rear fork s/a					
Frame front & rear A10SF					

APPENDIX 16 PART NUMBERS

1952	1953	1954	1955	1956	1957	1958	1959	1960	1961	1962	1963
←	←	←	←	←	←	67-790	←	←	←	←	←
←	←	←	←	←	←	←	←	←	←	←	←
←	←	←	←	67-1402	←	←	←	←	←	←	←
								42-0155	←	←	←
←	←	←	←	←	←	←	←	←	←	←	←
								42-153	←	←	←
←	←	←	←	←	←	←	←	←	←	←	←
	67-712	←	←	←	←	←	←				
←	←	←									
←	←	←									
		42-2760	←	←	←	42-2952	←	←	←	←	
		42-2763	←	←	←	42-2955	←	←	←	←	
←	←	←	←	←	←						
←	←	←	←	←	←						
		42-2766	←	←	←	42-2957	←	←	←	←	←
		42-2768	←	←	←	42-2959	←	←	←	←	
								42-2690	←	←	←
								42-2692	←	←	←
	67-2770	←								42-2635	←
										42-2644	←
										42-2640	←
←	←	←	←	←	←						
		42-2774	←	←	←	42-2963	←	42-2651	←	←	←
		42-2775	←	←	←	42-2964	←	42-2652	←	←	←
										42-2653	←
										42-2654	←
	67-2774	←								42-2649	←
										42-2627	←
←	67-4189	←	←	←	←						
←	←	←	←	←	←						
		42-4307	←	42-4335	←	42-4438	←	42-4483	←	←	←
								42-4677	←	←	←
										42-4688	←
		42-4102	←	42-4316	←	42-4450	←	←	←	←	←
	67-4141 & 42	←									

223

Pre-unit	1947	1948	1949	1950	1951
Front forks A7	67-5005	←	65-5400	67-5054	←
A7ST			65-5400	67-5054	67-5060
A10 pl				67-5049	←
A7, A10 s/a					
A7SS					
A10R					
A10SF, A10 Spitfire					
RGS					
RGS					
RGS					
Fork cowl/nacelle					
Front hub 7 in.	67-6021	←	65-5876	←	←
A10 pl				67-5547	←
s/a					
s/a					
brake drum	67-5530	←			
Rear hub rigid	67-6021	←	67-6136	←	←
pl			67-6126	←	←
s/a					
Drum and sprocket A7 solo	67-6040	←	67-6121	←	←
A7, A10 s/c	67-6050	←	67-6122	←	←
A7 pl solo			67-6123	←	←
A7, A10 pl s/c			67-6124	←	←
A10 rigid, solo				67-6149	←
A10 pl solo				67-6150	←
A7ST solo			67-6121	←	67-6154
A7, A10 s/a					
sprocket					
Front mudguard	67-6526	←	65-6605	←	←
			67-6543	←	←
A10SF, s/a					
RGS					
RGS					
Rear mudguard	67-6752	←	←	←	←
			67-6771	←	←
RGS					
Saddle	67-9050	←	←	67-9053	←
				67-9054	←
police					
Dualseat					67-9087

APPENDIX 16 PART NUMBERS

1952	1953	1954	1955	1956	1957	1958	1959	1960	1961	1962	1963
67-5077	←	67-5103									
67-5077	←	67-5103									
67-5077	←	67-5103	←	←	←						
		42-5005	42-5033	42-5048	←	42-5071	←	42-5127	←	←	←
		42-5005	42-5033	42-5047	←	42-5071	←	42-5127	←	←	
		42-5049	←	←	←	42-5069	←	42-5128	←	←	←
	67-5060	←						42-5314	←	←	←
										42-5146	←
										42-5147	←
										42-5148	←
	67-5084	←	←	←	←	42-5094	←	←	←	←	←
←											
←	←	66-5556	←	←	←						
		67-5547	←	42-5600	←	42-5805	←	←	←	←	←
						42-5807	←	←	←	←	←
←	←	←	←	←	←						
		67-6136	←	42-6088	←	42-6309	←	←	←	←	←
←	←	←									
←	←	←	←	←	←						
←	←	←	←	←	←						
←	←	←									
		67-6149	←								
				42-6069	←	42-6333	←	42-6331	←	←	←
←	←	←						42-6544	←	←	←
←	←	←	←	←	←	←	←	42-6553	←	←	←
	67-6556	←	←	←	←	←	←	42-6555	←	←	←
										42-6535	←
										42-6536	←
←	67-6841	←	←	←	←						
←								42-6904	←	←	←
			42-6841	42-6856	←	←	←	42-6906	←	←	←
	67-6861	←						42-6885	←	←	←
										42-6911	←
←	←	42-9032	←	←	←						
←	←	←	←	←	←	42-9032	←	←	←	←	←
								42-9134	←	←	
←	←	67-9104	←	←	←						
		42-9072	←	←	←	←	←	42-9230	←	←	←
								42-9210	←	←	←

Pre-unit	1947	1948	1949	1950	1951
Petrol tank A7	67-8010	67-8015	←	67-8045	67-8047
A7ST			67-8016	67-8046	67-8047
A10				67-8072	←
(4 gal) A7 s/a					
A7SS					
A10 s/a					
A10R					
(2 gal) A7, A10R					
A7SS					
A10					
A10SF, 1960 opt.					
(Alloy) RGS					
RGS					
(4 gal) RGS					
(5 gal) RGS					
Oil tank rigid, A10SF	67-8320	←	←	←	←
pl.			67-8334	←	←
s/a					
Centre stand XA7-101 to 1100	67-4821				
XA7-1101 on	67-4843	←	←	←	67-4816
s/a					
(siamezed pipes)					
Chainguard lower	67-7765	←	←	←	←
top rigid	67-7725	←	←	67-7726	←
pl.			67-7777	67-7778	←
s/a					
Spitfire					
RGS					
Toolbox rigid	65-9080	←	←	←	←
pl.			67-9007	67-9002	←
s/a					
inc. RGS					
A10SF					

APPENDIX 16 PART NUMBERS

1952	1953	1954	1955	1956	1957	1958	1959	1960	1961	1962	1963
←	67-8104	67-8126									
←	67-8104	←									
←	67-8105	←	←	←	←						
		42-8046	←	←	←	42-8102	←	42-8118	←	←	
		42-8047	←	←	←	42-8103	←	42-8118	←	←	
		42-8048	←	←	←	42-8102	←	42-8118	←	←	←
		42-8046	←	←	←	42-8102	←	42-8118	←	←	←
		42-8043	←	←	←	←	←	←	←	←	←
		42-8044	←	←	←	←	←	←	←	←	
		42-8045	←	←	←	42-8043	←	←	←	←	←
	67-8114	←						42-8125	←	←	←
										42-8055	←
										42-8056	←
										42-8107	←
										42-8090	←
	67-8362	←									
←	←	←	←	←	←						
		42-8367	←	←	←	←	←	←	←	←	←
←	←	←	←	←	←						
		42-4725	←	←	←	42-4736	←	42-4761	←	←	←
								42-4762	←	←	←
←	←	←	←	←	←						
		42-7701	←	42-7730	←	←	←	←	←	←	←
								42-7732	←	←	←
										42-7706	←
←	←	←	←	←	←						
		42-9038	←	←	←	←	←	←	←	←	←
								42-9262	←	←	←
	67-9014	←									

227

Unit	1962	1963	1964
Cylinder block A50	68-0048	←	←
A65	68-0043	←	←
Cylinder head A50	68-0089	←	←
A65	68-0069	←	←
Rocker box lid	68-0139	←	←
Inlet valve A50	68-0168	←	←
A65	68-0156	←	←
Exhaust valve A50	68-0169	←	←
A65	68-0157	←	←
Two port head A50			
A65			
Crankshaft	68-0175	←	←
A70			
Flywheel A50	68-0177	68-0201	←
A65	68-0177	←	←
A70			
Connecting rod – right	68-0053	←	←
left	68-0053	←	←
A70			
A70			
Crankcase	68-0006	←	←
A70			
Drive main race	67-1240	←	←
Timing main bush	68-0015	←	←
A70			
thrust washer			
A70			
Timing cover inner	68-0212	←	68-0529
(rpm)			68-0534
outer	68-0227	←	←
Points cover	68-0320	←	←
Oil pump	68-0283	←	←
			68-0282
Primary chaincase	68-0240	←	←
side cap			
Frame	68-4008	68-4128	←
A70			
(right hand chair)	68-4009	68-4129	←
(comp)			
A65L/R			
Rear fork (cable brake)	68-4201	←	←
(rod brake)	68-4220	←	←
(comp)			

APPENDIX 16 PART NUMBERS

1965	1966	1967	1968	1969	1970	1971	1972
←	←	←	68-888	←	71-1196		
←	←	←	68-886	←	71-1195	71-1464	←
←	68-0713	68-848	68-881	←	←		
←	68-0704	←	68-844	←	←	71-2307	←
←	←	68-830	←	←	←	71-2333	←
←	68-0661	←	←	←	←		
←	68-0665	←	←	←	←	←	←
←	68-0662	←	←	←	←		
←	68-0663	←	←	←	←	←	←
68-0467	68-0695	68-846					
68-0465	68-0700	68-834	68-879	←	←	71-2309	←
68-0179	68-0734	←	←	←	←	71-1346	←
							71-2669
←	68-0680	←	←	←	←		
←	68-0676	←	←	←	71-1153	71-1347	←
							71-2687
←	←	←	←	←	71-1105	←	←
←	68-0649	←	←	←	71-1106	←	←
							71-2677
							71-2673
←	67-0726	68-863	70-7707	70-9097	71-1108	←	←
							71-2713
←	68-0625	←	←	←	←	←	←
←	68-0636	68-657	←	←	←	←	←
							71-2697
	68-0685	←	←	←	←	←	←
							71-2681
←	68-0774	68-868	←	70-9482	71-1118	71-2277	←
←	←	←	←	←	71-1131	71-2280	←
←	←	←	←	70-9126	←	←	←
←							
←	←	←	68-941	←	71-1135	71-2449	71-2413
←	68-0720	68-837	←	70-9112	71-1044	←	←
		68-839	←	70-9114	←	←	←
←	61-4188	68-4271	82-8281	82-9567	83-1576	83-2802	←
							83-4797
←							
68-4135		68-4275					
68-4146							
←							
68-4228	←	←	←	82-9532	←	83-2513	←

229

Unit	1962	1963	1964
Centre stand	68-4705	←	←
(siamezed pipes)	42-4762	←	←
(comp)			
Oil tank	68-8302	←	←
Hornet			
Side cover A50	68-9212/33	←	68-9254/6
A65	68-9213/4	←	68-9254/6
A65T/R			
A65L/R, A50C			
A65L			
A50C, A65SH			
A50W			
A65T			
A65L			
A65S			
A65H			
A65S (USA)			
A65L (USA)			
A65T (USA)			
A64T (USA)			
A50 (USA)			
A65F			
A65F			
Exhaust pipe A50, A65	68-2706/12	←	←
siamezed, A50, A65		68-2734	←
A50C, A65SH, A50W			68-2742/4
A65H, A65F			
A50			
A65T, A65L			
A65F			
A65F			
Silencer A50, A65, A65R	68-2728	68-2732	←
A50, A65L, A65T			
A65S			
USA			
A65S USA			
A65F			
megaphone A65T, A65L			
Chainguard	68-7702	←	←
Seat	68-9024	←	←
		68-9047	←

APPENDIX 16 PART NUMBERS

1965	1966	1967	1968	1969	1970	1971	1972
←	68-4729	←	←	←	←	83-2627	←
←							
68-4719							
68-8340	68-8371	68-8378	←	←	←		
		68-8386					
←	68-9309/11	68-9345/8	82-8386/7	82-9850/1	←		
←							
68-9254/6							
68-9262/4							
68-9280/1							
68-9282/3							
	68-9308/35						
	68-9309/11	68-9494/5	68-9490/1	82-9846/7	82-9850/1	83-2502/4	83-4010/1
	{ 68-9307/281	←	68-9478/9	82-9805/6	←	83-2502/4	83-4010/1
	as A65L }	68-9496/7	68-9471/2				
		68-9471/2					
		68-9471/2					
		68-9478/9					
		68-9490/1					
		68-9480/1					
		68-9474/5					
			68-9471	82-9724	←	83-2502	
			68-9472	82,9472	82-9806	83-2504	
←	68-2789/91	←	←				
68-2761/3	←	68-2796/7					
		68-2821/2	82-8418/20				
				68-2789/91	←		
				70-9127/30	←	71-2043/5	←
				70-9198	←	70-2580	
				70-9200	←	71-2581	
68 2733	←	68-2732	←	←	←	71-1710	←
	68-2785	68-2732	←				
		68-2733	←				
		68-2785	←				
			42-2660	70-9206	←	71-2654	
						71-2382	←
68-7722	←	←	←	82-9192	←	83-2640	←
←	68-9331	68-9330	←	←	←	83-3633	←
			19-5599				
68-9056				68-9047	83-1684		

231

Unit	1962	1963	1964
Front hub	42-5807	←	←
	42-5805	←	←
Hub disc	42-5843	←	←
	42-5844	←	←
Rear hub	68-6005	←	←
Sprocket	42-6331	←	←
A50 s/c			68-6034
Drum and sprocket			
Drum			
Front mudguard A50, A65	68-6501	←	←
A65R			68-6526
A65R (USA)			68-6527
A50, A65 (USA)		68-6502	←
A50C, A65SH			
A65S			
A65S (USA)			
A50W			
A65F			
A65L (USA)			
Rear mudguard A50, A65	68-6752	←	←
A50, A65 (USA)	68-6753	←	←
A65L/R (USA)			68-6765
A65L/R (USA)			68-6766
A50C (USA)			68-6766
A50C (USA)			
A50C, A65SH, A50W			68-6764
A65L/R			68-6764
A65S			
A50, A65T			
Home			
USA			
A65F			

APPENDIX 16 PART NUMBERS

1965	1966	1967	1968	1969	1970	1971	1972
←	42-5569	←	37-2236	37-3404	←	37-3848	←
42-5538	68-5535	←	←				
←			37-1992	37-3460	←		
←							
67-6136	41-6022	68-6114	←	←	←	37-3985	←
←							
42-6361	68-6088	←	←	←	←	37-3747	←
67-6149							
42-6360	68-6090	68-6116	←	←	←		
←	68-6536	68-6535	←	←	←	97-4097	97-4272
←							
←							
←		68-6536	←	←	←	97-4065	97-4270
42-6544	68-6544	←					
	68-6539	68-6535	←				
		68-6539	←				
	68-6544	68-6536					
			68-6539	97-3795	97-3896	97-4065	
				68-6539	←		
68-6761							
68-6818	68-6828						
68-6819	68-6826						
68-6810							
68-6811							
68-6815	68-6836	←					
	68-6836						
	68-6828						
		68-6857	←	←	←	83-3565	←
		68-6856	←	←	←		
			68-6856	←	←	83-3565	

233

Unit		1962	1963	1964
Petrol tank (4 gal.)	A50	68-8003	←	←
	A65	68-8003	←	←
	A65R			68-8003
	A65T/R			68-8003
	A65T			
	A65L/R			68-8065
	A65L			
	A65S			
(5 gal.)	A65S			
(2 gal.)	A65S			
	A50, A65		68-8042	←
	A50			
	A50C			
	A50W			
	A65SH			
	A65H			
	A65F			
	A65T, A65L			
	A65T/R			
	A65L/R			
	A65S (USA)			

APPENDIX 16 PART NUMBERS

1965	1966	1967	1968	1969	1970	1971	1972
←	68-8065	←	68-8199	←			
←							
←							
	68-8065	←	68-8189	←	←	83-2881	83-4316
←							
	68-8065	←	68-8189	←	←	83-2881	83-4316
	68-8065	←	68-8189				
		68-8165	←				
		68-8095	68-8145	68-8188			
←	68-8107						
	68-8105	68-8145	68-8188	←			
68-8066							
	68-8093	68-8150					
68-8082							
	68-8094	68-8147					
			82-8446	82-9609	82-9801	83-2262	
	68-8105	68-8145	68-8188	←	←	83-2262	←
68-8042							
68-8066							
		68-8095	←				

235

Picture indexes

These are compiled in date order, by machine and by item to give the maximum benefit. Because of space restrictions it is not possible to have a picture of each side of every model for every year, but by using these indexes it is often possible to find a picture that helps. This is because the cycle parts were often common for several models in any one year, so any picture from that year will help.

Thus one of an A65L can help with an A50 except around the carburettor area, and an A7 and A10 will help one another.

So look for your model and year but also check other models of the same year. It can also be worth looking at the same model in the years before and after as the feature you are checking may not have changed.

Some of the references are for detail parts only so check the index, list the relevant pages and have a look at each to see if it helps.

Picture index by year

1947	A7	2, 11, 37, 67, 171
1948	A7	129, 196
1949	A7	195
	A7ST	12, 40, 139
1950	A10	13, 36, 92, 198
1951	A7	42, 116
	A10	13, 14, 41, 117, 142, 179, 193, 197
1952	A7ST	43
1953	A10	138, 187, 188
	A10SF	14
1954	A10	14, 83, 140, 148, 157, 166, 187
1955	A7SS	43, 69, 96, 174, 189, 194
	A10RR	97
1956	A7	79, 118, 166, 180, 191
	A7SS	15
	A10RR	44, 86
1957	A7SS	16, 45
	A10	118, 182
	A10RR	46, 153, 160, 174
1958	A7	47
	A7SS	119
	A10	16
	A10SR	10, 16
1959	A10	17
1960	A7	72
	A7SS	169
	A10	18
	A10SR	147
1961	A7SS	18
	A10	78
1962	A10RGS	20, 119
	A50	21, 48, 144
	A65	158
1964	A50	121
	A65	71, 170
	A65R	22, 108, 122, 175
	A65T/R	190
	A65L/R	50
	A65S/H	22
1965	A50CC off	121
	A50C US	123
	A50C	23
	A65LC	9, 88, 91, 122, 150
1966	A50	106
	A50W	24
	A65T	52, 149, 162, 164
	A65L	80, 110, 123
	A65S II	24, 50, 84
	A65H	87
1967	A65T	54, 125
	A65L	25
	A65S III	55, 85, 126, 156, 175, 176, 184
1968	A50	56, 105, 128, 143, 151
	A65T	26, 152, 177, 181
	A65L	127
	A65S IV	27, 163
1969	A50	28
	A65T	59, 99, 139, 168
	A65L	58, 89, 100, 153, 192
	A65FS	28
1970	A50	146
	A65T	29, 63
	A65L	28, 61, 90, 185
	A65FS	29, 185
1971	A65T	131
	A65L	30, 98, 134, 149, 167, 178
	A65FS	31

Picture index by model

A7	1947	2, 11, 37, 67, 171
	1948	129, 196
	1949	195
	1951	42, 116
	1956	79, 118, 166, 180, 191
	1958	47
	1960	72
A7ST	1949	12, 40, 139
	1952	43
A7SS	1955	43, 69, 96, 174, 189, 194
	1956	15
	1957	16, 45
	1958	119
	1960	169
	1961	18

A10	1950 13, 36, 92, 198	A65	1962 158	
	1951 13, 14, 41, 117, 142, 179, 193, 197		1964 71, 170	
		A65R	1964 22, 108, 122, 175	
	1953 138, 187, 188	A65T/R	1964 190	
	1954 14, 83, 140, 148, 157, 166, 187	A65L/R	1964 50	
	1957 118, 182	A65S/H	1964 22	
	1958 16	A65T	1966 52, 149, 162, 164	
	1959 17		1967 54, 125	
	1960 18		1968 26, 152, 177, 181	
	1961 78		1969 59, 99, 139, 168	
A10SF	1953 14		1970 29, 63	
A10RR	1955 97		1971 131	
	1956 44, 86	A65L	1966 80, 110, 123	
	1957 46, 153, 160, 174		1967 25	
A10SR	1958 10, 16,		1968 127	
	1960 147		1969 58, 89, 100, 153, 192	
A10RGS	1962 20, 119		1970 28, 61, 90, 185	
A50	1962 21, 48, 144		1971 30, 98, 134, 149, 167, 178	
	1964 121	A65LC	1965 9, 88, 91, 122, 150	
	1966 106	A65S	1966 24, 50, 84	
	1968 56, 105, 128, 143, 151		1967 55, 85, 126, 156, 175, 176, 184	
	1969 28		1968 27, 163	
	1970 146	A65H	1966 87	
A50CC off	1965 121	A65FS	1969 28	
A50C US	1965 123		1970 29, 185	
A50C	1965 23		1971 31	
A50W	1966 24			

Component picture index

Air filter 86
Alternator 106
Amal Concentric 83
Amal Monobloc 82
Amal Type 6 81
Badge 184
Battery 113
Bench stand 32
Brake drum trueing 159
Brake relining 165
Breather 57, 96
Cable lubricator 172
Cafe racer 141
Capacitors 109
Chaincase 73, 154
Clubman's twin 146
Clutch 70, 71, 73
Clutch tool 35
Condensers 109
Connector 114
Corrosion 113
Crankshaft 39, 45
cvc 103, 104, 105
Cylinder head 44, 50, 51, 52, 53, 55
Dynamo 102
Engine bench stand 32
Engine breather 57, 96
Engine internals 38, 40, 42, 46, 47, 49, 64

Exhaust pipes 88
Extractor tool 33
Feelers 35
Forks 135, 136
Frame 130
Front brake 166
Front hub 162
Gearbox 74, 75
Gearchange 77
Headlamp 111
Heat sink 107
Horn 112
Light unit 110
Magneto 101
Oil filter 93
Oil level 76, 77
Oil pressure switch 94
Oil pump 93
Oil system 95
Oil tank 97
Petrol taps 186
Pillion seat 189
Piston clamp 34, 60
Points 109
Primary drive 66, 68, 69
Pushrod tool 62
Racing twin 146
Rear hub 161, 168

Rear number plate 151
Rearset 156
Rear unit tool 140
Record engine 65
Regulator 103, 104, 105
Rev-counter drive 177
Silencers 90
Soldering 172
Special 150
Sprocket 79
Stand 132, 133
Steering lock 137
Strobe 109
Sump plate 93
Switch panel 114
Tail lamp 112
Tank badge 184
Tank cap 183
Tank mounting 180
Taps 186
Timing marks 59
Toolroll 153
Trials A7 144
Two leading shoe brake 166
Wall of Death 154
Workshop 32
Zener diode 107

Index

Ability 18
Addresses 10
Air cleaner body 152
Air filter 86
Alignment 129
Alternator 106
Alternator checking 106
Alternator control 107
Alternator housing 65
Alternator voltage conversion 108
Amal numbering 81
Amal restoration 81
Amal settings 210
Ammeter 113
Ammeter fitment 218
Assembly 65, 193
Assets 17
avc 103

Badges 185
Balance pipe 89
Bars 173
Basket case 34
Battery 113
Battery carrier 152
Bearing improvements 62
Big end 43
Block 48
Block finish 48
Block gasket 60
Block types 49
Brake diameters 216
Brake drums 161
Brake pedal 155
Brakes 165
Breather system 96

Cable 171
Cable making 173
Camshaft bushes 65
Camshaft fitment 209
Camshaft gear 57
Camshaft part numbers 209
Camshafts 57
Carburettor settings 210
Carburettor types 81
Carrier 157
Centre stand 132
Chaincase 73
Chaincase oil grade 99
Chaincase types 154
Chainguard 154
Chain lubrication 99
Chains 215
Chain sizes 215
Changes 9
Checking 35
Chemical cleaning 120
Cleaning 116
Clutch 70

Clutch bearing 71
Clutch centre 70
Clutch housing 71
Clutch hub 70
Clutch mechanism 73
Clutch plates 72
Clutch shock absorber 68
Clutch spring cups 72
Clutch springs 72
Clutch sprocket 71
Coil ignition 108
Colours 205
Connecting rod 46
Connectors 114
Controls 171, 173
Crankcase 60
Crankcase types 61
Crankshaft repair 42
Crankshaft types 44
Crash bars 158
Cut-out checking 104
Cut-out setting 104
cvc 103
Cylinder block 48
Cylinder block types 49
Cylinder head 51
Cylinder head types 52

Damper 137
Data 26
Dating 9
Detergents 116
Dismantling 32, 35
Drip shield 145
Drums 161
Dualseat 190
Dualseat types 191
Dynamo drive 58
Dynamo service 102
Dynamo tests 102
Dynamo types 102

Earthing 115
Electric systems 100
Electronic ignition 109
Energy transfer ignition 109
Engine dismantling 39
Engine numbers 200
Engine oil grade 99
Engine plates 141
Engine removal 38
Engine shock absorber 68
Engine sprocket 67
Engine torque stay 142
Engine types 37
Equipment 23
Exhaust pipe bracket 145
Exhaust pipe collar 91
Exhaust pipe types 88
Exhaust system 87

Fibreglass 128
Filler cap 183

Filling 124
Filter 94
Final drive chain 79, 215
Final drive sprocket 79
Finish codes 204
Finish 116
Finishing 36
Flywheels 43
Footrest 155
Footrest rubbers 155
Forks 134
Fork shrouds 145
Fork yoke types 137
Frame 129
Frame alignment 129
Frame numbers 200
Frame types 130
Front brake types 165
Front fork capacity 212
Front forks 134
Front hub types 161
Front mudguard 147
Front number plate 150
Front stand 147
Fuse 115

Gaskets 60
Gearbox 74
Gearbox assembly 79
Gearbox bearings 75
Gearbox capacity 212
Gearbox covers 76
Gearbox internal ratios 213
Gearbox oil grade 99
Gearbox plates 141
Gearbox shafts 75
Gearbox shell 76
Gearbox speedo drive 78
Gearbox sprocket 79
Gearbox sprocket cover plate 79
Gearchange mechanism 77
Gears 75
Gudgeon pin 48

Handlebar clamps 137
Handlebars 173
Handrail 192
Headlamp cowl 145
Headlamp data 218
Headlamp shell 147
Headlamp types 110
Head races 132
History 11
Horn 112
Horn position 112
Horn type 112
HT clip 145
Hub 161
Hub bearings 164
Hub types 161

Ignition points 108
Ignition timing 109

INDEX

Induction bias 87
Information 10, 26
Inlet manifold 53
Inner tube 170
Instrument bracket types 177
Instruments 173
Insurance 31, 197
Internal ratios 213

Kickstarter 78
Kneegrips 185

Layshaft 75
Legshields 158
Lifting handle 147, 157
Lighting 110
Lining 127
Lists 31
Local Vehicle Licensing office 198
Log book 197
Lower chainguard 154
Lubrication system 92

Machine test 195, 198
Machine year 9
Magneto repair 101
Magneto service 101
Magneto types 101, 209
Main bearings 62
Mainshaft 43
Mechanical cleaning 117
Mending 36
Model alterations 203
Model chart 202
Model choice 15
Modern regulators 105
Modifications 9
MoT 195, 198
Mudguard 147
Mudguard stays 147
Muffler 91

Nacelle 145
Nipples 168
Number plate 150, 151

Oddments 158
Oil filter 94
Oil grade 99
Oil pipes 93
Oil pressure switch 94
Oil pump 93
Oil release valve 93
Oil system 92
Oil tank 96
Oil tank capacity 212
Oil tank types 97
Overall ratios 213

Paint colour 125
Painting 124
Paint matching 125
Paint spraying 125

Panniers 158
Part numbers 220
Pedal 155
Petrol pipes 83
Petrol tank badges 185
Petrol tank capacities 212
Petrol tank caps 183
Petrol tank finish 180
Petrol tank types 181
Petrol taps 186
Pillion pad 190
Pillion rests 155
Pipe bracket 145
Pipes 95
Piston 47
Piston part numbers 208
Piston pin 48
Piston types 47
Pivoted fork frame 130
Planning 28
Plastic coating 126
Plates 141
Plating 126
Plug 110, 209
Plug cap 110
Plug equivalents 209
Plug lead 110
Plunger frame 130, 137
Powder coating 126
Pressure switch 94
Primary chain 68, 215
Primary chaincase capacity 212
Primary chain tensioner 68
Prop stand 132
Pushrods 56

Rear brake rod 157
Rear brake types 168
Rear carrier 157
Rear chain 79, 215
Rear chain lubrication 99
Rear fork 130
Rear hub types 163
Rear mudguard 148
Rear number plate 151
Rear sprocket 161
Rear suspension springs 140
Rear units 139
Receipts 21
Rectifier 107
Registration form 197
Registration number 197
Regulator – electronic 105
Regulator function 103
Regulator oddments 104
Regulator service 104
Regulator unit 103
Release valve 93
Repair 34
Restoration 34
Rev-counter 177
Rev-counter drives 59
Rigid frame 130

Rim fitments 216
Rim offset 159
Rim part numbers 216
Rims 169
Rim sizes 217
Rim tape 170
Rocker 56
Rocker box 54
Rocker box oiling 94
Rocker box types 56
Rod 46
Rubbers 155
Rust 120

Saddle 189
Saddle types 189
Seat handrail 192
Secondary chain 79, 215
Security 31
Security bolts 217
Shell 76
Shock absorber 68
Shrouds 145
Side panel 149
Silencer 91
Silencer bracket 145
Silencer types 91
Skill 10
Sludge trap 43
Small end bush 47
Soldering 172
Sparking plug 110, 209
Specifications 10
Speedometer bracket types 177
Speedometer drive 78
Speedometer types 175
Spoke 168
Spoke pattern 159
Sprocket 79
Sprocket cover plate 79
Sprocket sizes 213
Stainless steel 128
Stand 132, 147
Stays 142, 147
Steering crown types 137
Steering damper 137
Stop and tail light 112
Sump plate 62
Surface repair 120
Suspension springs 140
Suspension units 139
Swinging fork frame 130
Switches 115
Switch fitment 218
Switch types 110

Tail light 112
Tape 170
Tappet guide 51
Tappets 56
Taps 186
Telescopic forks 134
Telescopic fork types 135

239

Test certificate 195, 198
Timing cover 58
Timing cover points 108
Timing gears 57
Toolbox 153
Tools 25
Torque stay 142
Transfers 32, 127
Transmission 66
Transmission oil grade 99
Transmission types 66
Tubes 170
Tyre equivalents 217
Tyre fitments 217

Tyres 170
Tyre sizes 217

Undershield 145
Units 139
Upper chainguard 154

V5 197
Valve caps 54
Valve collars 54
Valve cottars 54
Valve cups 54
Valve guides 53
Valves 53

Valve spring lengths 209
Valve springs 53
Voltage conversion 108
VT20 197

Wheel bearings 164
Wheel building 170
Wheel rims 169, 216
Wheels 216
Wheel truing 170
Wiring 114
Work plan 28
Workshop 23